STILL RUNNING AFTER ALL THESE TEARS

A RUNNER'S JOURNEY THROUGH GRIEF

LISA JACKSON

To Graham: I will miss you. And never forget you.

*To Dad: I love you from the 'borrom'
of my heart, and always will.*

To Mommy: I am who I am because of you.

*To Loren: My friend, my friend,
my beloved childhood friend.*

Disclaimers

This is a true story. To respect the privacy of the people involved, I have changed some names, personal details and identifying features. In a few cases, events have been combined or adjusted slightly for clarity. But the heart of what is shared here is an accurate portrayal of my experiences.

Not all of my friends who have experienced cancer are comfortable with the term *cancer thriver*, which I've chosen to use throughout this book instead of *cancer patient* or *cancer survivor* (and certainly not *cancer victim*). I've used *thriver* because I believe it carries a sense of hope and strength. I trust that, if the term doesn't feel right for you, you'll understand the spirit in which it's intended.

Neither myself nor the publisher can be held responsible for any injury, loss or claim – be it health, financial or otherwise – arising out of the use, or misuse, of the suggestions made herein. This book is not intended as a substitute for the medical advice of a doctor or physician. If you are experiencing problems with your physical or mental health, it is always best to follow the advice of a medical professional. Always consult your doctor before trying any new complementary therapy or any new form of exercise if you have a medical or health condition or if you are worried about any of the side effects. The information in this book is applicable to the United Kingdom and may not apply if you live elsewhere.

Every effort has been made to trace copyright holders and to obtain their permission for the use of copyrighted material. The publisher apologises for any errors or omissions and would be grateful if notified of any corrections that should be incorporated in future reprints or editions of this book.

Contents

Foreword by Kathrine Switzer..10

Foreword by Vassos Alexander..12

Prologue..15

Chapter 1: 100 not out..21

Chapter 2: Take my breath away...33

Chapter 3: The solo big 5-oh...45

Chapter 4: The 'C' word and the 'D' word............................55

Chapter 5: Wanted: lab rat...65

Chapter 6: 'He had me at red wine'......................................77

Chapter 7: Choosing to live in hope, not fear......................89

Chapter 8: Chemo sabe...103

Chapter 9: Trials by fire..117

Chapter 10: Love in the time of Covid................................129

Chapter 11: A bag-of-marbles brain.....................................141

Chapter 12: The longest day..155

Chapter 13: Hanging up my carer hat.................................163

Chapter 14: Unbearable pain and a visit from a poltergeist.....173

Chapter 15: No place like home..185

Chapter 16: Till death us do part..197

Chapter 17: A celebration, a cremation and a crow...........207

Chapter 18: Where did my mojo go?..................................219

Chapter 19: Forget me not..227
Chapter 20: Flying by the seat of our pants..........................237
Chapter 21: Care-home comforts..247
Chapter 22: Oh sister, where art thou?.................................257
Chapter 23: Our father, who art in heaven............................269
Chapter 24: Ashes to ashes..279
Chapter 25: Farewell to all that..291
Chapter 26: Living with living losses......................................301
Chapter 27: 'Awful, thanks for asking'...................................311
Chapter 28: Love me Tinder..323
Chapter 29: All about my mother..335
Chapter 30: The flamingo rises from the ashes......................347

Epilogue..363
Acknowledgements..407
About the author..412
Book club questions...413

Foreword by Kathrine Switzer

The problem with being human is knowing we are going to die. Even worse – for me, anyway – is knowing that sooner or later, the person we love most in all the world is also going to die.

Lisa and Graham enjoyed a truly wonderful marriage, full of daring travel exploits, hilarious high jinks and lots of marathon running. Then, one day, the dreaded cancer monster appeared, slyly, quite literally stopping Graham in his tracks when he went out for a run. 'I just couldn't breathe. I couldn't even run to the end of the road and had to stop and walk,' the veteran of 30 marathons and two ultras told Lisa, puzzled. Hearing about this incident from my good friend Lisa, my hair stood on end – this was clearly not just one of those 'off days' that us regular runners are all too familiar with.

After a battery of tests, Graham was diagnosed with terminal lung cancer and, in the months and years that followed, Lisa kept a journal to record this new phase of their life: the doctors, hospitals, surgeries, meds and treatments good and bad, and the sleepless nights spent reading countless books and articles as they desperately sought advice on how to navigate their new reality. Later, things got even worse, as Graham began to experience terrible pain – howling, screaming, agonising pain.

In the end, Graham sadly died. Only, it wasn't the end, it was only Chapter 16. Shortly afterwards, Lisa was slammed with the dementia decline and death of her father, while at the same time dealing with the shocking and untimely death of her beloved younger sister Loren. To top it all, her running mojo deserted her, too.

FOREWORD BY KATHRINE SWITZER

How *does* someone live on with a thrice-broken heart? Well, Lisa pulled on her trainers one day and puffed her way through a slow, one-mile plod. There were plenty of tears: running does that; it opens the demon box so the harpies can screech at the sunlight and then fly away. And in the empty space they left, Lisa discovered a quiet calm, and a roadmap to finding herself again. She returned to running, and she wrote this remarkable book.

Maybe the purpose of life is to learn things and become wiser. Lisa has done that, but at the same time, she has also done us a huge favour: she has given us this gritty account so that we have a survival guide, allowing us, perhaps, to prepare ourselves for life's many trials. But before this, Lisa teaches us that we must embrace living with everything we've got. Death is inevitable. But so is life.

Kathrine Switzer

Foreword by Vassos Alexander

Last summer, I was on stage at a book festival when I was asked about how to cope with the inevitable mental 'dark places' during a 100-mile ultra. The times when you're in the middle of nowhere in the dead of night, every single bit of you hurts like crazy and you're wondering why the hell you're putting yourself through it all. That made me think back to mile 24 of the 2025 London Marathon, where I was running in a 25kg weighted vest (don't ask!) and was very close to my physical limit. At that point, I saw our ten-year-old daughter Mary at the side of the road holding up a hand-painted cardboard sign displaying the simple words: 'You can do it, Daddy!' I stopped to give her a quick hug before battling on through the pain cave. The whole episode took about ten seconds. I was in floods of tears as I stumbled along the Embankment towards the finish line and, as I later learned, so was Mary. But my tears weren't tears of pain: they were tears of joy, verging on rapture.

You see, those moments when you think you're at your absolute limit are rarely wholly dark. Because whatever you're facing in life – whether that's dealing with decades-old traumas, being diagnosed with a life-threatening illness, losing your job, or experiencing the deepest, most heartrending grief – when you peel back the layers you'll often find a spark, a shard of light that will help you survive. Another word for that spark? Love. The same universal energy that flows through each and every one of us – and which is an incredible force for good.

Which brings us to Lisa. I've been lucky enough to know Lisa for many years after we met through running. While I was loudly

FOREWORD BY VASSOS ALEXANDER

obsessed with my marathon PB, she was frequently finishing last and quietly teaching the world – and me – that running is about so much more than your finishing time. Because over and above everything else, running is about resilience. About pushing through the pain even if, like Lisa, you're plodding along right at the back.

Not that long ago, Lisa lost her beloved husband, sister and father in cruelly quick succession. She doesn't spare us the brutal details. It hurt so much because she loved so much. We're all going to experience grief; we're all going to have to go through our own very tough times. Lisa has navigated the toughest of these and here she gently, bravely, even humorously, shows us a way through. What helped Lisa keep her head above water (just!) during her husband's terminal illness, her dad's dementia and her three successive bereavements, was the deep love she felt for her family, and also her love of running which, at one point, she thought she'd lost forever. Pain, love and running, then, are what this beautiful book is all about. The following pages should be prescribed reading for anyone feeling overwhelmed by life or engulfed by grief. Life is wonderful, but it can't half feel lousy sometimes. Running, however, can reconnect us to the joy of being alive. A way to lose ourselves and find ourselves.

Running. And love. There is no more authentic messenger to herald their redemptive power than Lisa.

Vassos Alexander

Hugging my darling dad

My sister Loren with our adorable niece Leoné

With my beloved husband Graham

Prologue

♪♪ Mood music: *Chariots of Fire* by Vangelis
The song for someone who runs in slow motion

The book you're about to read is sad. Eyelids swollen shut sad. Kilimanjaro-sized mountains of snot-soaked Kleenex sad. Really. Bloody. Sad. Because it's the story of how I lost Graham, my beloved husband, to cancer, and then went on to lose my sister, and then my father – three domino deaths – all in the space of 17 months. Then, to top it off, and make a shit pie out of three cowpats, my running mojo did a runner, too.

I understand if you're tempted to stop reading, or listening, right now. I also hate sad books. Whenever I get a book or film recommendation, I always ask: 'Is it sad?' If so, I generally want nothing to do with it as I'm fiercely protective of my happiness. But please get to the end of this Prologue before making up your mind – you just might decide it's worth it.

This book has 30 chapters – one for every year Graham and I were married – and in writing them my goal is to pass on the hard-won wisdom I've gained from my experiences, from slogging through every cancer and self-help tome I could lay my hands on, and from my hypnotherapy and hypnobirthing training. When Graham was first diagnosed, I'd often get up at 4am, bleary eyed, to continue researching tools and techniques to make our journey easier. I'm hoping that whatever challenges you're facing today – caring for a sick partner, a child with special needs or elderly parents; or going through a bereavement, divorce or redundancy – *Still Running After All These Tears* will be the survival guide I was looking for but failed to find.

STILL RUNNING AFTER ALL THESE TEARS

Inspired by some of the amazing books I've read, I've decided to try to turn my wounds into warnings, so that hopefully you'll be able to avoid some of the distressing things we went through. I know that only by facing my sadness head on will I be able to return to the exhilarating life I once led that was punctuated by bouts of helpless laughter and marathon adventures in far-flung lands. So, while this may not be a happy book, exactly, it most certainly is a hopeful one. It definitely isn't a 'mismem' aka 'misery memoir'. Because, in among the shock and sorrow, traumas and tragedies, there were also a surprising number of delightfully tender and downright hilarious moments. Yes, I'll be taking you to some uncomfortable places – oncology waiting rooms, chemo wards, a hospice, two deathbeds and a care home for those with dementia – but you'll also be accompanying me as I relive some of the most heart-warming and joyous times I've ever known.

In the end, my main coping strategy – during Graham's illness and after my bereavements – turned out to be running, which I've had a love/hate relationship with for over 20 years. Despite going from ultrarunner and multi-marathoner to barely being able to run between two lampposts, I eventually fell back in love with running and it returned my affection with compound interest by helping me heal my broken self, and rebuild my life, one step at a time. Not only did it provide me with sanity-saving stress relief, achievable goals and a writing project, it also helped me process the trauma of losing both my loved ones and my trust in the medical establishment.

You're probably familiar with the quote 'Good friends are like stars. You may not always see them, but you know they're always there.' For me, running was the friend I could always rely on – even if it couldn't always rely on me. When I lost my

PROLOGUE

running mojo, I knew it would be waiting whenever I was ready to return to it.

Running might not be your thing – yet! – and it certainly isn't a cure-all, but it did give me an escape route out of my trauma. I hope that even if you're not a runner, you'll come to see how moving your body in whatever way you choose can shift your mindset, too. Running is something you can do on your own terms, throughout your life. You can fit in a 30-minute session while your loved one has chemo, for example, or go for a two-hour cross-country run to give yourself the headspace to try to come to terms with your grief. Most importantly, it gives you an extra *identity*, so that when, at times, people view you simply as 'the cancer patient's partner', 'the widow' or 'the person who lost their job', you can see yourself for what you truly are: a runner. Just like athletes who prefer the description 'Olympian' to 'World Record Holder' because no one can ever take the title away from them, being a runner is a constant, whether you run seven times a week or seven times a year. What's more, almost anyone can be a runner, or rather a run-walker like me. No exam, no entrance fee, no qualification required. Whether you're super-shapely or stick-thin, on form or infirm, young or ageing like fine wine, running is a life-enhancing activity most of us can use to help us ride the snarling tiger that is life. Because, let's face it, life is often hard no matter how much we try to distract ourselves by bingeing on boxsets, booze or... fill in the blank.

What this book is really about, then, is having courage and loving life, no matter how long you have or what cards you've been dealt. It's also about appreciating the extraordinary in the everyday. Many of the things I believed would make me happy again, haven't. But my faithful friend running? It never lets me

STILL RUNNING AFTER ALL THESE TEARS

down. Pit-pattering alongside me, it brings me both solace and profound pleasure, reminding me that, when all is said and done, reconnecting with what we love returns us to our default factory setting: joy.

Graham flaunts his foxy feather-boa tail

The coveted 100 Marathon Club T-shirt and a 'baddy bag'

Joyfully wearing my 100 Marathon Club T-shirt for the very first time

The fabulous flamingo cake

I ran my 100th marathon with a photo of my late mum Leoné on my back

Chapter 1
100 not out

🎵 Mood music: *Hey Ya!* by Outkast
The only song that makes me run faster

I was half human, half Jelly Baby the day I ran my 100th marathon. In fact, my blood was so thick with sugary snacks that it would have given Dracula diabetes. Since entering my first marathon in London back in 1999, I'd run through a Surrey vineyard where a bull was on the loose, eaten oysters and ham mid-marathon in Médoc, without throwing up – and amassed an utterly awesome collection of novelty hats. All that remained for me to do was to run-walk a final 26.2 miles and then I'd have achieved a goal I'd been chasing for 17 years: joining the 100 Marathon Club. Or to put it another way, achieving the world's most unlikely ambition for a runner so genetically ungifted that she'd come last in 23 marathons. But that was exactly why I wanted to do it. I love surprises. And surprising people. But most of all, I like surprising myself.

Although I come from a family of runners, I stubbornly resisted becoming one until the age of 30. My father Anthony won the South African University Cross-Country Championship and even considered an international athletic career – my mother Leoné always joked that she fell in love with his muscular legs – and Mum became a runner way back when people who ran slowly, like her, were called joggers. Both of them tried their damndest to get me interested in running: Dad insisted that all three of us kids go for a 2km run every weekday after school, and even entered me

STILL RUNNING AFTER ALL THESE TEARS

into a 5K fun run at the Kyalami Grand Prix Circuit when I was ten. However, unlike my sister Loren, who would go on to run the 56-mile Comrades Marathon three times in her 20s, and my much younger brother Mark, who skateboarded and windsurfed his entire childhood, I simply detested sporting pursuits, much preferring sweating over my studies (I was an über-nerd until the age of 14) to sweating actual smelly sweat.

All of that changed when I ran my first marathon aged 31 with my Aunty Rosie after donning a pair of fairy wings and a tutu and high-fiving my way to the finish line of the London Marathon. As I sat, utterly spent, on the grass in St James's Park, almost seven hours after I'd set out, I recall being bitterly disappointed. It wasn't because tens of thousands of other entrants had beaten me. Or that I'd finished just ahead of Jenny Wood-Allen, at 87 a woman almost three times my age and the race's oldest participant (a feat I only managed, by the way, because she stopped at a red traffic light while I jaywalked). It was because, despite the severe pain I was in, all I could see when I removed my trainers were a few small blisters, not the impressive torrents of blood I'd expected to spurt out of my throbbing feet.

'Never again!' I said that day, little knowing that marathon running would totally transform – and later save – my life. It would enable me to forge wonderful friendships and give me the courage to change my career by becoming a hypnotherapist, author and *Runner's World* columnist. It would even give me the confidence to run two races stark naked – except for my socks and trainers – one in Orpington and the other in London Zoo.

But, much like all the chatting I've done during marathons and ultras, I digress. Let's return to my momentous centenary marathon, which only came about because of a chance encounter with a man in a yellow-and-blue T-shirt during the 2010 Brighton

Marathon. I spotted him just after doing an emergency pee between stacks of wooden pallets at Shoreham Power Station, the most spectator-sparse section of the route. I never learned his name, but his T-shirt made a lasting impression. His words – and attitude – more so.

'I'd like one of those,' I panted, pointing to his shirt emblazoned with a laurel wreath and the words '100 Marathon Club'.

'Well you *can* have one,' he replied.

'Oh, but I've heard you need to do quite a bit of running to earn one,' I laughed.

'That's true! How many marathons have you done?' he asked.

'This is only my eighteenth so I have a long way to go,' I replied.

'Oh, we've *all* been there once! Good luck!' he grinned, before accelerating away.

That 20-second exchange was all it took to sow the seed for my next major running ambition. That anonymous runner gave me the permission slip to aspire to join a club so elite that, at that time, eight times more people had summited Mount Everest than had been admitted as members. I know better now. Today I understand that no one has to give you permission to do anything in life except yourself. But then, back when I was still a nervous marathon newbie (relatively speaking), other people's opinions mattered to me. A lot.

What I admired about this remarkable runner was that he'd made it to the castle on the hill and hadn't drawn up the drawbridge. He'd climbed the tallest tree in the forest, yet left the ladder propped up against it. He was proof that although the 100 Marathon Club most certainly was elite, it wasn't elitist. He wanted others to treasure the trek to the T-shirt, to relish the quest for the vest. He didn't want to hog all the glory but encouraged me to join the club.

STILL RUNNING AFTER ALL THESE TEARS

Time now for some 'monkey maths', as my sister Loren dubbed the kind of complex calculations that make your eyes glaze over when you're trying to work out your pace during a race. Stay with me, this bit will be over soon! At the point I decided to chase my 100 Marathon Club dream, aged 42, I'd done 18 per cent of the required qualifying marathons and ultras over a period of 11 years. If I continued at my average marathon quota of 1.6 a year, I calculated, it would take me another 51 years to reach my goal. Blimey, I wasn't sure I'd live to 93, and besides, I wanted to actually *run* in my 100 Marathon Club T-shirt, not be wheeled round or cremated in it. So I redid my monkey maths. Five marathons a year would mean I'd become a member in 16 years' time at the age of 58. Would I still be capable of running marathons by then? I couldn't risk it. I had no choice but to up the ante, and so I began setting self-devised challenges, such as completing 12 marathons in 2012, 13 in 2013, and so on.

Over the next four-and-a-half years I completed another 49 marathons and by the time fireworks welcomed in 2015 I was hellbent on concertinaing my timescale and joining the 100 Marathon Club more than four decades earlier than I originally thought I would. Starting with the sun-drenched Fort Lauderdale Marathon in Florida and ending with the marijuana-scented Reggae Marathon in Jamaica, both of which I ran with my very reluctant marathon-convert husband, Graham, my total in 2015 came to an astonishing 28 marathons. When I completed the Race for Life Marathon in October that same year – my 90th – I finally entered what 100 Marathon Clubbers call the 'nervous nineties' because of how carefully one has to plan the races leading up to the one you've chosen to be your 100th celebration. Anything can go wrong: from suffering a major injury or a race being cancelled to failing to complete a marathon before the cut-off, or one of your races being disallowed by the club member tasked with vetting your marathons and making sure you actually ran them. If you missed a race, your 100th could easily turn into your 99th. Do too many to ensure you had 'insurance' marathons in case there was a mishap, and your 100th could become your 102nd instead. In addition, it's tradition to ask an esteemed member of the club to present you with your medal and T-shirt: I'd gone the whole hog and asked both the former and current chairs to do the honours, and so risked having a lot of egg dripping from my face if I didn't hit my target at the right race. To complicate matters further, I decided to launch *Your Pace or Mine?*, the running book I was writing about my chat-running adventures, at my 100th celebration. This meant I had to write a lot faster than I ran!

So it was that in late March 2016, with only three weeks to go, I threw myself into planning my 100th, the Fabulous Flamingo Extravaganza, named in honour of the flappy-winged headgear that had become my trademark ever since I wore it at my first 56-mile Comrades Marathon in South Africa back in 2009. I'd initially thought of doing my 100th at the London Marathon, where I'd run my first, but Traviss Willcox, the chair of the 100 Marathon Club and co-founder of the running-events company Saxons, Vikings & Normans, advised against it.

'London is such a special race for so many people that you'll be just one of thousands celebrating,' he said. 'My advice is to enter a smaller marathon as that way the race can be all about you!'

Well, that did sound appealing, and meant I wouldn't have to throw a massive charity fundraising project into the mix to get a London place, so after much deliberation I chose one of the races Traviss organised: the Fowlmead Challenge at Fowlmead Country Park near Dover. What clinched the deal was that he said he'd customise the medal ribbons in my honour by matching them exactly, via a Pantone reference, to my pink flamingo hat.

My next priority was race nutrition. Despite the fact that the race website promised aid stations stocked with Jelly Babies, home-made Rocky Road, crisps and chocolate, I was determined that, in addition to these undeniably delightful goodies, my guests were going to have the chance to enjoy every single race snack I'd ever loved. Off to Tesco I went to fill a trolley with sackloads of mini KitKats, cheek-puckeringly sour Tangfastics, moreish Mini Cheddars and Mini Eggs. Oh, and South African red wine, in honour of my homeland, to be enjoyed mid-race as well as at the finish.

It's tradition that the 100 Marathon Club inductee provides a magnificent cake to share at the T-shirt presentation, but I ran out of time to order a customised one. Instead, I settled for a shop-bought chocolate sponge, but decorated it with a '100' candle, fold-out flamingo cocktail stirrers and a blue plaque like the ones affixed to London buildings where famous people once lived. It read: Lisa Jackson, chat-runner & Comrades finisher, joined the 100 Marathon Club on 16 April 2016.

The final consideration? What to wear? I chose a wedding-tradition theme as both my wedding and my 100th marathon were once-in-a-lifetime events (or so I thought). Something old was my trusty flamingo hat. Something new was a pink T-shirt printed with angel wings framing a photo of my late mother Leoné. Something borrowed was a rainbow-coloured tulle bustle, and something blue was the word 'Congrats!' on a helium balloon a friend had sent me. Graham, as usual, was less keen on running in costume.

'You are *not* going to wear that grungy T-shirt you wore at the Médoc Marathon,' I admonished him, recalling the way he'd refused to dress up as a butterfly, preferring to wear a worn-out greyish T-shirt, the kind that looked as if a blue sock had accidentally sabotaged it in the wash.

'Why ever not?' he challenged. 'I fitted in perfectly well with the Butterfly Ball theme of your outfit… my grubby T-shirt made me look like a grub.'

'Ha, ha, that's my joke, not yours,' I replied. 'At the very least, will you wear a pink wig? Or pink shorts? Or a pink feather boa? This is a *very* big day for me.'

'I'll think about it,' he said.

Sue Cesarini, my Italian 'marathon bridesmaid', was the first of my two international guests to arrive. She'd been my pacer at the Turin Marathon, where she'd cracked me up by singing opera arias and demanding Martinis and sponges soaked in Chanel No5 at the aid stations. René Kujan, aka the Czech Forrest Gump, was next. An amazing ultrarunner whom Graham and I had befriended at the Prague Marathon, he'd not only run the entire 828-mile Ring Road in Iceland but had also traversed the country from north to south and east to west. I felt so honoured to have them join me as they represented just two of the dozens of friendships I'd formed during my many marathon miles. I've been heard to say on more than one occasion, 'A race don't mean a thing if it ain't got bling,' but I can truly say, hand on heart, that these friends meant more to me than any medal.

STILL RUNNING AFTER ALL THESE TEARS

Our drive from south London to Dover was almost as much fun as the marathon itself. Graham was in good form and dubbed the race the Foul-*mouth* Challenge. 'That's actually weirdly appropriate,' he joked. 'Swearing helps you tolerate pain, and pain is one thing that won't be in short supply today as I've barely done any training so am going to find running 26.2 miles tough.' His other nickname for the event was the 'celebration on a slagheap' as he'd researched the venue and discovered Fowlmead Country Park had been created on the mine dump of a former colliery. Graham could always be relied on to lower the tone.

On reaching the venue, I was delighted to be met by dozens of well-wishers. The day was rather chilly, but the atmosphere was anything but as old friends and new complimented each other on their pink wigs and flamingo get-ups. Many, I was glad to see, were already tucking into the race snacks I'd crammed into their candy-striped goody bags, which I'd renamed 'baddy bags' in reference to the tooth-dissolving sugary treats they were filled with.

Round and round and round the 3.2km circular course we went, sometimes running, sometimes walking, always chatting. Graham, I was pleased to see, had given in to my request to 'respect the theme' by dressing up in a pink tutu and tucking a fuchsia feather boa he'd loaned from one of my friends into the waistband of his shorts, giving him a rather foxy-looking tail. My constant companion was Roger Biggs, the former chair of the 100 Marathon Club, who'd promised to not only present me with my medal but stick with me every step of the way, a vow he later had cause to regret when he found out I was intending to take almost nine hours to get to the finish – 'in order to get maximum value for money' I cheerfully told him. At one point I asked Luke, my youngest guest, to guess how many marathons and ultras Roger had done. Not surprisingly, it took about a mile for him to get it right – an astonishing 841. 'He's mental!' declared Luke cheerfully, before adding, 'And you're mental, too!'

Finally, after eight hours and 41 minutes, it was time to run the final 100m of the journey that had started 17 years before. Holding hands with several friends, I ran sobbing across the finish line to where Graham was waiting to give me a bear hug, having finished his own race several hours before. I'd done it! The woman who still struggled to call herself sporty had just completed her centenary marathon. I couldn't wait to get home and call my dad back in South Africa to tell him my dream-come-true news. His unathletic daughter had dared to do what she was worst at, and had won the right to wear the T-shirt she'd coveted for six long years. He'd inspired our whole family to run and had always encouraged me to persevere (Dad's favourite motto was 'If at first you don't succeed, try, try and try again') so I knew he'd be proud of the way my tenacity had won out over my lack of running talent. I grinned so much, my cheeks ached as much, if not more, than my legs. And then it was time for the presentation of my medal and club T-shirt emblazoned with my name on the back (and a mouthful or two of chocolate cake), before I commenced an al fresco book signing.

The question almost everyone asked me as they left was 'What's next?' The answer? Running my 101st marathon, wearing my box-fresh 100 Marathon Club T-shirt, in Brighton, the very next day. Another common question was, 'Will you continue running lots of marathons?' to which I jokingly replied, 'No, I want to stay married.' I was acutely aware that my marathon mania had taken a toll on my marriage and that I couldn't continue shooting off to races every second weekend as I'd done the previous year. I felt

STILL RUNNING AFTER ALL THESE TEARS

it was only fair that Graham got his wife back once my goal had been ticked off.

'It is good to have an end to journey toward; but it is the journey that matters, in the end,' the science-fiction author Ursula K. Le Guin once wrote in *The Left Hand of Darkness*. She was right, I thought, but what she really should have added is that it's not only the journey that matters, but the people who accompany you. Little did I know on that joyful day that two of the runners who'd come to cheer me on did not have long to live. And that after reaching my 100 Marathon Club journey's end, my running mojo would soon desert me.

Wearing my 'intellectual' glasses...

... and my 'leftie' yellow fez

In Graham's studio flat

Hippie chic in Cape Town

Lovers' tiff at a uni ball

On the Stellenbosch Wine Route

Our wedding day – before the sparklers caused chaos

Chapter 2
Take my breath away

♪♪ **Mood music: *O Mio Babbino Caro* by Kiri Te Kanawa
(from *A Room with a View*)**
The soundtrack to the first film Graham and I watched together

'I just couldn't breathe. I was so out of breath, I had to stop and walk,' Graham said, his face deathly pale after returning home from a run. In the 16 months following my 100th marathon I'd stuck to my promise of 'staying married' and limited myself to five marathons, during which time Graham had done only two, including the Transylvanian Bear Race, where the chance to run through a Romanian forest inhabited by real live bears accompanied by a wife dressed as Dracula, had been too tempting to resist.

'Graham, you know you never do enough training,' I retorted smugly. 'That's the first run you've done in months, so quite frankly, I'm not in the least bit surprised that it was hard.'

'No, you don't understand, I couldn't even run to the end of the road.'

Now it was my turn to look worried.

'You'd better see your GP – that's really weird.'

The next day a chest X-ray revealed something was indeed amiss, so shortly afterwards we were asked to come in to our local hospital to discuss the results. At this point, neither of us was particularly worried, especially since we knew that Graham, who'd always only been a very occasional social smoker, had quit decades ago. What's more, Graham was generally fit and capable of running marathons with the bare minimum of training due to his habit of fast-walking two miles a day as part of his commute. Having done some preliminary research, we suspected Graham's extreme breathlessness was due to tuberculosis as he frequently travelled to Pakistan, which has the world's fifth highest incidence of the disease. Coming from South Africa, which also has a high infection rate, I knew that it was serious but treatable. I took along a notebook, just in case, however, as I'd read it was vitally important to take notes in consultations or else you risked forgetting what had been said. 'We're not sure what it is yet,' said the stern-faced, dark-haired doctor seated opposite us behind the large wooden desk she'd barricaded herself behind. The scuffed wall behind her was painted a bilious shade of green, as if it felt queasy after hearing too much bad news.

'What job do you do?' the doctor asked. Graham explained that he was a research analyst at the Foreign Office, specialising in Pakistan, and that he often flew there for work.

'Show me your hands,' she said abruptly.

Graham held out his hands like a boy at my Pretoria nursery school who'd misbehaved and was now going to be smacked with a ruler as punishment.

The doctor glanced at his outstretched hands, seemed to notice that there was nothing unusual about them, and then scribbled down some notes. We waited patiently for an explanation, but none was forthcoming. (With the help of Dr Google I later solved the mystery myself: she was probably looking for finger clubbing, a thickening of the fingertips which can be a sign of lung cancer.)

'We'll have to conduct further tests,' she said, 'and collect a sample of fluid from your lung.'

'Are there any dos or don'ts?' Graham asked.

TAKE MY BREATH AWAY

'I can't say any more until we analyse the sample,' the doctor said without looking up.

'So, it's okay for Graham to fly to Georgia with me to celebrate my fiftieth birthday?' I asked, feeling relieved. The doctor shot me an alarmed look.

'With a lung like this,' she said, jabbing her finger at an X-ray, 'he could *die* if he flew anywhere.'

In other words, there *were* some *really* important dos or don'ts.

I felt sick to the stomach. At that moment I realised we couldn't assume anything – not even that a highly trained doctor would warn us of things that could be potentially fatal unless we specifically asked about them. From now on it was up to us to second guess the medical fraternity. My worst fear – losing Graham – was at very real risk of coming true. We'd just entered the scary world of medicine without any training or a map.

You have to rewind our lives 26 years before you can begin to understand the love affair that became a love story that became a life story. How I went from being a love-struck teenager in South Africa to a journalist and hypnotherapist in London fearing for the health of her soulmate. Fate had a big hand to play in this, and many stars had to align in order to bring us together. Firstly, it had to put Graham in South Africa, because aged 18 I was far too timid to travel. Fate engineered this crucial step by giving him a tutoring job at the University of Cape Town while he did his Master's in Philosophy. Secondly, fate had to ensure Graham had broken up with his girlfriend in England, which had happened the month before, as he was no love rat. And thirdly, the Universe had to pluck me from French Intensive

STILL RUNNING AFTER ALL THESE TEARS

– a course designed to teach us five years of schoolgirl French in a single year – and persuade me to study philosophy instead. This third prerequisite was met when I missed several weeks of uni during my first semester after contracting hepatitis A, most likely from contaminated food. Unable to teach myself French, I quit and signed up for a single semester of philosophy instead as I'd been assured by a fellow student that it was a 'Mickey Mouse course'. I had a choice of several philosophy tutors and I have no idea why I chose Graham's tutorial, but even to this day I can see myself struggling to make my pen work as I etched my name into the sheet of A4 pinned up on a noticeboard in the philosophy department lobby.

When I walked into the tutorial room, a man wearing John Lennon spectacles that resembled the ones I'd worn at high school caught my eye. Only mine had plain glass lenses as the teenage me only wore them to appear bohemian and intellectual. Similar sentiments had led to the 'leftie' look I cultivated on campus, where I'd stroll around in an ankle-length tasselled skirt and a paper-thin Blue Diamond T-shirt topped off with a canary yellow fabric fez, or sometimes go out, barefoot, dressed in a black petticoat I'd bought at a flea market.

'He looks super cute and interesting,' I thought, before the man dashed all my hopes by introducing himself as our tutor, Graham Williams. Things went from bad to worse when it became apparent how difficult studying philosophy actually was. Far from being Mickey Mouse, it made me feel like Dumbo. I'd been expecting it to involve discussions about ethics but instead we pondered mind-bending topics such as 'What is the meaning of meaning?' and 'What is truth?'

'WTF?' I thought, for once speechless. I simply couldn't think of a single intelligent thing to say, so kept my eyes firmly lowered, occasionally peering out from underneath my blue-mascaraed lashes to see whether anyone else was similarly embarrassed.

One week, we moved on to discussing abortion, a topic I had strong views on. Once I'd started, there was no stopping me, and Graham and I continued the lively debate out in the corridor for three more hours. Despite our very different upbringings, it felt as if Graham and I had known each other our whole lives. As the American author Jandy Nelson put it in her book *I'll Give You the Sun*: 'Meeting your soulmate is like walking into a house you've been in before – you will recognise the furniture, the pictures on the wall, the books on the shelves.' Graham, I discovered, had been born in Ghana to diplomat parents 23 years earlier and by the age of 11 had spent half his life abroad before attending boarding school in England. I, on the other hand, had set foot outside South Africa precisely once and had lived in Pretoria with my parents until uni. What we did have in common, however, amazed me: our values were identical and, most incredible of all, Graham viewed women as equals, something almost unheard of in patriarchal South Africa.

'I've just met the most amazing man,' I told my friend Lyndall when I got back to halls. 'Although he's my tutor and comes from England, I feel I've known him my whole life.'

'Don't get your hopes up,' Lyndall cautioned.

After the next seminar – one on the ethics of suicide, during which I again found myself expressing my beliefs at length – rather than stand outside the seminar room, Graham suggested we grab a seat in the canteen. As we sipped sour coffee from polystyrene cups, the conversation, for some inexplicable reason, turned to poltergeists.

'Do you believe in them?' asked Graham.

'There's a part of me that actually does,' I said.

STILL RUNNING AFTER ALL THESE TEARS

'That's ridiculous,' he said.

At that precise moment, a white plastic chair skidded across the terracotta tiled floor, coming to rest a few feet away from us. We turned to see where it had come from and noticed that the canteen's external glass door was open. Graham insisted the chair had been blown across the room by a gust of wind. But with impeccable timing like that, I just *knew* our first date had been gate-crashed by a poltergeist.

'We should go to a movie sometime,' suggested Graham. 'How about tomorrow? Or perhaps next week?'

The thought of waiting even a day to see Graham again was unbearably painful.

'Tomorrow's fine!' I blurted out. So much for playing it cool.

After going to see the romantic film *A Room with a View*, our second date involved sipping sundowners on Camps Bay Beach, where we snuggled up under my grey Paddington Bear duffle coat and ate brie from a box, olives from a bag and ham from a tin. We got back to Graham's studio flat long after my uni residence's curfew that night, so I had to stay over. As Graham returned from the bathroom with an armload of clean sheets to make up a bed on his sofa, I blocked his path.

'Are you going to let me pass?' he smiled.

'No,' I said, kissing him.

The next morning, Graham answered the door to find the warden of my residence standing outside.

'I'm here to see if you know where Lisa Jackson is,' she said. I hardly dared breathe. From where I was sitting on his sofa, wrapped in a towel, I could see the tips of her shoes.

'Yes, Lisa was here, but she's gone shopping,' Graham fibbed.

'Thank goodness she's okay. Please ask her to come and see me when she's back.'

Graham assured her he would, and I resumed breathing.

An hour later I nervously knocked on the warden's door.

'Graham's my tutor and was helping me with some emotional issues,' I lied.

The warden's face softened. 'My dear girl, I'm so sorry to hear that. You know you can always talk to me if you need to.'

I nodded. 'What happened to your face?' she enquired. 'It looks like you fell off a motorbike.'

Blushing furiously, I raised a hand and touched the biscuit-sized stubble-rash scab on my chin. 'I tripped on some stairs,' I lied again.

'You'd better get that looked at by a doctor – you might need antibiotics.'

Unsurprisingly, my philosophy grades did improve once I started dating Graham, but not because I received extra tutoring. He asked a colleague, who turned out to be a more generous marker, to assess my essays so there could be no claims of favouritism. Thankfully, his department didn't have a ban on students dating staff – if it had, I would have ceased my philosophy studies immediately as I didn't technically need the credit to get my degree. In fact, the minute I could ditch the course, I did: there's nothing worse than looking like Dumbo on what's supposed to be a Mickey Mouse course in front of a new boyfriend.

Falling in love with a penniless philosopher was everything it's cracked up to be. We had virtually no money, and no telly, but that made us appreciate what little we did have all the more. We drank cheap red wine in a box that Graham called a 'glad bag' because its contents made us so happy. And we spent hours lying on a foam mattress in front of a fire he'd lit in the tiny grate of his studio flat while reading novels and poetry to each other. He cooked me meals made from root vegetables, stock cubes and a single rasher of bacon. He penned me love poetry and I wrote him love letters decorated with crayon rainbows sprayed with hairspray to stop them from smudging. We completed a magazine personality quiz that decreed he was a 'Frisky Fergie', and I a 'Demure Di'! Our love deepened with each passing day – and every raging row – for we were two of the most stubborn people ever to enter into a relationship, and neither of us backed down if we thought we were right. Whatever you're thinking, this was no Professor Oppressor situation – Graham was only four years older than me and had met his match.

Four years after meeting we got married in a seventeenth-century Cape Dutch farmhouse. The white-gabled, thatched-roof venue with its mountain backdrop was perfect, except for one thing: it was run by a fearsome event organiser called Topsi aka The Dragon Lady. Canapés? No, far too tricky to make. Trifle? No, it wasn't wedding food. Imagine my surprise then, when one day, completely out of the blue, Topsi said 'yes' to us giving our guests sparklers. It was a decision she'd live to regret.

All I wanted for my wedding was for the day to go as smoothly as possible. Alas, it was not to be. As I'd run out of time to organise the wording of our civil ceremony, on my wedding day I dispatched my siblings to a local priest who gave them a copy of the Christian marriage service. The only problem was, the wording contained many references to God, which we had to redact as Graham was an atheist, prompting my 14-year-old brother to proclaim: 'This is a *bizarre* wedding. And you're a *bizarre* bunch of people!' Just what a nervous bride-to-be in too-tight new shoes with Elastoplast on her heels that kept peeling off needed to hear. But the best was yet to come. After dinner, the guests began lighting the clover-leaf sparklers my mother had laid out beside each place setting and within seconds the room filled with clouds of dense smoke.

'GET OUT! GET OUT!' roared Topsi, emerging from the kitchen in her chef's whites, fire extinguisher in hand, convinced we'd set the thatched roof alight. Mum rushed to open a window to allow the sparkler smoke to escape with an enraged Topsi hot on her heels. Dropping the fire extinguisher, Topsi grabbed my mother by both wrists and threw her outside, where the rest of our guests, by this time rather tipsy, were chasing each other round the garden shouting 'GET OUT! GET OUT!' I was utterly mortified.

The next day, Graham, bless him, proclaimed that ours was the best wedding he'd ever been to. And me? I agreed, but I still shudder every time I see a sparkler.

Once Graham had completed his Master's degree and PhD, it was time to decide where we were going to put down roots. Jobs were hard to come by in Cape Town so we took our chances in the UK, emigrating to London after backpacking for a year. I landed a job at *Cosmopolitan* magazine almost immediately, but it took Graham, who had no work experience, three-and-a-half long years before a research job at the Ministry of Defence materialised. Until that happened, he sold jewellery at H Samuel and cleaned an office. He also did a brilliant job renovating our house. I used to tag along in the evenings when he did his cleaning job, and it amused me to think that I was a Cosmo Girl by day… and a toilet cleaner by night, something that would no doubt have horrified my fashionista colleagues. A few years later, I jumped ship to the health and beauty magazine *Zest*, a life-changing decision as Sally, a colleague there, gifted me her London Marathon media place. The rest, as they say, is history (or, if you're not a historian, you can swot up about all my slow-running adventures in my previous book, *Your Pace or Mine?*). Running marathons, while claiming to hate running, became my favourite pastime, and Graham, despite hating running too, got so tired of being my 'baggage boy' that he started doing them as well. Eventually, he ended up doing 30 – plus two 56-mile ultras – entirely against his will, or so he said.

outside our much-loved Croydon home

Backpacking in Damascus, Syria

one of many fun times

Graham was always my guardian angel

Chapter 3
The solo big 5-oh

♪♪ **Mood music: *(Where Do I Begin) Love Story* by Andy Williams**
The song that speaks of sharing special moments

Turning 50 was bound to be challenging. This is because, in the final year of each decade, most people tend to give themselves a forensic life audit – and make significant decisions as a result. In my case, I'd experienced the Big Birthday Hex twice before: aged 29 I changed jobs and went through a time of great upheaval and upset as a consequence, and aged 39, my world was upended by the shocking death of my mother, who was killed by a driver who failed to brake at a stop sign. She had been out training for a marathon we'd signed up to run together. Aged 49, I was determined to break this negative cycle and instead welcome in a new decade by going on a trip to the Caucasus, a region I'd never been to before.

I felt I'd already done all the soul-searching I needed to do the year before when, as so many of us do before attending a high-school reunion, I'd given my life an MOT and concluded that I was exactly where I wanted to be. It had come as no surprise that, on reflection, my proudest achievement wasn't fulfilling a lifelong dream of becoming an author or retraining as a hypnotherapist. Nor was it becoming a marathon runner against all odds and completing the 56-mile Comrades Marathon, twice, despite being, let's put it politely, spectacularly untalented at running. My proudest achievement was my 25-year marriage, which had

STILL RUNNING AFTER ALL THESE TEARS

survived our emigration from South Africa to the UK, financial hardship – at one point, when we had £70 in our bank account, we used to refuse dinner invitations because we couldn't afford to buy a £3.50 bottle of Chilean Pinot Noir to gift to our hosts – and my working nine till nine at *Cosmopolitan* for many years. It had even survived Graham's inability to organise surprises or outings and my entirely justifiable aversion to housework.

'I'm just not that *interested* in housework, Graham,' I told him after being berated, yet again, for not pulling my weight.

'Lisa, I don't think *anyone's* that interested in housework. Most people view it simply as something rather unpleasant that has to be done, like clipping their toenails,' he replied.

'Anyway, how hard can it be to go online and research fun things to do as a couple?' I'd retort.

Most of the time I got away with dodging the dusting because I worked such long hours at both my day job and my side hustles that Graham would do it on my behalf, but every now and again tensions would flare up again and we'd have an argument. The same one we'd been having ever since the day we were married.

'When was the last time you polished the bathroom tiles?' Graham would say accusingly, knowing full well I'd never polished a tile in my life.

'Forget the tiles. Why don't you ever surprise me and arrange a weekend away?' I'd counter, knowing this suggestion was entirely futile.

After a decade or so spent arguing till 3am, having realised we could get a lot more sleep if our arguments could be shortened, we learned to speed-fight, which resulted in the following exchange:

Graham: 'Tiles.'
Lisa: 'Surprises.'
The End.

THE SOLO BIG 5-OH

The decision to go on my 50th birthday trip alone was not an easy one. Four weeks before we were due to depart, Graham underwent a procedure at our local hospital to remove some of the fluid surrounding his right lung. As I sat anxiously in the waiting room, a nurse in blue scrubs exited the operating theatre pushing a steel trolley bearing a plastic cup of amber liquid. It was a surreal sight as she looked like a flight attendant going to serve a passenger a pint of beer.

'Apparently there's loads more fluid on my lung,' Graham told me later. 'I asked them why they didn't just remove it all today but they said that would send my body into shock.'

A few days later, we were informed that Graham needed to have a procedure where a biopsy would be performed, the remaining fluid would be drained and some kind of talc would be injected into the resulting cavity to prevent liquid accumulating there again. The operation was due to take place the day after our trip ended but Graham had been warned by his doctor not to fly. Or more accurately, been told flying could kill him.

'I really think you should go,' he said. 'We can't get a refund on the holiday and it's a very minor procedure so let's not ruin your birthday over it.' Reluctantly, I agreed. As no one had mentioned the dreaded 'C' word, we still weren't unduly worried and, as we'd both gone on solo travel adventures before, I tried to tell myself this was just another one.

When I'd imagined my 50th, I'd pictured a romantic dinner for two eating lamb, aubergine and flatbread washed down with Georgian wine and Ararat cognac in one of the outdoor restaurants Yerevan is famed for. Instead, I was on the phone

STILL RUNNING AFTER ALL THESE TEARS

to Graham, seated on the floral polyester bedspread of a stale-smelling, windowless hotel room that fellow travellers told me was a 'knocking shop', looking at the red illuminated numerals of a cheap plastic alarm clock as it blinked away the final seconds of my 40s. It felt more like a wake than a celebration, except it didn't feature sausage rolls and daytime-drinking-inebriated relatives. Although turning 50 was certainly something to be celebrated – many people don't live long enough to have the privilege of doing so – I could no longer kid myself that I wasn't middle aged. Even though I'd met people well into their 80s who were still running marathons and were teenagers at heart, I knew this wasn't the norm, and that from here on in I was no longer going to be able to take feeling young for granted. I remember Robbie 'Red Hat' Wilson, with whom I ran two marathons, telling me how difficult that challenge was: 'Now I'm eighty-one,' he said, 'I'm fighting old age all the time by walking everywhere, working on my allotment and continuing to run 5K parkruns and the odd marathon.' I hoped I'd prove as much of a prize fighter as Robbie.

Though I enjoyed the trip, travelling without Graham wasn't the same. I desperately wanted to share every experience with him, as I'd done so often. This was my first-ever group tour and it made me realise how hard it was holidaying with strangers, no matter how interesting, well-travelled or kind they were. The tedium of 14 hot and dusty hours stuck at the border between Georgia and Abkhazia, a pocket-sized breakaway state recognised by only a handful of countries, was immeasurably worse without him. I especially missed the humour he'd have brought to the way I'd retched while squat-peeing in a deserted building we'd had to use as a makeshift toilet, narrowly avoiding toppling over onto the excrement-covered floor. Graham always relished a good 'poo story'. And when we visited Nagorno-Karabakh's Museum of

Remarkable and inspiring, and a salutary account of just how often doctors fail so miserably in the all-important art of communication.

Henry Marsh, author of *And Finally*

It's rare for a book to be both heartrending and inspiring but Lisa's account of how running helped her through the darkest times of her life is such a thing. As she unflinchingly shares her journey through the unimaginable loss of her loved ones, Lisa offers us a roadmap to help navigate life's most devastating circumstances.

Andy Dixon, editor-in-chief of *Runner's World* UK

Heartbreaking, hopeful and profoundly human, Lisa's story is a testament to the strength of the human spirit. This book is not just about running, it's about what keeps us moving when everything else falls apart. A must-read for anyone facing grief, searching for healing or simply needing a reminder that joy is still possible after unimaginable loss.

Paul Sinton-Hewitt, parkrun founder and author of *One Small Step*

Heartbreaking, honest and hilarious.

Vassos Alexander, author of *How to Run a Marathon*

Throughout my career I've witnessed first-hand how running can give women strength, resilience and hope in the hardest of times. Lisa's memoir captures this beautifully and her courage, honesty and humour shine through on every page.

Leanne Davies, Run Mummy Run founder

Deeply honest, poignant and painful, but deftly sewn together with the golden thread of Lisa's signature wit and sense of humour, this is an important manual for anyone facing a major life challenge.

Esther Newman, editor of *Women's Running*

Only Lisa could write a book about grief that's so full of laughter and hope. A brave, uplifting testament to love and the healing power of running.

Anna McNuff, author of *Barefoot Britain*

This poignant and often amusing book reveals running as a powerful source of solace when every other aspect of life feels broken. Its blend of heartfelt narrative, humour and practical guidance makes it a deeply enriching read.

Sophie Power, author of *The Power Within*

A love letter to freedom, running and self-discovery that will have you laughing and crying – sometimes at the same time.

Allie Bailey, author of *There Is No Wall*

Lisa Jackson has written something entirely new: it's a heartrending love story that ends in death, and a heart-warming women's running book that ends in life. When grief deprives you even of your sense of self, read this book, and follow its pragmatic advice about how running, and love, can save you.

Professor Roger Robinson, author of *Running Throughout Time*

Lisa has managed to turn a desperately sad story into a book of hope full of resources for anyone navigating cancer, dementia, bipolar disorder and grief. As a former GP, my toes curled at some of her healthcare experiences. Of course, with Lisa, there's always running, and this book is a wonderful reminder of its power to help you cope and heal.

Dr Juliet McGrattan, author of *The Runner's Guide to Menopause*

This heartfelt, inspiring and moving read tells you everything you need to know about resilience. This book is for anyone – whether a runner or not – who wants to know exactly how to dig deep when you feel like you want to give up. Brilliant.

Viv Groskop, author of *How to Own the Room*

Funny, sad, brave and brilliantly written, this book is tragic but life affirming, and made me want to run and live forever. Lisa Jackson writes from her very big heart; reading this expanded mine.

Paul Tonkinson, *Running Commentary* podcaster and author of *26.2 Miles to Happiness*

A heartbreaking, heart-warming and inspiring story.

Damian Hall, author of *In It for the Long Run*

This is a book for the broken-hearted who think they may never be happy again. Lisa's memoir is a moving exploration of loss, love and the quiet courage it takes to choose joy again. Raw, honest and ultimately uplifting.

Suzy Walker, editor-in-chief of *Platinum*

When her beloved husband died, and then her sister and her father, Lisa could have sunk into despair. Instead, she decided to dig out her running shoes, run yet another marathon – and write a book. Still Running After All These Tears *is an incredibly moving account of her attempts to deal with devastating grief. It's gripping, it's funny and it's hugely inspiring. Whether you like running or don't, this book will cheer you up, buck you up and make you want to raise a glass to Lisa's energy, exuberance and life. It will make you want, in fact, to raise a glass to life itself.*

Christina Patterson, author of *The Art of Not Falling Apart* and *Outside, the Sky is Blue*

I was diagnosed with stage four prostate cancer 11 years ago and reading Lisa's book made me appreciate just how hard it is for those around me to deal with my cancer. It made me laugh, cry and everything in between.

Kevin Webber, author of *Dead Man Running*

A deeply moving story of love, loss and the power of putting one foot in front of the other.

Jen Benson, author of *The Path She Runs*

STILL RUNNING AFTER ALL THESE TEARS

Copyright © Lisa Jackson, 2026

All rights reserved.

No part of this book may be reproduced by any means, nor transmitted, nor translated into a machine language, without the written permission of the publishers.

Lisa Jackson has asserted their right to be identified as the author of this work in accordance with sections 77 and 78 of the Copyright, Designs and Patents Act 1988.

Condition of Sale
This book is sold subject to the condition that it shall not, by way of trade or otherwise, be lent, resold, hired out or otherwise circulated in any form of binding or cover other than that in which it is published and without a similar condition including this condition being imposed on the subsequent purchaser.

An Hachette UK Company
www.hachette.co.uk

Summersdale Publishers
Part of Octopus Publishing Group Limited
Carmelite House
50 Victoria Embankment
LONDON
EC4Y 0DZ
UK

This FSC® label means that materials and other controlled sources used for the product have been responsibly sourced

www.summersdale.com

The authorised representative in the EEA is Hachette Ireland, 8 Castlecourt Centre, Dublin 15, D15 XTP3, Ireland (email: info@hbgi.ie)

Printed and bound by Clays Ltd, Suffolk, NR35 1ED

ISBN: 978-1-83799-737-4
eISBN: 978-1-83799-738-1

Substantial discounts on bulk quantities of Summersdale books are available to corporations, professional associations and other organisations. For details contact general enquiries: telephone: +44 (0) 1243 771107 or email: enquiries@summersdale.com.

Fallen Soldiers commemorating those who'd died during the early 1990s war with Azerbaijan, I just knew he'd have squeezed my hand when viewing the haunting portraits of the combatants lining the walls. Many of them were young men who'd been deprived of marriage, children, and turning 50, whose mothers had set up the museum to keep their memories alive using heartbreakingly humble treasured possessions such as cigarette lighters. And when, my vision blurred with tears, I'd mistakenly donated £100 to the museum instead of the £10 I'd intended to, I knew Graham would have smiled and said it was worth it to help validate those grief-stricken mothers' loss.

As soon as I got back from Armenia, I called Graham in the hospital. It was late at night and I was worried I'd woken him.

'I'm fine, everything went according to plan,' said Graham, his voice sounding strangely hollow.

'Well, it's all over now,' I said, trying to be cheerful in spite of the fact that Graham didn't sound at all like himself.

'Except it's not,' said Graham quietly. 'They found suspicious cells.'

The room spun, exactly as it had ten years before when I'd heard my father say down the phone 'Mommy's been killed'. I felt as if I'd left my body and was looking down at myself from above. The rest of our conversation is a total blank, but I do recall phoning my friend Sarah, even though it was now almost midnight, and blurting out the terrible news to her.

'Stop catastrophising, Lisa!' she said soothingly but sternly. 'Don't get upset until the doctors have told you for sure what's going on.' It was advice that would prove invaluable in the years to come when every single one of Graham's treatments came with a health warning a mile long and I could have driven myself crazy imagining all the potential horrendous outcomes and side effects.

STILL RUNNING AFTER ALL THESE TEARS

I hung up and turned in circles in my kitchen. I just didn't know what to do with myself. What *do* you do when – potentially – your greatest fear, the one thing you dread more than anything, is about to become a kicking-and-screaming reality? In my case, thankfully, the long flight had tired me out so when I went to bed, my heart fit-to-bursting with horror, I, miraculously, slept.

I felt a wave of happiness at the thought of seeing Graham again when I woke the next day, followed almost instantly by a sickening surge of fear once my brain updated itself on the previous evening's conversation. As I sat on the bus to the hospital to visit him, I reflected on our relationship and how, over the years, despite our many disagreements, it had deepened and matured and been strengthened by the many hardships we'd faced together: Graham not being able to get a full-time job for over three years; the death of my mother; and the obscene amounts of unpaid overtime and many challenges I'd been subjected to while a journalist (working in glossy magazines, I like to joke, is nothing like *The Devil Wears Prada* – it's ten times worse). When we'd met, we'd both been passionate about what we were studying and had both harboured ambitions of going into academia. And yet, strangely, once he had his doctorate, Graham never picked up a philosophy book again and, after uni, I seldom had time to read novels. Instead, we developed joint interests in travelling, camping and marathon running, things we never dreamed of doing when we first got together.

The Russian president Boris Yeltsin once said: 'We don't appreciate what we have until it's gone. Freedom is like that.

It's like air. When you have it, you don't notice it.' And I'd read that when the honeymoon period is over, most couples start to take each other for granted, like a new dress you couldn't wait to wear that now hangs unloved in a cupboard. Happily, I can say this was definitely *not* the case with us. To my surprise, I'd realised that I was far more in love with Graham now than I had been as a lovestruck teenager. I knew how special Graham was the minute I set eyes on him, and I never missed an opportunity to let him know how much I appreciated him, often by listing the things I loved doing with him. I took inspiration for this from the famed writer Vita Sackville-West. She used the term 'through leaves' as shorthand for the small but intense pleasures relished by both her and her beloved husband Harold who, like Graham, worked for the Foreign Office and was utterly devoted to his wife. Inspired by the joy she got from kicking up dry leaves as she walked through them, Vita said for her it was 'through leaves' to suddenly remember a word or name she thought she'd forgotten; to run a stick along an iron railing; to write with the perfect pen; to draw a cork with a good corkscrew, and to feel sand between her toes at the beach. For Graham and me it was 'through leaves' to sit and stare at the variegated maple tree we'd bought as a sapling that later towered over our pocket-sized garden, its white and green leaves breezily waving a greeting like the royal family on the Buck House balcony; to eat perfectly cooked al dente broccoli and comment each and every time how delicious, and uncannily like butter, it tasted, and to lie in bed last thing at night and burst into a fit of uncontrollable giggles we'd worry would wake – or alarm – the neighbours.

'Shhhhh!' I'd urge Graham, tears streaming down my face. 'The neighbours are going to think we're having some sort of fit.'

STILL RUNNING AFTER ALL THESE TEARS

'You shush!' Graham would reply, barely able to breathe, his full-body laughter causing our headboard to bang against the wall, giving our neighbours yet another thing to speculate on.

It was also 'through leaves' for Graham to say 'I'm proud of you!' every time I returned from a training run. Another running 'through leaves' was getting back from a run and performing our post-run stretches on our shagpile rug in the living room, all the while sipping steaming mugs of tea and moaning our heads off about how hard the run had been.

'I hate running,' Graham would groan.

'I hate it more,' I'd reply.

'I hate it most,' he'd say with a grin, trumping me in an inversion of the verbal exchange we often also used:

'I love you.'

'I love you more.'

'I love you most.'

I also derived immense pleasure from never using my own front-door key when Graham was home, cherishing the way my heart swelled with love when I heard his footsteps in the hallway as he came to let me in. Then there were the magic words Graham often uttered late at night when he thought I'd been overdoing it: 'Stop working and come and drink wine with your hubs.' This was one of our very favourite 'through leaves' moments. I'd switch off my computer while Graham turned off the telly, and then we'd settle companionably into our respective corners of the sofa, bucket-sized wine glasses in hand, and chat about niff-naff and trivia, everything and nothing, ranging from the untrustworthiness of politicians ('How do you know a politician is lying? His lips are moving') to extremely contentious topics such as 'What's the world's cutest small furry animal?' After much heated debate, Graham had voted for raccoons, cheeky-chappie animals that, like him, loved getting up to mischief, whereas I'd settled on big-eyed bushbabies, simply because they are adorable.

Perhaps the absolute best 'through leaves' for me, however, was spending weekend mornings in bed drinking tea with Graham. He'd often attempt to multitask by getting up and putting away laundry but I'd always say: 'This is my favourite part of the week: sit down and talk to me.'

Graham and I were looking forward to the next three decades together which I envisaged being full of moments like these, along with many more backpacking and camping trips and the odd marathon. We didn't hanker after fame and fortune. All we asked for was something very simple: to be able to grow old together. Was that really going to be snatched away from us?

Running the 56-mile Comrades Marathon taught us stamina and perseverance…

… and to laugh at ourselves

Hopeful words on the way to a hospital appointment

Chapter 4
The 'C' word and the 'D' word

♪♪ Mood music: *Eye of the Tiger* by Survivor
The song that reflects Graham's determination to survive against all odds

Death moved in with Graham and me the year I turned 50. And he was the houseguest from hell. The kind of visitor who arrives uninvited, wipes his arse on your towels, pees on your carpets, pukes on your pillow, writes his name in excrement on your walls and plays banging Death Metal music that wrecks your sleep till 5am. While we'd been appalled by the dismissive doctor who'd only warned Graham not to fly once we specifically asked about it, nothing could have prepared us for what happened when we returned to the same green-tinged room to hear Graham's prognosis. Until that point, we'd still been hoping that Graham had TB and had joked how weird it was to be wishing he had an illness that, if left untreated, kills over half of its victims.

Pushing open the door, I mentally adopted the brace position. Much to our relief, the stony-faced doctor had been replaced by a kindly white-haired consultant.

'How much have they told you?' he asked after inviting us to take a seat.

'Not much,' said Graham, shifting uncomfortably in his plastic chair.

STILL RUNNING AFTER ALL THESE TEARS

After knocking on the door, a nurse let herself in. 'Couldn't she have waited till we'd finished speaking with the doctor?' I thought with annoyance.

'I'm sorry to have to tell you that it's malignant pleural mesothelioma, a type of lung cancer caused by exposure to asbestos,' said the doctor, ignoring the nurse. I looked over at Graham. He was dumbstruck and staring at the doctor in disbelief. A nauseous feeling surged through my body as the desk and piles of medical files seemed to expand in my vision, as if someone was playing with a zoom lens that brought certain objects much closer and into sharp focus. The doctor kept on talking but he sounded different, as if he was speaking through a periscope.

'How long has Graham got?' I eventually plucked up the courage to ask.

'Eighteen months to five years.' I wanted to vomit. That single sentence obliterated our entire future. We'd intended spending at least another 30 years together but now there would be no retirement, no sharing of knee rugs, no staying in hostels while backpacking in our 70s. In fact, we might not even get to celebrate our 30th wedding anniversary in three years' time.

The nurse led us to another room and pressed a sheaf of leaflets into our hands.

'I'm Denise,' she said. 'Do you have any questions?'

'Could I have surgery?' asked Graham in a croaking whisper.

'Yes,' said Denise, 'they can remove the cancerous lung.'

My heart sank as I pictured Graham in a wheelchair, unable to breathe.

'Does that mean I'll be disabled?'

'No, strangely most people function almost as well with one lung as they do with two,' she said, smiling encouragingly.

THE 'C' WORD AND THE 'D' WORD

As we stood up to leave, Denise placed a reassuring hand on my arm and threw us a crumb of hope: 'I know loads of people with mesothelioma who've lived longer than five years. Can I give you a hug?' Tearfully, we both embraced her.

I wouldn't be here today if we'd done what we intended to do in the dark days after Graham's diagnosis. I'd been traumatised by the death of my sparrow-like, 93-year-old neighbour Ivy, who one minute was jokingly telling me how 'disgusting' it was that she'd lived to such a ripe old age, and the next was hospitalised after a massive stroke. Ivy had been put on the now discredited Liverpool Care Pathway where the terminally ill were denied food and water, and when Graham and I returned from a two-week holiday to South Africa, she was still alive, and didn't die for another week (don't ask me how she survived without water for all that time, all I know is that she did). A storyline in *Brookside*, in which a character faced murder charges for smothering his terminally ill mother-in-law to death when she begged him to help her die, was also etched indelibly on my mind. In desperation, Mick had bought Gladys heroin from drug dealers to ease her agonising cancer pain after her doctor failed to prescribe sufficient morphine. In a soap that had included a child molester buried under the patio, incest, a sex-crazed cult and police sieges, these scenes were the most harrowing I'd ever watched. Would Graham be dehydrated and starved to death like our friend Ivy? Would I be forced to break the law to get him enough pain relief? Would I face the agonising dilemma of helping Graham to die if he asked me to?

Back then I knew nothing about dying. Sudden death, like when my mother was killed, yes. But terminal illness and end-of-life care? Nothing at all. With only these two tragic examples of appalling palliative care to go by, I raised the subject with Graham a couple of days after he'd got his diagnosis.

'We need to talk about what we'll do if the pain becomes unbearable,' I said.

'I don't want to die in pain,' said Graham so quietly I could barely hear him.

'I know. I'd never let that happen.'

'You may not have a choice.'

'I read a book about euthanasia once,' I responded. 'There was something in it about suffocating yourself with a plastic bag.'

'Not being able to breathe is my biggest fear,' said Graham.

'Mine, too,' I said. 'But I'm sure it had some other useful information in it – that can't be the only way to die painlessly.'

We sat in silence for a little while, tears trickling down our cheeks. I simply couldn't imagine life without Graham. I'd loved him since I was a teenager. For close on three decades, he'd been my best friend, cheerleader, counsellor, travel buddy and reluctant running companion. I'd grown up with him by my side, how could I grow old without him?

'If you go, I'll go with you,' I sobbed. Graham didn't say anything. He knew exactly what I meant as, strangely, suicide had for many years been joked about in his family. In fact, the first time I heard about Beachy Head wasn't when I signed up for the gruelling off-road marathon that's held there every year, it was when Graham's dad proclaimed at a summer barbecue: 'If I ever go senile, I'm going to commit suicide by driving over Beachy Head.'

'Don't you dare do that, Dad,' Graham had joked. 'I want to inherit your Merc, so you'll have to walk and throw yourself off the cliff instead.'

THE 'C' WORD AND THE 'D' WORD

I remember finding this 'banter' about suicide really unsettling, even if it was spoken mostly in jest, little knowing this was something we, too, would contemplate one day. In the event, when he developed heart failure at the age of 72, Graham's dad passed away peacefully after a two-week stay in hospital, though for the entire fortnight Graham lived in fear of his father asking him to help end his life.

For several weeks, as I lay in bed trying to get to sleep, I wrestled with the practicalities of a suicide pact, my preliminary research having shown that achieving a painless death was a lot harder than I'd realised. In many cases, those who attempted to take their own lives ended up with zero quality of life when their failed attempts left them with liver failure or brain damage. TV crime dramas had shown us, too, how shocking it was for those who discovered the bodies of people who'd taken their own lives: we couldn't allow anyone we loved to experience something as horrific as that. But if we told friends what we were about to do, would they try to stop us? And would they be implicated in our deaths if they knew our intentions and did nothing?

'While there's life, there's hope,' said Cicero. And, we found, the reverse was just as true: while there's hope, there's life. Hope, Graham and I discovered, was the only thing strong enough to inspire us to keep on living. Graham's diagnosis was the equivalent of falling overboard from a cruise ship in the middle of the shark-infested Pacific. We had the option to exhaust ourselves by keeping on paddling for as long as we could in the – perhaps vain – hope of rescue, or we could stop swimming and sink beneath the waves almost immediately, sparing ourselves a lot of suffering in the process. Our suicide-pact discussion indicated we were both leaning towards the latter option, when we were tossed a lifebuoy.

I found an article called 'The Median Isn't the Message' by the evolutionary biologist Stephen Jay Gould. Back in 1982, Stephen was diagnosed with peritoneal mesothelioma – the same cancer as Graham's, except his affected the lining of his abdomen, not his lungs – and was appalled to discover his illness had a median mortality of only eight months after it was discovered. Most people would interpret that to mean 'I will probably be dead in eight months,' but with his training in statistics, Stephen knew that the median is simply the middle value in a range, and therefore that half of the people with his type of cancer would live longer than that. When he evaluated his chances of being in his preferred half, he concluded they were excellent: 'I was young; my disease had been recognised in a relatively early stage; I would receive the nation's best medical treatment; I had the world to live for; I knew how to read the data properly and not despair,' he wrote. The hairs on the back of my neck stood on end: except for the bit about being able to read data properly and not despair, I may as well have been reading about Graham.

Nervously, I Googled Stephen's name to find out how valid his optimistic assessment of his chances had proved to be. By how much had he managed to outlive his expiry date? At first, I thought I'd made a mistake with the maths, but then it hit me: he'd lived for 20 *years*, not months, after being given eight months to live. Imagine if he'd given in to despair and killed himself. He'd have needlessly shortened his life by two decades and not written the dozens of books he became world-renowned for.

Stephen stressed the importance of attitude, which he theorised influenced the immune system: 'In general, those with positive

THE 'C' WORD AND THE 'D' WORD

attitudes, with a strong will and purpose for living, with commitment to struggle, and with an active response to aiding their own treatment and not just a passive acceptance of anything doctors say tend to live longer,' he wrote. I couldn't believe it: in our darkest hour, I'd been given a detailed action plan. Graham and I never mentioned what we'd spoken of again, and even Dignitas, the Swiss clinic providing doctor-assisted suicide, never came up. In fact, 'dying' and 'Dignitas' became the second and third forbidden 'D' words in our home, joining our other long-standing prohibition on the word 'divorce'.

When I desperately needed a rock to cling to in the tempest that had just engulfed our lives, my thoughts turned not to family or friends, as few of them had any experience of cancer, but running. I realised the skillset marathons had given me translated into a DIY toolkit I could use in this latest, terrifying challenge. When I'd run my first half marathon, full marathon and ultra, I'd read every book and magazine I could lay my hands on to help me prepare, so I knew the answer would lie in research, something I, as a journalist, and Graham, as a research analyst, excelled at. With a thoroughly researched plan in place, much like a training schedule, Graham and I would know where we were going and, more importantly, the steps it would take to get there.

The most terrifying thing about cancer, I realised, is that it robs you of control. Hospitals can suddenly summon you to appointments, keep you waiting for hours, prod, poke and puncture your skin, slice you open, inject you with toxic chemicals and blast you with radiation, all with your gun-to-your-head 'consent'. Graham and I most definitely had what Stephen

STILL RUNNING AFTER ALL THESE TEARS

Jay Gould called a 'commitment to struggle', but if we were to cultivate 'an active response' to helping Graham's treatment and not passively accept everything the doctors said, we'd need to arm ourselves with facts. Accordingly, the first cancer book I purchased was the optimistically titled *Surviving Mesothelioma and Other Cancers* by Paul Kraus, the world's longest-surviving mesothelioma patient. As a primer on how to navigate a terminal-illness diagnosis it was invaluable, especially in its advice to 'accept the diagnosis but reject the prognosis' and not allow negative thoughts to contaminate our mindset.

The second thing that running had taught Graham and me was stamina. Perseverance. Endurance. There hadn't been a single race where I hadn't thought of quitting, but I'd never not finished, unless I'd been badly injured or chucked off the course for being too slow. Even when my toes blistered up badly right at the start of my first Comrades as a result of wearing three pairs of socks, I'd gone on to finish the 56-mile race with a grin on my face. Graham, in finishing Comrades twice despite being a self-confessed 'running hater', was the same. By heck, we could do this thing!

And finally, the biggest lesson that running had taught us was that it equips you for the vicissitudes of life. As the late, great South African two-time Comrades winner Lindsay Weight so eloquently wrote about death in her blog, but which is equally applicable to getting a terminal diagnosis: 'When I think of the sadness and the pain that comes with death, I realise that as runners we are very privileged to have a way of coping. We can run and be alone and live with our thoughts and fears and pain because we've done that many times in races. We know how to focus, to distract, to accept fatigue and pain as inevitable but transient. We have learned to cope mentally with the unknown and the uncomfortable and to

THE 'C' WORD AND THE 'D' WORD

keep looking towards the finish, knowing that it ends, it always ends.'

I knew that no matter how bad I felt during a race, that feeling was never permanent. Bad times simply don't last for ever, as Lindsay observed. Neither do good ones, sadly. Positive self-talk and visualisations, mantras, distraction and connecting with other runners had all propelled me across countless finish lines. I would dust off these strategies and use them again in this challenging journey where we didn't know the distance, but we did know the terrifying end point.

In *The Shawshank Redemption,* Tim Robbins' character, wrongly sentenced to life imprisonment for the murder of his wife and her lover, memorably talked about how he and his buddy, played by fellow lifer Morgan Freeman, had a stark choice: whether to focus on living or focus on dying while spending the remainder of their lives in prison. Graham and I realised we had to stop thinking about death and instead start making the most of the time he had left to live. Which is why, unlike the poor woman we read about who, on hearing she had a terminal illness, went home and threw all her clothes in a skip, Graham defiantly rushed off to TK Maxx and bought himself half a dozen flamboyant patterned shirts, including one festooned with flamingos, along with two stunning Orla Kiely duvet sets. It was his way of proving he was getting busy living. And that we were going to treat cancer as a word, not a sentence.

In the New Forest coming to terms with the dreadful news of Graham's cancer diagnosis

Chapter 5
Wanted: lab rat

♪♪ **Mood music: *Not Afraid* by Eminem**
Actually, we were

One to four years; 12 to 21 months; four to 18 months. Every website I went onto while researching Graham's treatment options revealed an even bleaker prognosis. 'Two in 100 people diagnosed with mesothelioma in England survive their disease for ten years or more,' reported Cancer Research UK. What's more, when I researched what were referred to as the latest 'promising' drug trials, I discovered they extended patients' lives by weeks or months, not years. Without exception, mesothelioma was described as 'aggressive', 'devastating' or 'deadly' – the disease equivalent of a rabid dog. Or a tornado. I took on the task of confronting these soul-destroying statistics single-handedly, something I found terrifying, as I wanted to shield Graham as much as possible from the horrifying information that kept cropping up.

I have to admit I often put off doing the research as I dreaded it so much, but one day I made a huge breakthrough about whether or not Graham needed to have his whole lung removed while working on, of all things, *The Official Ferrari Magazine*. I'd been hired as a freelance sub-editor despite the fact I'd confessed I knew next to nothing about cars and found it hard to distinguish my windscreen wipers from my indicators.

'Don't worry,' said the editor, Jason Barlow, a former *Top Gear* presenter who owned half a Ferrari ('I always say I own the bit with the engine in it,' he once said in an interview). 'All of us are petrol-heads so we'll be able to pick up most of the errors. We just need you to fact check and fit the copy.'

And so I found myself in the world of supercars, Kimi Räikkönen, Sebastian Vettel, Maranello and the Prancing Horse logo, astonished that any car could cost the equivalent of half our house.

When I reported for work a week into my contract, I was still in shock from Graham's diagnosis and thought it best to inform my colleagues about what had happened.

'If you find me crying in the loos it's because my husband's just been told he has lung cancer,' I told Jason. 'It won't be because of anything anyone here has said or done.'

'If you find *me* crying in the loos, it'll probably be because of something someone here has said or done,' he joked kindly.

One morning I found myself with nothing to do as the copy I'd been hired to edit would only be arriving that afternoon so, with my boss's blessing, I steeled myself and began to research Graham's surgery options. In much the same way as I'd previously spent hours researching wish-list marathons I hoped to run abroad, I'd spent every spare minute of the past couple of weeks desperately trying to gain clarity on whether it was indeed necessary to remove Graham's entire lung. Each article and research paper I read seemed to contradict the previous one, so I decided to assess the credibility of each piece of information and compile a spreadsheet listing my findings. Mesothelioma.com and Asbestos.com? Probably not the best sources, I decided, as these sites were sponsored by American law firms that were perhaps likely to encourage the pursuit of expensive treatments requiring their equally expensive legal services. Cancer Research UK and the American Cancer Society? Credible charities, so worth taking seriously.

WANTED: LAB RAT

On and on I went, methodically clicking through to different websites, feeling sick whenever I encountered yet another dismal life-expectancy estimation. Once I'd typed everything up, I printed out my spreadsheet and rushed down to the basement, where the toilets were located and where staff often went if they wanted to make private phone calls.

'Hi my love, it's me,' I said breathlessly to Graham. 'I know *exactly* what operation you need to have. The latest research shows it's only necessary to remove the outer lining of your lung – you don't have to have your whole lung removed after all.'

At that moment, Jason stepped out from the stairwell on his way to the toilets. Startled, I dropped the printouts I was holding.

'I'm just chatting to my husband,' I said, blushing guiltily – even though I knew full well I'd done nothing wrong – as he handed me the sheets of paper he'd scooped up off the floor. Jason smiled a wordless, encouraging smile. I knew he'd seen what was on the printouts, and that they had absolutely nothing to do with V8 engines or Formula One, but I also knew he understood.

'Who in their right mind would design a room like this?' I thought as Graham and I sat nervously in the hospital's circular waiting area, which wasn't so much a waiting room as a mental torture chamber. Like one of those dreadful in-the-round comedy shows where the audience sits facing each other, forcing them to experience not only their own terror at the thought of being singled out or hauled onstage, but the squirming embarrassment of their fellow comedy-goers, too. The building itself was no better: I'd expected a gleaming glass-and-chrome edifice but instead we walked into a drab building that looked like the municipal offices of a down-at-heel seaside town. I mentally gave the architect F for effort, and myself an A, as I'd got dressed up specially for the appointment in a smart outfit, full make-up and hellishly uncomfortable patent-leather shoes in which I could barely hobble. I practically sleep in trainers, but Sophie Sabbage's book *The Cancer Whisperer*, another of the books I'd purchased and found particularly helpful, made me realise that in order for Graham and me to put ourselves on an equal footing (pun intended) with the doctors, we needed to dress the part. Sophie, who was diagnosed with stage four terminal lung cancer at 48, shared how she'd always worn something fabulous to her oncology appointments. When I worked at *Cosmopolitan* magazine in the 1980s, I used to scoff at power dressing, but I could now see Sophie's point: we needed to impress upon the oncologists that we were equal partners in Graham's treatment, not submissive patients who'd let them make all the decisions, and we weren't going to do that wearing scruffy jogging bottoms or mud-spattered trail shoes.

Directly opposite us, slumped in a chair equally as uncomfortable as mine, sat an emaciated woman holding her head despairingly in her hands. A sallow-skinned 20-something woman next to her, eyebrow-less and wearing a headscarf, nervously played with a silver necklace that spelled out her name. A man, whom I assumed was her partner, was holding her hand and staring miserably at the floor. Each time one of the doors leading to the consultation rooms opened like the lid of a red box on *Deal or No Deal* there'd be a collective intake of breath as everyone wondered whether it was their turn to have their fate revealed by the white-coated medics.

Our wait gave me time to reflect on how much our lives had changed since I'd heard the words 'suspicious cells'. One minute I'd been daydreaming about what 'bucket list' races I still wanted

WANTED: LAB RAT

to do with Graham – the Cambridge Half Marathon, Florence Marathon and Two Oceans ultramarathon in South Africa had all been contenders – but now the words 'bucket list' had taken on an entirely different meaning, one devoid of joy and tinged with dread. My thrice-weekly runs had been replaced with frantic cancer research: nothing mattered except getting Graham the very best treatment and I felt that I didn't have a second to waste.

Twenty minutes later, we were led into an empty, windowless room and took our seats on a pair of plastic chairs sandwiched between two examination couches. More minutes ticked by. I wondered what was worse: avoiding eye contact with the cancer patients outside or staring at a blank wall. My anxiety was heightened by the fact that we'd decided to make a covert audio recording of all our medical consultations after our previous disastrous encounter with the doctor who said there were no dos and don'ts – another tip I'd gleaned from my reading – but decided not to reveal this to the medics in case they refused us permission to do so. (I was unaware then, that it's perfectly legal under British law to do so, and that the British Medical Association advises doctors not to decline such requests.)

Eventually an oncologist arrived and I scrambled to push the record button on my phone. Pale faced and clean shaven, with shoulder-length raven hair, he resembled Severus Snape, the Potions Master played by Alan Rickman in the *Harry Potter* movies. Although he looked extremely serious, it was hard to take him seriously as he'd taken a seat on one of the examination couches, so his legs dangled from it like a child's on a playground swing.

'So you were recently diagnosed with mesothelioma,' he said in a super-cheerful voice, as casually as if he were telling Graham he had bunions. Or a bad case of flatulence.

STILL RUNNING AFTER ALL THESE TEARS

'Yes,' said Graham.

After a brief discussion of Graham's medical history and symptoms, Severus dropped a bombshell: 'Normally there are very few, rare situations in which surgery would be considered for the stage of the cancer you've got. Based on the appearances of your CT scan, we'd usually offer you chemotherapy alone.'

My stomach lurched. I knew that patients who'd had surgery had by far the longest survival times, but that surgeons wouldn't operate if a patient's cancer had already spread to other parts of their body. We hadn't been told what stage Graham's cancer was at – whether it was just in the lining of his lung or had metastasised elsewhere – so from what the doctor had said I assumed the worst. Horrifyingly, Graham's cancer must have been too far gone for them to offer him surgery. But then, as the doctor kept on speaking, and I continued taking notes, it became clear that *he* didn't know what Graham's staging was either. In fact, Severus had to pop outside to check. What's more, he didn't know whether a surgeon had or hadn't been present when Graham's case was discussed by the medical team, demonstrating clearly that his categorical statement that surgery would be inappropriate was not based on all the factual evidence.

Graham explained that we'd done our research and that he couldn't understand why they wouldn't offer surgery, as well as chemotherapy and radiotherapy, as people who'd had all three appeared to live the longest.

'Surgery isn't evidence based,' countered Severus. 'The researchers are probably picking their patients really carefully. They include the very fit patients where they've had really good results and ignore the patients who did really badly. But,' he added, 'if you sign up for our clinical trial – where half the patients get randomly selected by a computer to have surgery and chemo and half get only chemo – we can still consider surgery.'

Repeatedly Graham and I tried to discuss surgery, and time and time again the oncologist returned to the clinical trial. We just couldn't fathom why he couldn't understand our logic: Graham was a young, fit, otherwise healthy runner and therefore, if anyone was going to do well by having surgery, the chances were it would be him. As the symptoms can take several decades to develop, most people with mesothelioma are elderly, and so are more likely to have other illnesses, making surgery more risky. In fact, for many, a mesothelioma diagnosis wouldn't actually shorten their lives as they'd have a fair chance of dying in the next five years anyway.

Throughout our discussion I remembered to use the assertive questioning technique I teach my hypnobirthing couples. It's handily summarised by the catchphrase 'use your BRAINS', where B stands for asking about the Benefits of a treatment, R represents the Risks, A stands for Alternatives, I for Intuition (what do you intuitively feel is the best course of action?), N stands for what would happen if you did Nothing and S stands for Smile, as building a collaborative relationship with your caregivers is essential. It was a really useful way to keep the discussion on track.

'I can't believe how hard that oncologist tried to convince us to sign up for that trial,' said Graham, holding my hand as I hobbled back to the car. 'If we hadn't done our research, I'm sure he'd have persuaded us.'

'I know,' I said. 'It seemed his main goal was recruiting enough trial participants. He was treating you like a lab rat.'

A few days later, we were summoned back to the hospital, where a friendly nurse we hadn't met before greeted us.

STILL RUNNING AFTER ALL THESE TEARS

'Hi, I'm Judith, one of the clinical nurse specialists,' she said. 'I believe you're here to give consent for the clinical trial?'

Graham and I looked at each other in disbelief.

'No,' said Graham, 'we told the oncologist we wanted to explore the surgery option.'

The nurse looked puzzled. 'Well that's what I was told.'

Just then Severus strolled in.

'Hi Graham and Lisa,' he said. 'How are you?'

'Fine,' said Graham. 'But Judith is under the mistaken impression that we're here to give consent for the clinical trial and we never agreed to that.'

'Oh yeah, sorry about that,' said Severus unconvincingly and way too quickly. 'There must have been some mistake. I'm sorry for wasting your time.'

We'd both taken the day off work, so I was seething, especially as my feet were killing me after I'd once again limped across acres of car-park tarmac in my shiny 'torture shoes'. Did that oncologist really think we'd instantly cave in when confronted with a clipboard and a consent form?

'You didn't waste our time,' said Graham graciously. 'We got to meet Judith, so that was a great use of our time.'

'No it fucking wasn't,' I said. To myself.

A smartly attired oncologist with dark, curly hair towered over us from her unsteady perch on the examination couch when we returned to the hospital for the third time the following week.

'I'd want you to start chemotherapy immediately,' she said, brushing a curl from her cheek. 'If you have surgery, you'll have half the cycles before it, and half afterwards.'

WANTED: LAB RAT

'That doesn't make sense to me,' said Graham. 'Wouldn't it be best to remove the tumours first, while I'm strong enough to survive a six-hour operation, and then have the chemo afterwards?'

'No,' she snapped impatiently. 'We need to know how you'll respond to the chemotherapy.'

'And what if Graham doesn't respond?' I asked. 'Are there other types of chemo you could try?'

'No, there aren't,' she replied. So what was the point of 'testing out' the chemo, I wondered?

'What are your views on Ukrain?' I plucked up the courage to ask, referring to an anti-cancer drug I'd read about that was developed by a Ukrainian scientist and was said to boost immunity and kill cancer cells while leaving healthy cells unscathed.

'Ukrain? What are *your* views on Ukrain?' she said sarcastically, raising an eyebrow. 'Why on earth would we use a drug that's not tested properly when we can use ones that have been thoroughly trialled and that can give you years of extended life?'

'I hated the way she answered a question with a question,' Graham said afterwards.

'Indeed. I wouldn't dare ask her any more – she's like a terrifying headmistress,' I said, feeling like a slapped child.

Thankfully our next consultation – this time with the thoracic surgeon who'd previously carried out Graham's biopsy – was a lot more amicable.

'I remember operating on you, Graham,' he said kindly. 'I'm just so damn sorry that it turned out to be cancer.'

I immediately warmed to this floppy-haired, bespectacled surgeon who treated Graham as a person, not merely a patient, and could immediately see why Graham thought so highly of him.

We discussed Graham's medical history and the biopsy results.

STILL RUNNING AFTER ALL THESE TEARS

'I've looked at your notes and I'm willing to operate on you,' said the surgeon. 'I think we need to throw everything – and the kitchen sink – at your cancer. I've done a few of these procedures before: the last one was six months ago, and then I did another three months before that. However, I have to warn you that it's an incredibly complicated operation: removing the lining of the lung is like peeling the skin off a grape with a scalpel.' Graham and I both winced at this graphic description. 'And you need to know there's a two to four per cent mortality rate – that means your chance of dying during surgery or thirty days afterwards – though considering that you're an ultrarunner, I'd say you'd fall into the lower category.' I looked at Graham reassuringly. 'Whatever happens, you're going to have a shit Christmas, if you'll pardon my language.'

As I struggled to digest this news, the surgeon went on to say something that surprised me a great deal: 'There are no egos in medicine,' he told us, 'so I suggest you shop around before making a decision.'

'Your surgeon was just as lovely as you said he'd be,' I remarked to Graham as I limped back to our car, cursing the fact that despite owning a dozen pairs of trainers, I had only one pair of serviceable 'smart' shoes, and that they'd by now practically severed my Achilles tendons. 'I really, really liked him – in fact, I was tempted to invite him round for dinner – but I suspect that he was hinting strongly that there could be a better surgeon out there.'

'I knew you'd like him,' said Graham. 'What makes you say that he didn't feel up to the job?'

'It's just the way he stressed that he doesn't do that operation very often. And the way he said it was so difficult to do.'

'I disagree,' said Graham. 'I really don't think he was saying we'd be better off with a different surgeon.'

WANTED: LAB RAT

'Well he told us to shop around, so that's precisely what I'm going to do,' I said. 'I don't think he could have made it any clearer that there are better surgeons out there than he is, and I'm going to find them.'

Thumbs up before surgery

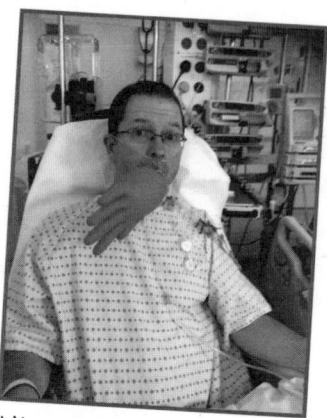
Joking around in ICU

Graham points out how the pain scale works

Dinner — with Graham's South African red wine prescription

Feeling victorious on Discharge Day

Chapter 6
'He had me at red wine'

♪♪ **Mood music: *Special Star* by Mango Groove**
The song that was a guiding light in Cancerland

'Am I being greedy?' Graham unexpectedly asked me on the drive back from the hospital.

'What do you mean?' I said.

'It's just that I've had such a rich, happy life already: I'm married to you, I'm doing a hobby I get paid for as a job, I've got fantastic family, friends and colleagues, I love our house and I've done pretty much everything I could possibly have wanted to do in life. I've already had much more than most people ever dream of. And yet I want more of the same.'

'Don't be ridiculous, Graham,' I said. 'Of course you want more, and so do I, even though I know I've also had an incredibly blessed life compared with lots of people. There isn't rationing on happiness you know: just because you've had a lot of it doesn't mean you can't have more, or that it's going to deprive others of joy. In fact, I *want* you to be greedy.'

When we got home, I immediately started searching for a holistic oncologist – someone happy to combine conventional medicine with complementary approaches – and an alternative surgeon. Despite knowing dozens of health journalists, I drew a blank on both, but then I stumbled across the website of a private mesothelioma clinic in London. I couldn't believe what I was reading: 'In more than 100 operations, no mortality occurred and there was a median overall survival of 32 months – one of the

STILL RUNNING AFTER ALL THESE TEARS

best ever reported in the field. After five years, more than a third of patients with epithelioid mesothelioma were alive.' Today, that clinic has closed, but at the time it felt like a lifeline. I raced downstairs to tell Graham but, much to my dismay, he wasn't keen to explore this option because he liked and trusted his original surgeon.

'I'm booking you an appointment – and I'll pay for it myself,' I insisted. 'Of course it's your decision, but I'm desperate to know what that clinic is doing differently.'

The surgeon who strode into the consulting room was smartly dressed in a charcoal suit and blue shirt and tie, and his blue eyes twinkled as he shook our hands.

'Graham, you are a mutant,' Professor Loïc Lang-Lazdunski declared in a wonderfully warm, French-accented voice after discussing Graham's diagnosis.

I let out an involuntary giggle, surprised that I felt able to laugh during a meeting where Graham's life was at stake.

'BAP1 is a gene that helps control cell growth but you have a BAP1 mutation meaning you're much more likely to get mesothelioma. There are various kinds of mesothelioma and, luckily, yours is epithelial, which responds best to treatment.'

The surgeon went on to give us lifestyle advice: 'I tell all my patients to have two oranges and a lemon blended in a liquidiser every day,' he smiled. 'I drink that myself. You also need to keep running, and drink red wine – about half a litre – daily. Garlic is also good, as is Turkey Tail, a type of mushroom supplement. Happiness is also very important: spend time with the people you love, do some meditation and, most importantly, reduce your stress.'

'HE HAD ME AT RED WINE'

Graham and I looked at each other in amazement: this was the first time anyone had mentioned anything other than the standard 'cut, burn, poison' approach. I smiled at the mention of garlic and red wine, wondering whether they'd been added to the mix because the surgeon was French.

'What I suggest is that we operate as soon as possible, and that you have chemo and radiotherapy after that.'

'But at the hospital we were told categorically that I had to have half the chemo before the operation and the rest afterwards,' countered Graham.

'No, I don't agree,' Professor Lang-Lazdunski said gently. 'Does that make sense to you?'

'No!' Graham and I both almost shouted in unison. 'I told the oncologist that didn't seem logical,' said Graham.

'It isn't,' continued the surgeon. 'And trying to get you onto that clinical trial doesn't make sense either. You're a young, healthy ultrarunner and it's obvious that surgery will give you the best possible chance of longer survival. I believe it's not appropriate to let a computer decide whether you have the operation or not. You have almost all of the prognostic factors associated with a good outcome from having the lining of your lung surgically removed. It's obviously your decision but I think it would be unethical not to offer you surgery followed by radiotherapy and chemotherapy.'

'How many of these operations have you done?' I asked.

'About two hundred,' he said. 'If anything goes wrong and there are complications, I've seen it many times before and can easily fix it. That's the other problem with this trial – they're using surgeons and doctors who aren't very experienced at this type of very complex surgery. They only have to have performed it a minimum of five times to be eligible to participate.'

'Do you offer surgery on the NHS?' asked Graham.

'I'm afraid not. I left the NHS in 2014.'

'How much would the operation cost?'

'Including the ten-day hospital stay, about twenty-five thousand pounds.'

Although this was a huge sum, we'd recently been given money by the government to aid those diagnosed with an asbestos-related disease, so we could afford it. My heart, my mind and every cell in my body was screaming 'Yes! Yes! Yes!' We'd finally found The One: someone I felt comfortable enough to laugh with, someone who wanted to empower Graham to take control of his own health, someone with the same courageous, can-do attitude we had. I didn't even look at Graham before speaking: 'We'd like to ask you to do the operation,' I said.

When I turned to face Graham, I wasn't sure how he'd feel about my impulsive decision. We had a rule in our house that neither one of us could buy so much as a scatter cushion or rug without the express approval of the other, let alone agree to expensive, life-changing lung surgery.

'Oh, Lisa,' was all Graham said with a grateful sigh.

Back in the crisp autumn air, we took a walk along the Thames, watching the sunlight reflected on the flowing water, as if shoals of glittering fish were skimming along just below its surface. I realised then that we'd been given three things that day: a date for Graham's surgery and a list of things he could do to aid his recovery, but most importantly, hope. 'Hope is one of the most precious drugs doctors have at their disposal,' the neurosurgeon Henry Marsh would later write in his wonderful book *And Finally* after being diagnosed with late-stage prostate cancer.

'You didn't mind me booking him without consulting you first?' I asked.

'HE HAD ME AT RED WINE'

'To be honest, Lisa,' said Graham with a gap-toothed grin I hadn't seen for weeks, 'he had me at red wine!'

On the day of his surgery, Graham sprinkled himself with unicorn poo. Or rather, that's what the tinkling Koshi wind chimes we'd strung up over our bed sounded like when he banged his head on them while springing out of bed. The sound was so joyous it lifted both of our spirits and gave me hope that the operation would go well. In the weeks since his diagnosis, Graham had got himself as fit as possible, both mentally and physically, by doing two half marathons and running laps of Ashburton Park near our Croydon home. Prof Lang-Lazdunski had been impressed by his efforts, saying the endorphins this released would boost his immune system. Graham was seemingly less keen, however, on my other endorphin-releasing idea: having sex every day until his operation. 'Can't I just wank into a hanky?' he'd asked jokingly.

After accompanying Graham to the hospital, I tenderly kissed his naked belly and back before taking my leave. On my way out, I saw Professor Hope, as I'd rechristened Prof Lang-Lazdunski, almost jauntily walking towards Graham's room, a leather satchel slung across his back, exuding such an air of confidence that I was able to leave the hospital without feeling the least bit anxious. Seven hours later, I returned. This time I was shown to the basement ICU where I was surprised to see a weakly smiling Graham, in a bay containing four beds, looking pale but otherwise well, considering he'd spent almost the entire day under anaesthesia. Prof Hope, his eyes bloodshot from the six-hour operation, informed me that he'd also found some cancer in Graham's oesophagus and diaphragm, but had managed to remove most of it. My stomach lurched at this news, but I told myself I'd worry about that later if it ever became a problem. I was only supposed to visit for ten minutes but when the staff saw all I wanted to do was sit with Graham while he slept, they let me stay with him for a couple of hours.

The very next day, Graham, while still attached to his drains, and sporting a 15cm-long stapled-shut scar, started doing slow and painful laps of the shiny linoleum corridor outside the ICU, which also happened to lead to the staff restaurant. Up and down he shuffled, past noticeboards festooned with photos of the hospital staff dancing and posing for tongues-out photos at a staff party. It was odd seeing nurses we recognised merrily draped across the shoulders of their colleagues like human feather boas, but we found these images immensely amusing. Whatever target he'd been set, Graham was determined to exceed it, until a physio rushed from her office warning that overdoing it could damage his heart. My own heart skipped a beat when she said that, but Graham was undeterred.

'Just one more lap? I promise that'll be it,' he begged, ever the impatient patient eager to do all he could to get well.

The next day I returned to the hospital and found that Graham had been moved to a private room. Exhausted by my commute up to central London, I asked the hospital if I could hire a camp bed, which was duly installed under the window next to Graham's bed, so that I could remain by his side 24/7. That night I curled up on it and listened to the gurgling of the pumps draining fluid from his lungs. It felt strangely soothing, like falling asleep inside an aquarium. Determined to follow Prof Hope's instructions to the letter, that evening Graham and I shared a bottle of South African red wine at dinnertime.

'HE HAD ME AT RED WINE'

'Let me see what you have bought with my prescription,' Prof Hope jested when he came to check how Graham was getting on the next day, turning over our empty bottle of Kanonkop Kadette so he could read the label. 'I went to a South African medical conference many years ago, so I know you have excellent wines. I met Chris Barnard – you know the South African surgeon who performed the world's first heart transplant? – on that trip, and two of my colleagues were mugged at the Cape Town Waterfront – one of them twice in a single day!'

'Cape Town is one of the most beautiful cities in the world – if not the *most* beautiful – but not many people know that it's also one of the most dangerous,' I said. 'Nyanga, a township on the Cape Flats just outside Cape Town, is the murder capital of South Africa. Your colleagues were lucky to have escaped with their lives.'

'This is like being on a cruise – they keep throwing food at us all day long,' said Graham happily as he tucked into his third crustless finger sandwich only two hours after having had lunch.

'They're trying to fatten you up,' I said, sitting on the chair next to his bed while nibbling on a macaroon he hadn't managed to wrestle away from me. 'Keep this up and you'll soon be outta here!'

During the day, while Graham was sleeping, I continued researching ways to help him. We'd already agreed that we would go for the 'marginal gains' approach adopted by the hugely successful British Cycling team at the 2012 Olympics: the theory went that if you improved everything about riding a bike by one per cent – such as wearing a wind-tunnel-tested riding suit, having a more comfy bike seat, and even handwashing to avoid illness – you'd gain a significant advantage when you put it all together.

Radical Remission by the researcher and psychotherapist Kelly A Turner was the book that became my bible during the quest for the marginal gains I hoped would enable Graham to become a medical miracle. Kelly studied over 1,500 instances of radical remission, where people recovered from cancer either without using conventional medicine, or after it had failed, and came up with nine factors all the cases had in common. These ranged from embracing social support, and radically overhauling their diet, to releasing suppressed emotions and increasing positive ones. Kelly would later say that exercise was the tenth factor (something we knew already) but explained that she'd omitted it from the book 'because many people are simply too weak to exercise when they first begin their healing journeys'. Reading Kelly's book was like taking tiny sips of courage every day, and I even recited the nine factors to myself just before falling asleep every night on my camp bed, which I found immensely comforting. My hospital lullaby.

The more I researched, the more I realised there were literally 1,001 things people claimed had helped them live longer or even cured them of cancer, some of which were legal, others that weren't, ranging from ketogenic or organic diets to mistletoe and cannabis, which was reported to result in cancer cell death but also to sometimes encourage the cancer cells to grow. Even though up to 40 per cent of people with cancer use complementary and alternative medicine, according to Cancer Research UK – and some hospitals even offer free acupuncture, reflexology, reiki, hypnotherapy and massage to patients undergoing treatment – I'd noticed people on cancer forums admitting they were lying to their oncologists about the complementary approaches they were taking. The common narrative was that Big Pharma knew of all kinds of cancer cures, such as mega-dosing with vitamin C but, as there was no money in them because they couldn't be patented, these 'cures' were being suppressed in favour of money-spinning drugs the big companies could make billions from. I could see the logic, but as a non-medic, I didn't want to do anything that could jeopardise Graham's health. I thought it scandalous that so many cancer patients didn't trust their doctors, but after our previous negative experiences, I could see why. Again I thanked our lucky stars that we'd found Prof Hope, who was open to exploring complementary options alongside the medical ones, and later never made us feel stupid when we ran ideas past him (even the more woo-and-wacky ones). In the years following Graham's operation, we learned to trust him more and more with each conversation and his word became law: if Prof Hope said no, it was a hard no, but one that, we knew, was inspired by a genuine concern for Graham, not one where he was scoring an ego point or treating Graham like a statistic. Prof Hope's words 'We must remain humble in the face of this disease,' had assured us of that.

'This is one of the biggest operations you can ever have,' a nurse called Georgia, whose own grandfather had died of mesothelioma, told a trainee nurse four days after Graham's surgery. 'It's bigger than open-heart surgery. But Graham looks amazing – he's exceptional – not all patients look this good so soon after their operation.'

Two days later, the anaesthesia had worn off enough for Graham to finally do a bowel movement. As he couldn't be unhooked from his drains, I fetched a kidney dish and locked the door to give him some privacy. The resulting stench was overpowering, and just as I was liberally spritzing the room with scented pillow spray, the only deodorising substance I could lay my hands on at such short notice, there was a loud hammering at the door.

'Open this immediately!' a muffled voice shouted. I rushed to unlock it and a furious nurse barged in.

'We have to have access to our patients at *all* times!' she ranted. 'Don't you ever, *ever* do that again!'

Afterwards, Graham and I began giggling at the thought of how lucky the nurse was that he'd been suffering from insomnia: without his sleep spray, she could easily have been gassed. Poo-gate most certainly cheered us up and helped us tick off one of Kelly's factors – increasing positive emotions – though we were sure it had had the opposite effect on Graham's enraged nurse. Twiddling each other's earlobes had a similar mood-boosting effect. I taught my hypnobirthing couples that nipple and earlobe stimulation released the feel-good hormone oxytocin during labour, so every evening Graham and I spent a few minutes doing this (just the earlobes, mind!), hoping we wouldn't be caught in the act by the nurses and wondering what we'd say if they walked in on us.

Finally, after ten days, it was time for us to be discharged and we tearfully bid farewell to the kindly nurses who'd taken care of Graham so well. When I saw the rows of thousands of tiny ticks marching like ants across the charts they'd had to fill in detailing all the medical checks they'd conducted day and night, I realised what a team effort it had been to get Graham to this point.

'HE HAD ME AT RED WINE'

'I don't want to blame anyone else if it's not done properly,' smiled Prof Hope, explaining why he'd insisted on removing Graham's stitches himself. I marvelled at the neatness of Graham's scar.

'I always tell my surgical students that they have to close up their patients very carefully,' Prof Hope told us as he gently unpicked the metal staples in Graham's back. 'It's the only bit of what we've done that the family ever gets to see. If we do a neat job on the outside, everyone's reassured that what we've done on the inside has been done properly, too.'

'When are you going to start taking out the staples?' asked Graham, wondering why Prof Hope was chatting away and not doing anything.

'I've just got one more to go,' said Prof Hope, laughing.

'Really? I didn't feel a thing,' said Graham.

After Graham had put his shirt back on, Prof Hope had some final advice for us. 'I want you to treat your mesothelioma as if you have a chronic disease like diabetes,' he said. 'It'll always be there, but you'll learn to live with it. Don't give up hope – there are lots of new treatments coming down the line. Many of my patients have lived way past their prognosis, remember that. Now go and live your life as normal.'

While those words gave us hope, I knew 'living our lives as normal' was going to be one of the hardest challenges we'd ever had to face. Because living life on Death Row was never going to be normal. Or easy.

Graham at an art class three weeks after his cancer operation

Happily the Christmas after Graham's surgery was far from shitty

Chapter 7
Choosing to live in hope, not fear

🎵 **Mood music: *The Way It Was* by The Killers**
The song that reminded us to enjoy life like we used to

'I'm scared, Lisa,' whispered Graham to me late one night as we lay in bed a week after we'd left hospital. I felt as if someone had reached into my chest and was squeezing the blood out of my heart. Graham always slept naked, and to feel his warm, vulnerable body next to mine in the dark brought to mind *Babes in the Wood*, the tale of two orphaned children who'd been abandoned in a forest and died of exposure before being covered with leaves by robins.

'I am, too, Graham, but we'll get through this together,' I whispered back, trying to find a way to give him courage that I wasn't sure I possessed myself. This was the first and only time Graham ever spoke openly of being afraid and I made him promise that if he ever experienced dark moments in the night, he'd wake me, no matter what time it was, and tell me about them. One of my greatest fears was him crying silently with no one to comfort him. It truly terrified me, and kept me awake at night.

The role of being Graham's protector was entirely new to me, though, on reflection we'd both been each other's tutors until that point. Graham had schooled me in philosophy (or rather, made a valiant attempt at doing so), how to drive (again, a daunting task as to this day I'm a white-knuckle driver), how to avoid 'knee-jerk reactions' (by responding calmly rather than reacting emotionally in challenging situations), and how to appreciate toilet humour ('I saw a sign today that made me wet myself. It said: "Toilets closed"' was the type of joke he taught me to enjoy). I'd taught him the value of thoughtful gifts and actions and that it was important to squeeze every last drop of living out of life by running marathons and backpacking as often as we could, even if that meant feeling exhausted because of all the planning it took – and the mountains of laundry it generated. Through the 27 years we'd been together, he'd always been my biggest cheerleader, telling me that of course I could realise my lifelong dreams of running Comrades and becoming an author 'because you're a stubborn so-and-so and always get what you want'. Now the roles were reversed, and I knew that I, as the healthy partner, would have to alternate between donning my boxing gloves and shaking my pom poms so I could repay all the protection and encouragement Graham had given me over the past three decades.

'I'm not yet ready to be pushed into a wigwam, smoke peyote and have hallucinations,' Graham warned me when I informed him that I was going to research every means possible to prolong his life.

'We'll see about that!' I replied.

Like the Gregorian calendar, the timeline of our lives had been split in two by a single, seismic event: BC (Before Cancer) and AD (After Diagnosis). In our AD life, I grieved for the carefree BC life we could never lead again. I often reflected that I now knew, first hand, the anguish, fear and sorrow Jesus felt in the Garden of Gethsemane shortly before his crucifixion when he prayed: 'O my Father, if it be possible, let this cup pass from me.' Every day I'd wake up, and for a few moments feel happy, until reality would suddenly wake up, too, smack me in the face and shout: 'GRAHAM'S GOT CANCER! YOU'RE GOING TO LOSE THE MOST PRECIOUS THING IN YOUR LIFE. GRAHAM'S GOING TO DIE!'

Despite Prof Hope's assurances, all was not well, Graham was not well, and unlike before, when we'd both been very content with our lives, we were now going to have to put in a helluva lot of work to be happy, because our minds had been infected with cancer and I didn't know if there was a cure. For many weeks after Graham's diagnosis, I awoke thinking about cancer, spent the day thinking about cancer, went to bed thinking about cancer and woke up in the night to think about cancer. I felt guilty doing anything that wasn't cancer related. How could I, in all conscience, enjoy crappy telly or read novels when I could be researching Graham's illness or watching educational YouTube videos? It was when Graham forlornly asked, after opening the door to yet another delivery of cancer tomes, 'How many more books are you going to read, Lisa?' that I realised how his illness had taken over not only Graham's life, but mine, too.

'Graham,' I said, my voice trembling with emotion, 'you're asking me to show you the way, but I don't know where to lead you. I've never done this before, so I need these books to guide me.'

Sophie Sabbage's book *The Cancer Whisperer* taught me many more things than avoiding wearing athleisure to oncology appointments. One of Sophie's most surprising assertions was that people diagnosed with terminal cancer often don't die from it, they die of *shock*. When I looked into it, I found research showing the risk of having a heart attack or stroke in the six months following a cancer diagnosis was more than *twice* that of people without cancer, which the researchers attributed to people undergoing cancer treatment having a substantially increased risk of developing blood clots in their veins. Nonetheless, I knew Graham and I were both moving through life like stunned fish so yes, the shock of his horrifyingly short life-expectancy prognosis needed to be addressed. During my hypnotherapy training, I'd studied Eye Movement Desensitisation and Reprocessing (EMDR), a technique that's often used to treat trauma survivors, so I asked Graham if he'd like to have a few sessions to see whether it would help. When something extremely traumatic happens, a part of your brain called the hippocampus sometimes doesn't process it like a normal memory and instead stores the memory in its raw, unprocessed form. This means the upsetting sights, sounds and feelings associated with the traumatic event can get stuck, almost like a video clip from a horror movie that keeps playing on loop making you relive the same overwhelming, negative emotions over and over again. The aim of EMDR is to help you reprocess that memory so that you're able to recall it without the intense emotions you experienced at the time. In Graham's case, we realised that the main source of his trauma was being told he had a maximum of five years left to live, so I asked Graham to recall that memory and identify the negative belief about himself associated with that while becoming aware of his thoughts and feelings. Next I asked him to follow my fingers as I moved them back and forth in front of his face. This bilateral stimulation is thought to enhance memory processing and is repeated until the memory feels much less distressing. After three sessions, Graham reported feeling a lot less fearful, and as a result, a lot more empowered.

CHOOSING TO LIVE IN HOPE, NOT FEAR

A second hypnotherapy technique I used with Graham was visualisation, during which Graham closed his eyes while I spoke to him in my low, slow, soft hypnotic voice while describing how his immune system was going to eradicate the cancer cells. Unlike some cancer thrivers who like to imagine themselves as Rambo shooting their cancer cells to death, we didn't use battle terminology. I'd read that talking about malignant cells 'invading' the body and patients 'bravely fighting' their illness was fear provoking and stress inducing as it made people feel they were under attack and that, if their disease progressed, they hadn't fought hard enough. I knew, too, that chronic stress can weaken your immune system, which plays a key role in killing cancer cells.

'We aren't going to *fight* the cancer, but *heal* it instead,' I told Graham. Just saying that out loud made me feel calmer. Instead of fighting a foe we couldn't see, we were going to nurture Graham back to health. In healing mode, Graham chose to see his immune system as foam that flowed over and covered his cancer, obliterating it completely, turning what had been something dark, sinister and malicious into healthy, positive whiteness.

'That sounds a bit like spunk,' I joked when he informed me of the metaphor he'd chosen.

'Thanks very much!' Graham responded indignantly. 'I'm not about to change this imagery as it works for me. The foam is life-giving, fluid and clings to all surfaces.'

'Hmm, a bit like spunk then...' I replied.

Another game-changing mindset shift took place when we came to the conclusion there was no point in asking 'Why us?' because the logical answer to that was 'Why *not* us?' Cancer isn't in the slightest bit picky or choosy: monk or millionaire, to it we are all the same. It was pointless trying to make the case that Graham didn't deserve to die young. Because who does?

STILL RUNNING AFTER ALL THESE TEARS

No matter what shit omelettes cancer threw at us, we vowed to be happy and positive. Haruki Murakami's book *What I Talk About When I Talk About Running* had mentioned the Buddhist saying: 'Pain is inevitable. Suffering is optional.' I knew this to be true of running, and realised it was equally applicable in our situation, too. While I couldn't end the pain, I knew there was something I could do about the mental suffering we were enduring. Graham and I had already sampled what it was like to live in fear, and hadn't much cared for it – discussing suicide had been the logical outcome of that – so now we took the decision to live in hope. We knew that if we didn't succeed at doing this, not only would cancer rob Graham of several decades of his life, but it would succeed in ruining the remaining precious time we had together. As Christopher '*Superman*' Reeve put it after considering suicide following a near-fatal riding accident that left him paralysed: 'Once you choose hope, anything's possible.'

There's a lot of talk about 'toxic positivity' these days: a mindset that stresses the importance of positive thinking and encourages people to deny or actively avoid negative emotions. In the case of cancer thrivers, many report feeling an almost unbearable pressure to remain cheerful at all times. However, in our case, because we'd already done a 'try before you buy', we knew the fear option wasn't for us, even though some friends and family members obviously preferred it, and later told me they'd thought we were 'too positive'. I wondered how they'd have coped with our suicidal selves, as spending even just a couple of weeks feeling like that had been intolerable, and would have turned us into the most horrendous dinner-party guests.

CHOOSING TO LIVE IN HOPE, NOT FEAR

'What have you been up to lately?' I could imagine them asking as we tucked into our roast dinner.

'Nothing much. Just planning our funerals and working out how best to kill ourselves. Did you realise how hard it is to do so painlessly? And that many people don't succeed and so end up in a vegetative state? Otherwise, just the same old, same old.'

The bottom line was this: while we didn't know whether staying positive would help Graham live *longer*, we knew for certain it would help us live *better*. Quality of life trumped quantity of life. After discussing how we were going to stay optimistic, Graham said he wanted to carry on working at the Foreign Office, a decision I fully supported. Without the banter, kindness and intellectual stimulation his amazing boss and colleagues could provide, I knew he'd have spent every waking hour contemplating his fate, and what he was going to leave behind. He ended up working, full time, until a month before his death.

Continuing to work was definitely going to help, yes, but would only go so far. We needed a way to keep negative thoughts at bay, something I called Thought Management. It was a concept inspired by the legendary runner and winner of four Olympic medals Sebastian Coe who, while pointing to his head, once said: 'The nine inches right here; set it straight and you can beat anybody in the world.' I realised Graham and I had to find ways to get in the habit of focusing on the positive, something humans are not programmed to do as it's way more important to remember that salivating lions are dangerous than it is to remember that baby rabbits are fluffy.

The first idea I came up with was to create a Positivity Book in which we could write everything positive or hopeful that happened, as well as document our efforts at bolstering Graham's immune system.

STILL RUNNING AFTER ALL THESE TEARS

'Whenever we're feeling low, we can refer back to it to give us courage,' I told Graham.

In it we listed everything Prof Hope had told us was a plus as far as Graham's prognosis was concerned: Graham had epithelioid mesothelioma which Prof Hope had said was 'the most important factor for long-term survival' as it was less aggressive and more treatable than the other kinds; Graham had been one of only five out of 200 of his patients not to need a blood transfusion during surgery; his immune system was extraordinarily healthy and the cancer had not spread to his lymph nodes. The only negative factor, in fact, was Graham's gender, as men with mesothelioma didn't live as long as women with the disease.

'We're working on that, too,' wrote Graham in the book. 'I'm getting in touch with my feminine side by wearing anti-DVT compression tights and learning how to sashay!'

The Positivity Book was also used to write each other little messages every day. Graham's first entry read: 'You are my rock and my life. With you by my side I will win through! I love you passionately and so deeply and am blessed to have you standing beside me. You are so very dear to me that I want to cry hot tears of love thinking of you. You are the love of my life and my best friend.'

I dubbed our approach 'authentic positivity' as I was determined that even our optimism be evidence-based. Every tiny thing was written up in that raspberry pink journal decorated with cupcake stickers, from the hug we'd been given by the nurse immediately after Graham's diagnosis to how lucky Graham would be to receive free chemo on the NHS, and even how, in moments of black humour, I thought the term 'meso patients' made them sound like a Japanese menu item. Prof Hope's immensely encouraging words got pride of place: I truly don't know if our Positivity Project

CHOOSING TO LIVE IN HOPE, NOT FEAR

would ever have succeeded without his presence in our lives as he was one of the few doctors who was always on our side, someone who was prepared not only to share our hopeful outlook but to turbo-charge it. As the palliative care doctor Rachel Clarke writes in her remarkable book *Dear Life*, '… even when a patient's fate seems hopeless, a doctor, if they care, through their basic humanity, can always make things more bearable…'

The Positivity Book was also a place where we could practise gratitude journalling, which I knew would reduce stress and anxiety and help prevent depression. Each day we challenged ourselves to come up with three things we were grateful to be ('in love, runners and alive,' I wrote), three things we were grateful to have (Graham once touchingly wrote, 'Lisa, **bold**, <u>underline</u>, *italic*; my family and my friends'), and three things we'd done well. One entry read: 'What Graham did well today was learn how to eat raw garlic, as Prof Hope suggested. He tried chomping on a few cloves but that made him throw up, so from now on he's going to chop it up and try to gulp it down with water.'

While the Positivity Book went some way to helping me manage my fear, negative thoughts ambushed me like guerilla fighters when I least expected it. 'How much pain is Graham going to have to endure when he's dying?' I'd suddenly think while waiting for the kettle to boil. 'I'm going to grow old and die alone,' I'd think while brushing my teeth. 'Will Graham eventually suffocate to death?' I thought while lying in bed listening to his noisy 'puh, puh, puh' breathing that was keeping me awake. Graham, too, was plagued by dark thoughts: 'When I lie in bed at night, I feel powerless, vulnerable and out of control,' he shared. In my hypnotherapy training we'd learned to call these thoughts ANTs, an acronym for automatic negative thoughts, a term I thought far too cutesy for something that could wreck your mental wellbeing. The psychotherapist Julia Samuel's term – the Shitty Committee – was far more apt.

It was then that I remembered the STOP Technique I taught my clients, which I often used myself when I was plagued by pre-marathon jitters.

Whenever he became aware of a negative thought, I instructed Graham to imagine a giant red stop sign rearing up in front of him, and someone with a megaphone (preferably a fierce Little Lisa with a South African accent) shouting 'STOP!' very loudly. He was then to recite the mantra 'All is well. All is well. All is well,' or a more hopeful thought, until he began to believe it and feel calmer.

'It's like playing the arcade game Whack-a-Mole,' I explained to Graham. 'If you whack each pesky mole on the head quickly it won't have time to breed more mini-moles. We simply cannot allow what may or may not happen in the future to ruin what we have together right now.'

After practising the technique for several weeks, Graham told me he was worried that by Whack-a-Moling negative thoughts we risked being in denial.

'We're not in denial,' I told him. 'If we were, you wouldn't be doing all the things you're doing to boost your immunity like eating fermented foods and having freezing cold showers. Remember, there's no such thing as "false hope". There's either hope, or there's not, and we've decided to live in hope, not fear.' Interestingly, several studies have shown that denial is often a positive coping strategy as it allows patients to gradually face the reality of their illness, bit by bit, without feeling overwhelmed. As the grief experts Elisabeth Kübler-Ross and David Kessler put it in *On Grief and Grieving*, 'Denial helps us to pace our feelings of grief… It is nature's way of letting in only as much as we can handle.'

To imprint our hopeful approach on Graham's unconscious, we came up with positive affirmations that he could recite in the shower every day, concluding with the age he hoped to be when he died: 'All is well. I am fit, I am strong, I will win this meso marathon. I love my life, I love my wife, I am going to lead a very long, healthy, happy and productive life. In with courage and conviction, out with fear and doubt. Each day, in every way, I'm getting better and better. Hungry for life! Greedy for more! Eighty-five!'

Something else that transformed our approach to fearful and negative emotions was the Waterfall Technique, which Graham, in typical fashion, instantly renamed the Turd Flushing Technique. The technique, which I found described in a single paragraph in a cancer book, suggested that instead of avoiding or suppressing emotional pain, we actually acknowledge and lean into it, and then let it go. In my case, I knew I was numbing my pain through binge-watching boxsets, overeating and, in particular, overworking. Like Graham, I'd resolved to continue working full time, which often involved editing and writing by day and conducting hypnotherapy sessions in the evenings and at weekends.

'I'm terrified of losing Graham as I don't know how to live without him,' is how I once verbalised my fear. The next step was to ask whether my feelings were justified. 'YES! Losing my best friend and soulmate is a horrifying thought,' I remember thinking. The final step was to allow myself to fully experience these feelings – the terror, the anguish, the grief, the unfairness of it all – and then to surrender to the urge to howl, cry or punch things (preferably not people!). The key thing was to fully feel these feelings but not to let them stay lodged inside me – they had to be swept away as if by a thundering waterfall… or a very satisfying toilet flush!

I was initially reluctant to try this technique as I feared, as many people do, that if the tears came, they would never stop. But after an initial long, animal-like howl, followed by about a minute of full-body, uncontrollable crying, I felt the emotions subside and a new peace and calmness within me. I was taken aback by the brevity of my emotional episode and smiled to myself as I realised that this type of speed sobbing was a time-efficient and enormously helpful way to face down difficult emotions rather than expending untold energy suppressing or running away from them. From that day onwards, whenever I noticed Graham was having a bad day or mentioned he'd been having 'dark thoughts', I'd pull up a chair and hold both of his hands in mine and then we'd 'turd flush' together.

Graham's wholehearted endorsement of our Positivity Project became apparent when he wrote the following in our Positivity Book, acknowledging its role in helping us find Prof Hope: 'Living in this new state of peace and joy meant Lisa's intellect and intuition were not drowned out by wild and terrified shrieks of fear. This enabled her to research my surgery options without being afraid of encountering dire prognoses and led us to making rational decisions, such as seeking a second opinion when I was dead against it.' It was a stark reminder of how damaging living in fear could be: not only was it deeply unpleasant, it could switch off the rational part of our brain at a time when it was vitally important for us to use it.

Waiting for chemo

With our 'book babies' *Travel Seekness* and *Travel Agents*

Graham at the start of the Karlovy Vary Half Marathon

The medal photo we sent to Prof Hope's wife

Sipping a (free!) post-race beer

Chapter 8
Chemo sabe

♪ Mood music: *Days* by The Kinks
The song that helped us recall our 'endless days' backpacking abroad

'I just can't face having my chemo at the hospital where those oncologists tried to bully me into that clinical trial,' Graham said as he brought me my morning tea in bed. I knew he was right. We simply couldn't trust doctors who'd tried to strongarm us into what we wholeheartedly believed was an inappropriate clinical trial. A call to Prof Hope established that we could indeed change hospitals, so we did.

The waiting room of our new hospital couldn't have been more different. Nurses with Christmassy tinsel in their hair were bustling around and there was a café selling hot drinks and snacks, lending it the air of a noisy school canteen. While this hospital had a much nicer atmosphere, we were still wracked with anxiety as we'd decided to continue surreptitiously recording our consultations. 'When would be a good time to press "record" on my phone without being spotted?' I wondered as we waited in a small consulting room for the medics to appear.

In preparation for this meeting, Graham and I had written a letter to our new medical team outlining how we wanted them to treat us. It felt impertinent telling them how to behave – like cheekily informing a headmaster how much discipline we were prepared to accept – but our previous experiences had been so upsetting we thought it best to risk it. The main messages we wanted to get across were that we had accepted the diagnosis, but not the dire prognosis, and that Graham would not be a passive passenger in his treatment, but a co-pilot.

'We're doing everything in our power to avoid the "nocebo effect" so I would respectfully ask that you do not mention life-limiting prognoses because this would make me anxious and thereby undermine my immune system,' said the letter.

The nocebo effect was something we'd read about in Dr Lissa Rankin's *Mind Over Medicine*, in which she referred to it as 'medical hexing'. She called it the placebo effect's evil twin, and said it was probably most obvious in voodoo deaths, where people who were cursed and told they would die, did indeed die. However, tribal cultures are not the only ones susceptible to voodoo death, she noted: 'The literature shows that patients believed to be terminal who are mistakenly informed that they have only a few months to live have died within their given time frame, even when autopsy findings reveal no physiological explanation for the early death.' Dr Rankin had also mentioned two fascinating studies. In the first, patients in a control group for a new chemo drug were given saline but were warned that it could be chemotherapy. Thirty per cent of them lost their hair simply because they *believed* chemo had that side effect. In the second study, 80 per cent of hospital patients given a drink they were told would make them throw up, did so, despite the drink being sugar water. No way were we going to have our doctors put a spell on us, we decided.

Our letter had gone on to list all the exercise, diet and complementary approaches we'd researched together and agreed Graham would adopt, ranging from a low-sugar diet and eating turmeric and raw garlic to having acupuncture and hypnotherapy and attending live stand-up comedy, pointing out that many of them had been suggested by Prof Hope.

CHEMO SABE

'I've taken on board what you've written here,' said the oncologist who'd be in charge of supervising Graham's chemotherapy, an extremely tall, moustachioed man whom we instantly, with some amusement, dubbed Dr Seuss as, if he'd been wearing a red bow tie and candy-striped top hat, he'd have been a dead-ringer for The Cat in the Hat. 'There's nothing that's contraindicated if you're having chemo, but I simply can't say whether any of it will make any difference.'

We had been excited to talk about our plan but it felt as if Dr Seuss was unimpressed by our proactive approach. The very opposite of Prof Hope. Talk about popping our party balloons.

I'd never read the word 'chemotherapy' without the adjective 'gruelling' preceding it. I believed it would help to prolong Graham's life, but I also assured him that I'd respect his decision not to have it, or to stop having it, if he found the side effects intolerable. The two types of chemo he'd been prescribed – pemetrexed and cisplatin – were unlikely to cause hair loss, but did have a long list of possible horrifying side effects ranging from mouth ulcers and anaemia to sepsis, blindness, heart attack and stroke.

'We're just going to have to forget about the nasty side effects,' I told him. 'You'd never use paracetamol if you kept reminding yourself that taking too much has the potential to cause serious liver damage.'

Another thing we hoped would help Graham get through chemo was something I'd learned from my friend Sue, my 'bridesmaid' at my 100th marathon, who'd been told she had stomach cancer around the same time Graham was diagnosed.

STILL RUNNING AFTER ALL THESE TEARS

'Tell Graham to welcome the chemo into his body, not fear it,' she said in a Skype call from Milan in which she 'introduced' me to the packets of chemo pills she was taking as if they were old friends. Sue called her chemo Chemo Sabe, like Tonto's nickname for the Lone Ranger, which means 'faithful friend'. She explained how avoiding viewing her pills as a deadly enemy and instead seeing them as allies made taking them a lot easier.

In the event, Graham's first chemo session was, in fact, gruelling, but not for the reasons we'd anticipated. On the advice of Prof Hope, Graham had decided to adopt a 'fast-mimicking diet' in which he'd mimic the effects of fasting by restricting the calories he ate for a day before his chemo, and a day afterwards.

'Cancer cells are dumb: all they want to do is feed on sugar so they can multiply,' Prof Hope told us. 'So, if you deprive them of sugar by fasting – just have a few lettuce leaves and skinless chicken with lemon juice – the cancer cells will weaken and be more likely than your normal cells to be killed.' When we researched the topic, we discovered that Cancer Research UK doesn't recommend fasting as it can lead to malnutrition and muscle loss, but as Prof Hope had recommended it, and Graham was at a healthy weight, we decided to give it a go.

Due to the sudden calorie restriction, Graham was already feeling a bit weak by the time we reported to the orchid-filled chemo ward at 9am. On arrival he was weighed and then the wait began. At five hours long, Graham had probably the longest chemo protocol of any cancer patient and yet, as time ticked by and we waited for him to be hooked up, it became apparent that patients who'd checked in hours after him had already been treated and discharged. It slowly dawned on us that we'd needlessly been forced out of bed at sparrow fart, and could have had a lie-in instead of spending several hours staring at other people's drips.

CHEMO SABE

The nurse who eventually came to administer the chemotherapy couldn't have been more lovely. She crouched down next to Graham and explained that as chemo is such a toxic drug, they had to be 100 per cent certain it was given to the correct patient, so she had to triple check his full name, date of birth and the two drugs she'd be giving him. She also explained that while they usually used buckets of warm water to help make patients' veins easier to locate, they were trialling a new machine that would warm his arm without water splashing all over the place. The chemotherapy infusion, once it got going a full three hours after we'd arrived, was a non-event, the only complication being that Graham had to wheel his chemo drip stand with him every time he wanted to use the loo. The one shining light during the day was the time we spent chatting to Amelie, a vivacious woman with breast cancer, and her husband Ben. Amelie, we learned, was mum to a two-year-old, who was being taken care of that day by Amelie's mum, who'd once been treated for breast cancer at the same hospital.

'I specifically asked to be treated here,' said Amelie, 'as Mum's alive and thriving thirty years later.'

Her husband Ben, whom I felt incredibly sorry for as I knew he must be worried sick about losing the mother of his child, was similarly upbeat, and even shared a few hilarious anecdotes.

'I once had a pet rabbit who used to assist me with my gardening,' he told us. 'He was so clever that he would help me plant vegetable seeds by digging a hole wherever I placed my trowel!'

After a while, all the other patients left, and then the lights were turned out as the staff must have thought everyone had gone home. Alarmed, I went in search of a nurse and, when I found one, she promised to get a doctor to come and weigh Graham to ensure the four litres of extra fluid he'd been given via a drip to flush the chemo from his body had been excreted, so it didn't put undue strain on his heart. We were utterly drained – Graham literally and figuratively – when we eventually got home 12 hours after we'd set out that morning. 'Gruelling', I now saw clearly, was an understatement.

What I loved most about being Graham's cancer champion was that we fully embraced a positive approach together. Unlike some of the inevitable married-life spats and disagreements we'd had over the decades, we were completely united in this regard and I'm so grateful that our resolve brought us closer as a couple.

Take our dilemma of how best to get through future chemo sessions if Amelie and Ben – or other friendly fellow chemo recipients – weren't there to boost our mood. Remaining positive for such a long time really would be a challenge, we reckoned. We considered downloading comedies to watch on Graham's iPad, and I thought of wearing a novelty hat from one of my fancy-dress marathons, but we were worried that our laughter might seem disrespectful to the other patients. And then I had a bright idea: we could write our travel memoirs together.

'Come on, it'll be fun,' I cajoled Graham, who wasn't keen on the idea. 'Besides, if you won't be my co-author, I'll include all the funny bits you wrote in our travel journals and pretend I wrote them.'

'You can't do that,' protested Graham. 'That's plagiarism.'

'Oh yes I can. Sue me.'

And so for the next five dawn-to-well-after-dusk chemo sessions, while Graham put his feet up in a squishy recliner, I sat in a chair beside him and read aloud from our travel journals. We winced as

CHEMO SABE

we recalled nearly freezing to death in a flimsy tent when it was minus 9°C in the Grand Canyon. We laughed (quietly) reading about the time I insisted that Graham manually retrieve my grandfather's wedding ring which he'd accidentally dropped into a Portaloo at the start of the Giant's Head Marathon in Dorset. And we chuckled at how I'd once booked us into a dodgy Medellín hostel that Graham suspected was a *Breaking Bad*-like drug lab (turns out the white-suited staff were moonlighting as beekeepers, not meth cooks). Chemo session by chemo session the creation of our two book babies – *Travel Seekness* and *Travel Agents* – took shape. We'd managed to find an excellent way to kill time while the chemo did its work killing cancer.

All this time, running hadn't been far from either of our minds as my research had shown that it could play an important role in Graham's recovery. I'd read there was growing evidence that exercise might make chemotherapy more effective, and that it helped patients better tolerate treatment side effects such as fatigue, pain, nausea, vomiting, anxiety and depression, so throughout the four months of Graham's chemo treatment, we tried to run as much as possible. I also later learned something astonishing: when muscles contract, they secrete not only the mood-boosting 'happy hormones' dopamine and serotonin but chemicals called myokines that act as an antidepressant. The nickname scientists have given to these chemicals? Nothing other than 'hope molecules'! Turns out that by being runners – despite our complicated relationship with running illustrated by our frequent 'I hate running' outbursts – Graham and I had a significant head start in our Positivity Project.

STILL RUNNING AFTER ALL THESE TEARS

Many cancer patients are so exhausted during chemo that they can barely walk to the post box, but a day or so after each chemo cycle, once the chemo-induced fatigue abated, I was amazed that Graham could still outrun me. We'd start out together and within a minute he'd be at the end of the block, jogging on the spot like a sparring boxer, waiting for me to catch up.

'How ya diddling?' he'd always say when I reached him, red-faced and convinced I was having an asthma attack even though I don't have asthma.

'Shut up, will you!' I'd snap in mock annoyance. 'My legs feel like logs.'

'You know you only have to get through the first "toxic ten minutes" and then you'll be fine,' he'd laugh, evidently enjoying using the term I'd coined to describe the horrendous nature of the first 600 seconds of every run in my first book, *Running Made Easy*.

'Please don't spout my own advice back to me,' I'd snarl, casting desperate glances at my sports watch to see if the bloody ten minutes were up yet, knowing that it took that long to juice up my joints with synovial fluid. As Bella Mackie put it so perfectly in *Jog On*: 'The first ten minutes hurt, without fail. I have to push myself to get that first ten done, and I always feel lumbering and slow initially, like the Tin Man clanking down the yellow brick road.'

'Bloody hell, still three minutes to go.' Never had my sister Loren's favourite catchphrase felt truer: 'Life is short, running makes it feel longer.'

Dismayed at how unkempt our neighbourhood had become, Graham and I decided to try plogging – the Swedish craze that combines '*plocka uup*' aka picking up litter, with jogging. Channelling our inner Womble, we hit the mean streets of

CHEMO SABE

Croydon and soon came across the grisly sight of a pile of grease-and-tomato-stained pizza boxes and empty beer cans strewn around a park bench. After loading up the al fresco dining detritus in our arms, we continued our run, only to be met with some very strange looks from passersby. 'Oh, they're not ours, they belong to Dean Karnazes!' I was tempted to quip in order to clear up any confusion, but I didn't think anyone would get the admittedly niche reference to one of my all-time favourite running stories. Dean, in case you hadn't heard, is the legendary ultrarunner who, when faced with the problem of refuelling in the dead of night during a nonstop 200-mile race, hit on the genius idea of ordering a pizza using his mobile. Upon being handed his order, Dean deftly rolled his takeaway into a burrito-style log, and wolfed it down while continuing to run. Talk about thinking outside the (pizza) box!

Our favourite route was around Ashburton Park, a short distance from home, where a tunnel of overarching trees always made us feel that we were trotting along a Parisian avenue. It was also home to some very acrobatic squirrels and several squadrons of shrieking ring-necked parakeets, the descendants of exotic pets that either escaped from their owners or were deliberately released. They'd slice through the air as if performing a neon-green Red Arrows display, bringing a touch of the tropics to Croydon's gritty greyness.

Once at the park, Graham would let the brakes off and run at his own pace, usually lapping me before long. He always dressed the part in a smart, figure-hugging red jacket, black running tights and black baggy shorts, whereas I, despite my impeccable running pedigree, always managed to look scruffy, as if I'd carelessly selected my outfit from random charity-shop items loitering in the bottom of our laundry basket. During one of these runs, I watched

STILL RUNNING AFTER ALL THESE TEARS

Graham's figure in the distance, running in the distinctive way he always did, his upper body rigidly upright and his legs paddling furiously beneath him like a determined duck, and felt a huge surge of sadness. I knew that one day I'd be running round that park alone, with no one to ask me how I was diddling, and no one to annoy me by outpacing me.

Thankfully Graham seemed to sail through chemo and in fact only vomited once, after forgetting to take his anti-nausea tablets. In the middle of every three-week cycle, he'd feel fatigued and a 'little bit grotty' as his cancer nurse had warned him was likely to happen, but other than that he had very few side effects. Being a running evangelist, I, of course, wanted to credit the fact he went running regularly for this, and he was happy for me to do that as I suspect he really enjoyed our runs (though he never once admitted to this!).

At some hospitals, it's tradition for cancer patients to ring a bell to celebrate the end of their treatment. There wasn't one for us to ring at our hospital so, three weeks after Graham's final chemo session, and after being given the go-ahead to fly, we chose something far more celebratory: a spring half marathon in Karlovy Vary, formerly known as Carlsbad, in the Czech Republic. At the start, Graham shot off like a greyhound, appropriate for a race held in a town famously founded by a hot dog, or rather the owner of a hot dog. The hound in question was out hunting with the Holy Roman Emperor Charles IV, when it discovered a natural hot spring – by falling into the scalding water. Impressed by the healing properties of the water, which cured Charles's injured leg after he later decided to bathe in it, the emperor established a spa there, naming it Carlsbad after himself.

As the race started at 5.30pm, the tourists were out in full force along the route, mostly wandering along taking sips of medicinal spring water from the spouts of their porcelain spa cups as if smoking small pipes. A visit to the local museum had informed us that in former times, spa visitors had indulged in what was termed 'extreme drinking', which involved downing up to nine litres of spa water daily, which often led to extreme diarrhoea.

'We'll save our sipping for *after* the race,' declared Graham, anxious to avoid spending too much time in the toilets.

Leaving behind the cobbled streets and pastel-coloured gabled townhouses that the renowned architect Le Corbusier had described as 'a gathering of cakes', the route plunged into a fir forest. There I spotted a statue of Beethoven, who visited the town twice in 1812. Stepping out with his right foot, with his head lowered and his left arm bent, the great composer looked almost exactly like I did in a photo at a half marathon in 2004. Convinced I'd been hurtling down The Long Walk in Windsor Great Park like a greyhound, I'd ordered a pricey official photograph, only to find that I looked as if both of my feet were rooted to the road. If you hadn't been able to see the effort on my face, you'd swear my feet were superglued to the ground.

'You and me both, Beethoven, baby,' I grinned, wondering why he hadn't been depicted conducting or composing, rather than plodding along.

Back in town, when I was just about the only remaining runner on the course, Graham having left me for dust after about 200m, a cyclist in a Day-Glo tabard drew up alongside me.

'You need to stop,' he barked. 'You're running too slowly.'

'I'll speed up,' I promised.

STILL RUNNING AFTER ALL THESE TEARS

'I'm afraid you're already too far behind,' said the Grim Sweeper tasked with enforcing the three-hour cut-off.

Luckily our hotel was coming into view, so I grumpily exited the course and headed up to our room.

'You're back early,' said Graham with surprise.

'I got kicked off the course for being too slow,' I said. 'How did you do?'

'I finished in two hours and forty-six minutes! That's my third fastest half-marathon time,' he said, grinning. 'Not bad for an old man who's just finished chemo.'

'Wow, that's amazing!' I exclaimed. I suggested we send a photo to Prof Hope's wife Alexandra, who'd been corresponding with me after I'd discovered she was a fellow runner.

Minutes later we received a reply: 'That is FABULOUS!!!! Well done, Graham!' she wrote. 'I can tell you that your surgeon is very proud of you.'

I was keen to drown my sorrows, and celebrate Graham's outstanding performance, by going to a beer spa (yes, it's a thing, though you don't actually bathe in the stuff, you soak in water infused with yeast and hops). But he refused.

'Oh please, Graham, you get to bathe in vitamin-rich water. And loll about on hay bales eating beer bread afterwards. And you get to drink as much beer as you like for an hour,' I protested.

'I've already showered, and I'm lying on my own bed – I'm not sure I want to go and lounge in a manger.'

'Graham, you are always such a stick in the mud. I really, really want to go,' I begged.

'All right, how much does it cost?' he said.

'A one-hour session costs a hundred and twenty euros for two.'

'A hundred and twenty euros? Are you *mad*? We could drink a hundred and twenty pints of Pilsner for that. I haven't cut my own

CHEMO SABE

hair for twenty years to blow all the money I've saved at a beer spa. It's a definite no from me.'

'Please, Graham.'

'No.'

I knew from his tone that there was no point in arguing any further.

At our next consultation, Prof Hope congratulated Graham in person.

'I'm so impressed with what you have achieved,' he said, 'especially considering I removed twenty per cent of your lung.'

'What? That's news to us!' I thought, marvelling at how sneaky, but also supremely smart, our surgeon was. Until then, I'd been more than happy to bully Graham into participating in races he'd never have entered of his own volition. If we'd known about Graham's lung, I doubt that he'd ever have signed up for the half marathon, and I doubt, too, that I, for once, would have tried to persuade him otherwise.

Celebrating after one of Graham's all-clears

Group photo in Ghana, Graham's birthplace

With Faye, Sarah and Anthony at the Thames Meander Half Marathon

Posing at the PolarNight 10K in Norway

With my Italian 'marathon bridesmaid' Sue, who sadly died of cancer

The Jackson Two at RunFestRun

Chapter 9
Trials by fire

♪♪ **Mood music: *Seasons in the Sun* by Terry Jacks**
The nostalgic song that always made Graham cry

Russian roulette is the only way I can describe the months following the end of Graham's first six cycles of chemo. At every three-monthly scan-results appointment we never knew whether we'd hear a relief-inducing click, or a bang that would blow his brains out. Good news, or a death sentence. We'd sit in the waiting room, consumed by scan-xiety, passing a small kidney-bean-shaped pebble we'd picked up on Deal beach to each other, gripping it tightly in our sweaty hands, much as those in medieval London had once relied on bezoar stones – hardened lumps of undigested material taken from the stomachs of goats – to ward off bubonic plague. Our stomachs churned each time we heard Graham's name called and were led to the small, airless rooms where his oncologists, like the oracles of Ancient Greece, were waiting to reveal his fate. Most of the doctors we encountered were wonderfully caring and respected our wish not to be reminded of Graham's dire prognosis, but each consultation was nonetheless made more nerve-wracking as we never knew when Dr Seuss, whom we found incredibly intimidating and dreaded seeing, would be present.

As the months flew by, Graham, who was now completely back to normal, continued working full time and I kept myself busy with editing projects, writing and hypnotherapy. We went camping as much as we could, and visited Graham's birthplace in Ghana

STILL RUNNING AFTER ALL THESE TEARS

('If we don't go now, I fear we never will,' he told me). I also gave Graham the chance to beat me by miles at three more half marathons – the Queen Elizabeth Olympic Park Half Marathon, the Thames Meander Half Marathon and the Croydon Half Marathon – and we even managed to fit in a race in the Arctic Circle, the torchlit PolarNight 10K in Tromsø, after which we celebrated our 29th wedding anniversary in spectacular style with a sighting of the Northern Lights.

Running offered me another welcome escape from Cancerland when I was invited to speak at Chris Evans's inaugural RunFestRun, a festival with my name all over it as it featured teams dressed as bees and ladybirds led by running legends such as Paula Radcliffe and Steve Cram. After my onstage Q&A with *Women's Running* editor Esther Newman was over, I was free to shake a leg in the mosh pit where I came within sweat-spattering distance of Razorlight's Johnny Borrell (a tap on the shoulder from a friendly bystander informed me that I was filming him with a switched-off phone). When Colin Jackson strolled by, I just had to go and tell him that we shared the same surname, and how much I'd admired his fancy footwork on *Strictly Come Dancing*. Jo Pavey, whom I'd recently interviewed, greeted me warmly, as did Vassos Alexander, who came bounding over – that man has the infectious positive energy of a greyhound, as well as the speed – and asked whether he could interview me on his parkrun podcast and for his new book, *How to Run a Marathon*. It amused me no end that while most of the other VIPs were Olympians, or at the very least, hares, my own USP was coming last in 25 marathons.

TRIALS BY FIRE

After several all-clears, 14 months after his chemo ended, a radiologist broke the upsetting news that there was a small tumour in the centre of Graham's chest.

'Don't worry, we can zap it with stereotactic radiotherapy,' she assured us. 'You're a young, strong ultrarunner and I'm sure I can convince my colleagues to approve it.' The tumour wasn't the only bad news we received that month. I was due to fly out to Milan to visit my marathon-running friend Sue. 'It's going to be so much fun bathing in Chanel No5 and drinking Martinis for breakfast!' I emailed her.

'We'll celebrate the Summer Solstice together – I cannot wait to spend two days with you! Whoohoo!' she emailed back.

'You are such a ray of light that celebrating the Solstice with you will be entirely appropriate,' I replied. 'But if you aren't feeling great at that point, you must promise to let me know as I can just mooch around Milan for two days without visiting you if you're too tired or just not up to it.'

The day before I was due to fly out, Sue emailed me.

'I'm in hospital with a belly full of fluid, so sadly I am too sick to see you tomorrow,' she said.

I offered to come anyway in case she felt better by then, but she told me she was feeling really grim.

'Not to worry,' I wrote back. 'I'm sure I'll be able to see you next month – please spend all your energy on getting better. Sending huge hugs.'

A month later, her son Alex contacted me to let me know that Sue had died. My beautiful friend with legs like a teenager, my all-time favourite marathon pacer, was no more. Her will to live had been so strong, and yet fucking cancer had snatched her away. I didn't dare tell Graham as I knew the news would upset him, but he found out anyway when the sympathy card I'd sent Alex was returned to sender.

'Why did you post a card to Sue's son?' he asked me. I had no choice but to tell Graham the heartbreaking news.

Eight months later, the cancer, like a persistent stalker, was back, this time with a vengeance. While the tumour in the centre of Graham's chest had been zapped successfully, many more tumours, this time tiny ones resembling the snowflakes in a snow globe, had been detected, so Graham had more radiotherapy, but it wasn't enough to keep them in check.

'There's not much more we can do chemo-wise either,' said Dr Seuss when we returned to the hospital. 'Chemo is like weedkiller – the first time you use it, it gets rid of most of the weeds, but the ones that are left become resistant, so they're harder to kill the next time.' My heart sank. 'However, there's a trial that I'm going to put you forward for,' Dr Seuss continued. 'It's for an immunotherapy drug called nivolumab that helps your immune system find and kill cancer cells. Only twenty-six per cent of people respond really well to it, so they're trying to figure out how not to waste it on those who won't benefit.'

I immediately mentally put Graham in the 26 per cent.

'On this trial you have a sixty-seven per cent chance of receiving nivolumab, so the odds are in your favour.' Again, I put Graham in the 67 per cent, as if by willing this outcome fervently enough I could somehow make it happen.

I'd previously researched how Graham could get access to immunotherapy, which at the time wasn't approved to treat mesothelioma on the NHS, and found it would cost in the region of £68,000 a year to have it privately. Though it had been a daunting prospect, I'd already told Graham that I was willing for us to spend all of our life savings on treatment with one proviso: I didn't want to be homeless, so we couldn't sell the house.

'We were poor and happy before, so it doesn't worry me now,' I had told him.

However, I had known our savings wouldn't last long paying out for nivolumab, so I'd seriously considered getting hold of some cardboard and poster paint to make a placard I could wave outside Parliament while handcuffed to its railings to demand Graham receive access to the drug. At that time, the chemo was still working so I'd put that idea on hold. Now there was a chance – a good chance – Graham could get nivolumab for free.

Graham began to experience more frequent bouts of pain while we waited for the trial to start. His face would contort in agony and, after drinking several large glugs of the Oramorph liquid morphine he'd been prescribed, he'd have to pace around in circles until it abated. Deeply concerned, we booked a hospital appointment.

We were kept waiting in reception all afternoon, and finally led into one of the windowless consulting rooms where we waited for another hour.

'I feel like a disobedient schoolchild outside the headmaster's office awaiting their punishment,' I told Graham, who nodded a 'Me too'.

'Why are you here?' Dr Seuss asked when he finally arrived, seemingly annoyed that we'd insisted on having an unscheduled consultation. We'd clearly broken protocol, but what else did they expect us to do?

We told him about Graham's unbearable pain.

'As I understand it,' Dr Seuss said vaguely, 'patients are given liquid morphine and then, once the correct daily dosage has been worked out, they're switched to long-acting morphine tablets, I think.'

What? He had only a passing knowledge of what was involved. Was he really admitting that he was relying on hearsay?

'Anyway, you'll have to discuss this with the doctors conducting your clinical trial. You're no longer under my care.'

What? No one had bothered to inform us of this. It was like being broken up with by a bad boyfriend: at the end of the day, no matter how glad you are to be shot of him, *you* want to be the one who does the dumping.

And then, when we were still reeling from this news, completely out of the blue, Dr Seuss dropped the H-bomb.

'Or, of course, you could always go to a *hospice*.'

The word landed in the room with the same force as several tons of TNT. Stunned, we didn't say anything, and neither did Dr Seuss who, oblivious to the horrifying impact of that word, made it clear he was keen to head home as it was, by now, dark.

Graham stumbled out of the consulting room into reception: even though he'd been there many times before, he seemed not to know where the exit was; in fact, he seemed to have forgotten how to walk.

'Graham,' I said firmly, leading him to a chair and forcing him to sit down. 'Listen to me! Look at me!' His face was ashen and his eyes wide with fright. 'This doesn't mean you're going to die.' Graham nodded dumbly. 'People often go to hospices as outpatients for years and years as their staff are experts in pain relief.

TRIALS BY FIRE

I've researched this. Hospices don't just offer end-of-life care but help people to manage their condition, especially if they're in pain.'

Graham stood up unsteadily.

'Let's go home,' he said quietly.

In *Dear Life*, palliative care doctor Rachel Clarke recalls being shown *Wit* – a film about an American professor diagnosed with late-stage ovarian cancer – on day one of medical school. 'It compelled me to consider my future power as a doctor – my potential to dehumanise, distress and even hurt my patients,' she wrote. Dr Seuss had evidently bunked class that day. As the saying goes: 'The tongue has no bones, but is strong enough to break a heart. So be careful with your words.'

Graham did eventually go to the hospice, a full 17 months after Dr Seuss's callous 'Get thee to a hospice' remark. By then he really was dying, though we didn't know it at the time.

'Lots of nasty side effects last night, including vomiting, swollen ankles and itchiness,' I messaged my friend Sarah six days into the immunotherapy trial. 'We didn't drink any wine last night so it's definitely not a hangover. I really do believe Graham's getting the drug and not the placebo – hurrah!'

'Oh my God Lisa, I have never been so happy to hear that somebody has vomited and is itchy! That has literally made my day,' she shot back.

'Crazy, crazy times when you wish vomiting on a friend! Thanks for all your vomity, itchy thoughts!'

As the clinical trial – and the horrendous side effects that made it clear Graham was indeed receiving nivolumab – continued,

STILL RUNNING AFTER ALL THESE TEARS

another trial was waiting in the wings: a lawsuit against one of Graham's former employers for exposing him to asbestos while at work. We'd been having meetings for several years with Lacey St James, who worked at Irwin Mitchell, a law firm highly experienced in handling personal injury claims by this point, but the wheels were grinding incredibly slowly.

Part of the legal process involved Graham having a medical assessment with an independent oncologist, so off we went to London for what would turn out to be a train smash of a consultation that left us gasping in disbelief. The consultant, a portly, rosy-cheeked Toby Jug of a man, greeted us in the lobby of the hospital but refused to shake hands with us as the Covid pandemic was all over the news. After relating the history of Graham's illness for the umpteenth time – and wondering whether the pile of clinical notes in front of Toby Jug were only there to serve as an armrest as he patently hadn't read them – he blithely informed us that he'd heard a rumour that the government was going to cancel clinical trials due to the pandemic. We'd just been tossed a hand grenade with the pin removed and didn't have a clue what to do with it. Graham looked at me worriedly: we both knew immunotherapy was his best, and possibly only, hope. What would we do if his trial was called off?

'Is there anything you want to ask me?' said Toby Jug at the end of the consultation, stifling a yawn and casting a very obvious glance at his expensive watch.

'Yes,' I said, hoping to make the most of the exorbitant consultation fee we were paying. 'As the chemo options are so limited, is there anything we could do on the complementary front that has helped your patients in the past?'

'No!' he said bluntly. 'There's nothing you can do to keep mesothelioma at bay. In fact, I once had a twenty-three-year-old patient who thought carrot juice would cure his cancer. Can you imagine? He drank so much of it, he turned orange!' The doctor started to laugh, and then smacked us with the punchline: 'He was dead within three months!'

We couldn't get out of his office fast enough after that.

'What the actual fuck?' said Graham as we exited the building onto London's traffic-clogged streets. 'Was that doctor really *laughing*, in front of us, about a young patient who *died*?'

Now I understood why one cancer thriver on a cancer forum had described her visit to an uncaring oncologist to get a second opinion as 'the worst experience of my life – even worse than the day I received my terminal diagnosis'. How on earth could these doctors not understand the havoc such 'casual cruelties' could cause?

'The Fucker!' I said. 'I thought doctors were supposed to care about their patients, not mock them.'

That horrifying visit gave rise to a new coping technique: swearing. We remembered it could reduce the perception of pain while running, so now we applied the same strategy to emotional anguish. 'The Fucker!' we'd loudly say whenever a member of the medical fraternity let us down. By calling a medic who had power over us a Fucker, we reclaimed some of our power as it always resulted in a fit of stress-busting giggles.

When I related this story to my friend Iona, she shared a story of her own. I'd asked her for advice when Graham had been about to have chemo as her husband Matt had had non-Hodgkin lymphoma at the age of 26. Of all my friends, she was the only one who was also a 'cancer-thriver's wife'. Mercifully, Matt made a full recovery – but not before they'd developed a dark sense of humour that persisted long after he'd been given the all-clear.

STILL RUNNING AFTER ALL THESE TEARS

'Twenty years after Matt became ill, we still like to precede everyday sentences with the random use of "Well, I'm no oncologist but…"' she told me. 'For example, "Is that tap leaking? I mean, I'm no oncologist but I think we might need a plumber" or "I'm liking this pasta sauce you made… Now, I'm no oncologist but, if I were you, I'd add more basil next time…"'

Three years after Graham was diagnosed, when we'd pretty much given up hope of being successful in our legal claim, we received a most unexpected email: 'The defendant has just admitted liability,' wrote our lawyer, who went on to say she was confident we could now persuade them to cover the cost of any treatment Graham might need going forward. We couldn't believe what we were reading. In one sentence all our money worries evaporated. I could put away the poster paint, and cancel my Amazon order for handcuffs.

Rocking the London lockdown look

The magical fairy tree at Croham Hurst

Dad ran the virtual Comrades race inside his house

Our invite to the Zoom Killers concert

Uncle Ian as Einstein

Our final holiday at Loch Ness

Chapter 10
Love in the time of Covid

♪♪ **Mood music:** *Chasing Cars* **by Snow Patrol**

My heartbreak song

He'd once sat at my desk when I was freelancing at the parenting website Mumsnet and fielded webchat questions such as 'What's your favourite biscuit?', 'Are you a feminist?' and 'Does your mum tell you off when she sees you on TV with messy hair?' After he became Foreign Secretary, Graham gave him an expert briefing on Pakistan. And now, on 23 March 2020, Boris Johnson, that same blond man with a haystack on his head, was staring us straight in the eye from the telly and insisting: 'From this evening I must give the British people a very simple instruction: you *must* stay at home.' Even though the news was expected, thanks to endless media speculation, it came as a shock. Graham, having started the clinical trial a couple of days before, was fighting for his life, and now millions of other people would be, too. Looking back, it's hard to believe that the whole world came to a halt and that, for 16 months, we were all sent in and out of quarantine like part-time medieval lepers.

We embraced the 'new abnormal' as best we could. Graham had already been working from home several days a week, so it wasn't a big adjustment for him, but after being sent home by Condé Nast, where I'd been freelancing, I missed my water-cooler moments with my chatty colleagues.

'Talk to me, Graham,' I said, warming my bottom against the radiator in our dining room while waiting for the kettle to boil.

STILL RUNNING AFTER ALL THESE TEARS

'I can't, I'm working,' he said without looking up.

'Oh, come on! Are you telling me you don't chat with your colleagues while you're making tea at the office?'

'I do, but they don't drink tea seventeen times a day like you do! And besides, we tend to talk about work.'

'Oh, go on, Graham, I'm bored,' I said. 'Tell me a state secret. Just one – I promise I won't tell anyone.'

'Lisa, it's a privilege to be allowed to carry on working while I'm sick so I need to prove myself,' he said, his lips sealed tighter than an airlock on a nuclear submarine.

The only thing that could drag Graham away from his laptop, besides lunch, was Pecan, an adorable grey squirrel who'd taken to visiting our garden. He'd melted both our hearts and become used to Graham feeding him nuts, turning up at the same time each morning and dancing on his hindfeet outside our conservatory begging for food.

'Graham, stop feeding Pecan those Brazil nuts,' I said crossly. 'They're expensive and there's a worldwide shortage – I had to go to three shops to find them.'

'But he likes them,' said Graham, offering Pecan another. The squirrel stretched out his tiny paws and took the large nut straight from Graham's fingers, his furry tail quivering like silky grass seedheads.

'You need them more than he does,' I replied. 'Let him eat peanuts. They're much cheaper.'

'Only the best for my Pecan,' said Graham fondly, ignoring me.

Graham did make one concession for me, however: he began turning up at his desk at 10am every weekday so that we could spend time in the morning sitting in bed drinking tea, knowing that this formerly weekend-only ritual was the highlight of my week.

LOVE IN THE TIME OF COVID

'I'll make up the time at the end of the day or have a shorter lunch break,' Graham said as he placed a large mug of tea into my grateful hands.

'You haven't responded to the immunotherapy as we'd hoped so you're being withdrawn from the trial due to disease progression,' said the lead researcher two months after Graham started the immunotherapy drug. Progression. It was a word I'd always thought had positive connotations ('Lisa's piano playing is progressing well') but now it meant Graham's mesothelioma, after a period of dormancy when it must have regrouped and gathered reinforcements, was on the march with homicidal intent. The White Walkers from *Game of Thrones* were on the rampage inside Graham's body and no Wall was going to hold those murderous hordes back. Graham and I were beating a retreat and could no longer hold onto the hope of 'healing' his cancer: it had most definitely turned into a fight.

But we didn't have time to grieve what couldn't be helped. A new chemo regime at the same hospital was started, this time under the supervision of a different oncologist whom we nicknamed Dr Yes because he was always so kind and obliging and seemed to fully support our Positivity Project. Most of our interactions with him were on the phone due to Covid restrictions. Although we couldn't see Dr Yes's face, it was always comforting to listen to his friendly, soothing voice, and unlike Dr Seuss, we never dreaded speaking to him.

STILL RUNNING AFTER ALL THESE TEARS

I've heard the Covid pandemic described as a fever dream and, for Graham and me, it really was. Days blurred into weeks blurred into months. The experience comes back to me in a series of flashbacks…

- Having missed the boat when it came to panic-buying loo roll (and stockpiling paper napkins instead), reassuring each other that, when they too ran out, we could always wipe our bottoms with pages torn from paperbacks as we'd done when backpacking through India.
- Watching YouTube videos explaining how to quarantine your mail to ensure any coronavirus that had been sneezed or coughed onto your post and packages had expired by the time you opened it (and idly wondering whether this could be used as a defence in court to explain any delay in paying your bills).
- Using our rationed one hour of outdoor exercise a day to go running or walking – which meant we ran more often than we ever had before, going out religiously after work every day to make the most of our 'ration'.
- Becoming so obsessive about washing my hands with antibacterial handwash that they became red-raw and even bled in several places.
- Lying in bed listing what we were grateful for and concluding each session with a series of Oms – in the yoga classes we'd attended together at our running club, we'd been restricted to three, but now we took great delight in chanting as many as we wanted to, relishing the way the mind-soothing sounds vibrated through our bodies and our bed.
- Screaming at each other in frustration while writing our two travel books and then almost losing our voices – and

our minds – during the laborious process of recording the audiobooks in a hastily constructed home studio before having to edit out every sigh, snuffle and swallow. So much for avoiding stress!

- Visiting a magical fairy tree in the heart of Croham Hurst where we frequently went 'forest bathing' in order to boost Graham's immunity by exposing him to phytoncides, the natural defensive compounds trees emit. Someone had screwed a brass keyhole cover into the tree trunk wound at its base, turning it into an imaginary tiny door. Decorated with glitter, ribbons and little gifts for the fairies, it became a sacred site for us both. Pre-Covid, we'd hugged it before Graham's surgery. During lockdown, these healing hugs became one of our most treasured regular activities.

- Feeling as if we were on the set of the post-apocalyptic zombie film *28 Weeks Later* while driving to chemo sessions through a silent central London, staring in disbelief at the boarded-up pubs, empty restaurants and shops whose frozen-in-time window displays remained the same week after week.

- Chuckling away while listening to the American humourist David Sedaris's Radio 4 series in our sun-drenched conservatory. Graham and I were always laughing together and had exactly the same irreverent, dry sense of humour. The episode that had us in stitches was the one where he related a family shopping trip to the upscale clothing emporium Kapital in Tokyo. Here he described – in his little old lady voice – how impressed he was by the Japanese store's fashion-forward designs that looked like they'd been 'pulled from the evidence rack at a murder trial' and his sister's delight at a hat 'modelled on a used toilet brush'.

STILL RUNNING AFTER ALL THESE TEARS

He couldn't get enough of Kapital's bizarre clothes, and we couldn't get enough of him.

- Peeing standing up in a Soho alleyway like a lager-fuelled ladette while a platoon of policemen walked past because the hospital where I accompanied Graham to chemo sessions had started refusing to allow non-patients to use its toilets due to the Covid infection risk.

- Being jolted awake as Graham leapt out of bed in the middle of the night and paced our bedroom while crying out: 'Don't you dare tell me to fucking breathe through the pain! I need to walk it out.' We were subsequently told that the source of his unspeakable pain was a large tumour that, as his oncologist Dr Yes put it, was 'nibbling away' at one of his ribs.

- Hearing that my dad had completed the same Race the Comrades Legends 10K virtual event I'd done with friends – within the confines of his house. This was because South Africa had possibly the most stringent lockdown restrictions in the entire world meaning, along with the sale of alcohol and cigarettes, any outdoor activity was banned.

- Attending a virtual Killers concert on Zoom, when the live one we had tickets for was cancelled, staged by our friends Sarah and Anthony in Colchester, complete with mocked-up tickets, a stadium backdrop and snacks and drinks couriered round courtesy of Sainsbury's.

- Tossing fat balls made from bird seed and lard onto our lawn and watching a wood pigeon peck up every last oily crumb, until we feared his liver would turn into foie gras. We named him Sedaris, like our literary litter-picking hero David Sedaris, who'd had a garbage truck in Horsham named after him in recognition of his hobby of picking up roadside trash.

LOVE IN THE TIME OF COVID

Could you be prosecuted for bird cruelty if the death was due to self-inflicted greed? we wondered.

- Knowing that the one place I was most likely to contract Covid, and where anyone experiencing symptoms was pretty likely to visit, was the one place I simply had to go to at least twice a week: the pharmacy. Each foray almost always required a double-dip visit because not all of Graham's medications were available or he'd been issued with the incorrect dosage.

- Finding something Graham had written in our Positivity Book, without telling me about it: 'Leaving you alone scares me. I feel so guilty leaving you – you're just so lovely. If I die, I won't know about it, but you'll have to live with my absence. I know you feel I do a lot for you – I feel rotten that you'll have to make that adjustment, so I will live as long as I can. I so wanted to have a long old age with you, but there's a big question mark over that now.'

- Administering twice the usual dose of Oramorph – whose name conjures up an image of Morph, the little terracotta clay character from the children's TV show *Take Hart* – late one evening on the advice of Graham's nurse. Then, fearing I'd go to jail, sitting up with him until 2am to make sure I hadn't killed him after hospital hotline staff point blank refused to tell us what the maximum safe dose was and insisted we come all the way up to London to find out.

- Being WhatsApped a photo of Einstein with his white hair standing on end as if he'd stuck his finger in an electric socket then realising it was my Uncle Ian complaining that he hadn't had a haircut for six months.

- Switching Graham's chemo sessions from being administered at the hospital to having them delivered at home by masked nurses in white *Breaking Bad* coveralls who hooked Graham up to a drip and then remained out of shot as he participated in video calls with his Foreign Office colleagues.

- Making frantic early-hours calls to the hospice (yes, the dreaded 'H' word was now part of our lives after we'd been referred to them for help with pain control) to get guidance on how much Oramorph and fentanyl Graham could take without accidentally overdosing, because his pain was getting worse and worse, despite him taking long-acting morphine tablets.
- Searching for a seaside studio flat as I'd always fantasised about writing by the sea, and both being smitten by Worthing, a charming town 12 miles from Brighton. Then taking the truly momentous decision to move there from south London, where we'd lived for 27 years. 'If we could live in Worthing, why would we ever go back to Croydon?' said Graham while surveying the aquamarine ocean from our prospective property's balcony.
- Witnessing Pecan's tiny arms slowly sinking to the ground as he took his last breath on our decking after being savaged by a scowling fox. Then watching Graham wrap Pecan's limp, lifeless body in a carrier bag and tenderly place him in our dustbin to stop him being eaten by the murderous fox. And finally seeing Graham later return, slowly open the lid, and cry, when he thought I wasn't looking.

Just as the final lockdown was easing, Graham and I took what would turn out to be our last holiday together: a staycation in Scotland, to celebrate his 58th birthday. In Fort Augustus, on the shore of Loch Ness, we stayed, Rapunzel-like, in the stone tower of a former monastery. The visit was a combination of tranquil hours spent gazing at the mirrored waters of the loch, and high drama, because while we were there, South Africa went up in flames as rampaging rioters torched shopping malls and attacked homes and businesses in what would later be deemed the worst violence the country had experienced since the end of apartheid.

My sister Loren sent us daily dispatches from the frontlines, relating how she and her husband had grabbed whatever weapons they could find – golf clubs, walking sticks and kitchen knives – and joined a local civic defence group where they manned barricades to stop the rioters setting fire to their suburb. Her best friend Angie, she told me, was barricaded into her house in Phoenix, where some of the worst rioting took place, preparing to protect her paralysed mother armed only with curry powder and scalding hot water. Facebook kept me abreast of developments, too, coming up with a video showing quick-witted staff at one shopping mall thwarting would-be looters by pouring cooking oil on the marble floor, turning it into a skating rink.

'We *have* to get Dad out of South Africa *urgently*,' Loren told me. 'I need you to find out whether the UK will let him in without a visa, and what countries bordering South Africa are visa-free. Maybe we can ask his carer to drive him up to Harare and fly him out from there.'

My research showed that the UK was a no-go, but that the Zimbabwe idea could possibly work, provided our dad could endure hiding in the back of a car for 22 hours to escape detection by the rioting mobs. Graham and I thought it too risky for Dad to leave the security of his residential compound, so it was a huge relief when the riots finally petered out and we could try to relax and enjoy the final days of our trip. By now, Graham was experiencing agonising pain episodes increasingly often and also reporting worrying difficulties with his motor co-ordination.

'I don't know what's wrong but I just can't pick up this mug,' he told me, making several passes at it before finally managing to grasp it.

'We'll talk to Dr Yes about it when we get back,' I promised.

One evening, after reluctantly deciding to pull out of our Worthing property purchase because we'd been informed that all the apartment owners were about to be hit with a staggeringly high bill for external renovations despite the building only having been built six years before, we had dinner at Foyers Lodge, a newly renovated guest house overlooking the loch. At the end of our fantastic three-course meal, Graham upset the waitress by accidentally leaving a minuscule tip despite the excellent service (after I'd redone the maths, he adjusted the amount much to my, and the waitress's, relief). Then, during the drive back, he started driving extremely fast.

'Slow down, Graham!' I shouted.

'I can see oncoming traffic perfectly well,' he replied, going even faster.

'Stop it! I mean it! I didn't come to Scotland to die!' I blurted out, tears welling up in my eyes. 'If you don't slow down, I'll walk back.'

Graham eased off the accelerator. His behaviour puzzled me, but once he'd slowed down, I thought nothing more of it.

On the final day of our stay, Graham leaned heavily on my arm and shuffled along like a frail old man as we took a walk beside the Caledonian Canal. A gleaming white yacht called *Seas the Day* was making its way up the staircase of locks when the skipper turned on the yacht's sound system.

LOVE IN THE TIME OF COVID

I couldn't believe that out of the millions of songs he could have chosen, the skipper had selected *Chasing Cars*, a mournful song by Snow Patrol that was played on the radio almost constantly when my mother died. The lyrics reminded me of the way, as a child, I'd loved spooning with Oumie, my maternal grandmother, during our afternoon naps, and the way Graham and I fell asleep every night.

'Let's not go any further,' said Graham.

I thought it was because he was worn out, but then I noticed what looked like buttons jumping on the path ahead of us.

'I don't want to accidentally step on any baby frogs,' said Graham.

I looked more carefully and noticed there were indeed hundreds of tiny frogs struggling to hop through the stubby grass and cross the path to get to the canal. I didn't want to crush them either, so we turned and slowly walked back.

I tried not to think about the lyrics to *Chasing Cars* too much but couldn't help it. It was clear to me that Graham was becoming weaker and weaker. I didn't know *when* he was going to die, or *how* his death would unfold, but I did know that I'd never been more in love – or felt closer to him – than at that moment, touched by his concern for the vulnerable frogs when he was feeling so dreadfully ill himself. I knew, too, without a shadow of a doubt, that although everything was about to change, my love for Graham never would.

The Inflatable 5K where I slipped off an obstacle and injured my arm

Sporting my cat's-whiskers mask

The calm before the storming out

Chapter 11
A bag-of-marbles brain

♪♪ Mood music: *Hurt* by Johnny Cash
The song that captured our heartache

'I think we need to admit Graham to hospital to assess why he's having motor co-ordination issues and is struggling to walk,' said the specialist nurse who acted as Dr Yes's PA. 'It may be that he is suffering from morphine toxicity.'

'I really don't want to go into hospital,' said Graham, when I told him what the nurse had suggested.

'My love, it'll probably only be for one night and hopefully we'll find out why you're feeling so wobbly,' I said.

After spending the night in hospital, Graham called me early the next day, demanding to be discharged immediately.

'They confiscated my Oramorph the minute I arrived and then, when I pressed my call buzzer in the middle of the night because I was in pain, it took the nurses seventeen minutes to get to me,' he told me. 'Then they had to go and fetch the Oramorph because it was locked up somewhere, and then it took ages to work.'

'Oh my love, that must have been horrendous.'

'Trust me, it was. I'm absolutely livid. They say that I haven't got morphine toxicity but, you won't believe this, they didn't give me a blood test or a brain scan: all they did to test that was to ask me to touch my two index fingers together like you would a drunk driver! I'm not staying here another minute longer. I want to be back home with you. This whole hospital admission was a complete waste of time.'

STILL RUNNING AFTER ALL THESE TEARS

Thankfully Graham was discharged later that day, still none the wiser about what was causing his worrying symptoms, but mightily glad that he could get almost instant access to pain relief at home.

Graham and I had giggled like schoolkids when we first came across an advert for the Inflatable 5K, a race comprising two 2.5km laps and 15 blow-up obstacles.

'The Slapper? And The Growler? It's going to be bigger, bouncier and better than ever! What *were* they thinking?' said Graham.

'Graham, enough of the innuendos – do you want to enter it or not?'

'Well we loved watching *Total Wipeout* on TV, so I'm happy to give it a go,' said Graham in a very rare show of non-resistance. I duly signed us up, but then Covid hit and the race was postponed. By the time it was rescheduled, two weeks after our return from Scotland and ten days after his overnight hospital admission, Graham had been signed off work three days before and felt too unwell to attend. Nonetheless, he urged me to go along as he knew frolicking in the fresh air would do me good. I hadn't run at all for several weeks so I was a bit apprehensive, but when I arrived at Brands Hatch and saw everyone from pre-teens to pensioners gamely bouncing, swinging and sliding over all the enormous obstacles, my anxiety lessened and I vowed to stop worrying about my time and focus on having a great one. Goodness knows, I needed it, as Graham's pain episodes had been getting progressively worse, necessitating several phone calls to the hospice each

A BAG-OF-MARBLES BRAIN

night in order to ascertain what additional pain relief he could take to top up the high doses of long-acting morphine he was already on. Not only that, but he'd started waking in the night every 15 minutes or so, desperate to have a pee. As he needed help doing this, I hadn't had an uninterrupted night's sleep for several days.

Right from the start line – a hill fashioned from what looked like a pile of frankfurters – I started to laugh, and I just couldn't stop. Getting punched in the face by giant swinging rubber hammers, leopard-crawling on my stomach through narrow tunnels and clambering over what looked like a spiky, rolling pin, I found each fiendishly challenging obstacle funnier than the last. All around me, all I could hear were grunts and giggles as my fellow competitors hurled themselves through the inflatables, bouncing off the walls and often landing upside- or face-down. It was like being a kid again, and enormously enjoyable.

I was on my second, and final, lap, and within sight of the finish, when it happened. As I exited The Demon – a huge black-and-red mouth with red fangs – I slipped off the inflatable and crashed to the ground, landing heavily on my right shoulder.

'Arggggghhhhhh!' I howled. 'I think I've broken my arm!'

Two marshals immediately rushed over to get me on my feet.

'No, no, please leave me alone! I can't move!' I howled, pain raging through my body.

Concerned spectators and competitors crowded round me as hot tears spilled down my cheeks.

'Let's get you to the medical tent,' said one of the marshals.

'I just need a minute,' I sobbed, cradling my arm and suddenly realising how dumb I'd been entering this race. If I really had broken my arm, who was going to help Graham when he needed to pee or be driven to hospital?

STILL RUNNING AFTER ALL THESE TEARS

Cursing my stupidity, and with a lot of help from the marshals, I eventually staggered to my feet, realising with some embarrassment that my arm wasn't broken after all.

'I think I'm going to be alright,' I told the relieved marshals. 'In fact, I'm so keen to get a medal that I'm going to tackle the final obstacle.'

The drive home, though painful, was uneventful, and when I got back I went upstairs to see Graham who was resting in bed.

'Did anyone say "It's the Big Red Balls!"?' he asked me, referencing *Total Wipeout* presenter Richard Hammond's catchphrase on the TV show. Graham and I and, it turns out, Richard, had loved it when contestants faced the notoriously tricky Big Red Balls obstacle – four giant Swiss balls suspended on poles over a pool of water – as most people had spectacular wipe-outs almost the minute they attempted it.

'There you go again – lowering the tone!' I replied, laughing. 'No, there weren't any Big Red Balls, but I did balls it up by falling off an obstacle and landing on my arm. I think I've torn some tendons in my shoulder.'

'Oh no, you poor thing. Can I make you a cup of tea?' Graham said, struggling to his feet.

'No, my love, I think it's important that you rest. But that's a great idea, I'll make us both one.'

'Lisa, help me, please help me, I'm having a stroke!' Graham cried out early one morning three days later, his voice high pitched with panic. I'd been asleep when I'd suddenly felt his body shaking uncontrollably next to mine.

A BAG-OF-MARBLES BRAIN

'Lisa, do something! Call an ambulance!' he cried, deathly pale and visibly shocked by what was happening.

As I frantically fumbled with my phone, the convulsions increased in intensity until his entire body was jerking so violently that he fell to the floor, hitting his head on the bedside table as he did so.

'I'm calling them, my love, just hang on in there,' I said, my heart racing.

A few seconds later Graham stopped shaking and I attempted to lift him back into bed, an agonising task due to my injured shoulder. The ambulancemen arrived a short while later and, after taking Graham's vital signs, reassured us both that he didn't appear to have had a stroke and was going to be okay. Much to our relief, when they heard that we were due to see a doctor at the hospice later that day, they said it wasn't necessary for Graham to be admitted to hospital.

Our meeting with the hospice doctor was one of the best experiences we'd ever had with a medic. A middle-aged woman with short blonde hair and a kindly face, she listened intently to what we had to say, made suggestions for how Graham could adjust his pain meds and told us that Graham waking up every 15 minutes in the night to urinate meant he probably had a urinary-tract infection. Unbelievably, in my sleep-deprived state, this thought hadn't once crossed my mind. The doctor also advised Graham to have an MRI brain scan to determine, once and for all, what was causing his lack of co-ordination. Besides these practical pointers, what we appreciated most was that she respected our desire to remain positive and even found a way to suggest we discuss end-of-life options without using negative language.

'I like to call it "parallel planning",' she told us. 'It's important to consider what you'd like to do if things don't go the way you want them to.' It really is incredible what a difference a simple change in terminology can make. What would you rather talk about? Palliative care? End-of-life options? Or do a spot of 'parallel planning', a term free from fear?

The next morning, a violent seizure once again tore through Graham's body like a tornado and again caused him to fall out of bed. This time, although I was aware of how awful it was for Graham, I wasn't as concerned as I knew he'd made a full recovery the day before. Incredibly, seizures had already become the 'new normal'.

Like anyone who didn't live with a hairdresser during the Covid lockdowns in the UK, Graham's oncologist, whom we'd nicknamed Dr Yes, could have done with a haircut, I thought, when he greeted us with an elbow bump at the hospital. A tall man with a mop of blond hair, I noticed that his blue eyes almost matched the colour of his face mask. Although Graham had run into him a few times when he'd gone to the hospital to have chemo, I'd never met him as I'd had to remain in our car outside. Graham's specialist nurse, a bespectacled woman with long, bleached blonde hair caught up in a ponytail, was also in attendance, and acknowledged Graham but ignored me. Even though most of her face was covered by her face mask, I was aware of her glowering at me. I'd previously raised concerns with her about Graham's unbearable pain not being addressed, his sudden weight loss not being acted upon (meaning he could potentially not be eligible for further chemotherapy) and several medication issues.

'I almost feel that if I don't question things and follow them up, things could go horribly wrong,' I'd texted her. 'I've helped

A BAG-OF-MARBLES BRAIN

Graham dodge a few bullets but am concerned that there may be things I'm unaware of and hence can't prevent or rectify.' I'd ended the text with the words 'What's done is done but I need reassurance that going forward we can all work together and be proactive and give the next steps the best possible chance. Thanks for all you've single-handedly done to move things forward – we are really grateful,' so I was astounded by her attitude, which made it hard to focus on what Dr Yes was saying.

'Mesothelioma only spreads to the brain in three per cent of patients,' he said, 'but we'll give you an MRI scan today to check whether you've got any brain tumours.' I was surprisingly calm at this news, and even managed to ask a few questions though I was painfully aware of the nurse scowling in the corner. Three per cent was a reassuringly low number, I thought.

That evening, as Graham and I sat on the sofa in our living room, we got the call I hadn't been dreading, as I'd worked hard on not worrying about Graham's health until we'd heard incontrovertible facts.

'I'm afraid the cancer's spread to your brain, Graham,' said Dr Yes, his voice changing in that by now all-too-familiar way into periscope-speak as I struggled to come to terms with the horrific implications of the news.

'Whole-brain radiotherapy might be an option,' he said. When the short call ended, Graham and I sat looking at each other in shock. We didn't discuss what the news meant. We didn't cry. Or scream. We both felt too numb to react.

When Sophie Sabbage was told she had too many brain tumours to count, she'd resisted having whole-brain radiotherapy as it can change your personality. At that point I didn't even consider the fact that this treatment might rob Graham of everything that made him my special person, my beloved husband. All I could

STILL RUNNING AFTER ALL THESE TEARS

think of was that we hadn't reached the end of the road quite yet – there was still *something* the doctors could do.

'I've already got one,' I said, pointing to my mask made from a fabric festooned with flamingos when a young woman seated at a table at the hospital entrance tried to offer me a disposable one.

'It's hospital policy that everyone wears a fresh face mask,' she smiled.

'But the masks you have here are so *boring*!' I said, grabbing one from the box on the table in front of her. 'If you really want us to wear them, you should at least give us *designer* ones!'

'That's a great idea,' she laughed. 'Perhaps I should set up a business doing just that.'

Graham and I had come up to London again for a radiotherapy planning session in which they'd make a plastic mould of Graham's head to hold it still while he was having whole-brain radiotherapy. Once the mould had been cast, we had a brief meeting with the clinical oncologist who'd be supervising Graham's radiotherapy sessions.

'I wish I could do more to help,' he said. 'Do want to see your brain scan? Not everyone does.'

We nodded, and the doctor held up what looked like an X-ray of a bag of marbles. I couldn't comprehend what I was seeing. How on earth had Graham managed to drive us around Scotland with so many tumours crowding into his skull? No wonder he was driving so recklessly. And had forgotten how to do simple maths when calculating our restaurant tip. How had he managed to walk? Or talk? Or think? Again my own brain shut off from the horrible sight I'd just seen, so much so that I was able to draw

A BAG-OF-MARBLES BRAIN

a set of cat's whiskers on my hospital mask in the toilets before we left. On the way out we passed the friendly woman I'd spoken to before.

'This is the kind of thing you could put on your designer masks,' I said, pointing to my newly decorated one.

'Yes, I do think cat masks could be the next big thing,' she giggled.

At that point Professor Chris Whitty, the man who'd been on TV standing beside Boris Johnson advising us on the government's response to the pandemic almost every evening, walked past. We made eye contact and I smiled, though I knew my mask meant he couldn't see me do it.

'That was Chris Whitty!' I said to Graham. 'I can't believe I just saw the man himself. Did you see him?'

Unlike me, Graham never got excited when he spotted celebrities, even if they were super-famous ones, and found the fact that I keep a small notebook of stars I've encountered ridiculous. But I mean, Paula Radcliffe, Nelson Mandela (I shook his hand, no less), Jude Law, Bill Clinton, Steve Cram, Demi Moore, Princess Di, the Popé, Jack Nicholson, Stephen Fry, Kelly Holmes… c'mon, any normal person would need to make a note of that kind of thing.

Graham chuckled: 'Yes,' he said. 'It's just a pity that you were wearing a cat mask when you saw him!' My hand flew to my face.

'Oh no! But he probably didn't notice!'

'He noticed. Trust me, he noticed.'

It amazes me now that we were able to have this everyday conversation when Graham had so recently been delivered a death sentence, but we did.

STILL RUNNING AFTER ALL THESE TEARS

After a weekend off from whole-brain radiotherapy, we decided that Graham should stay overnight in the hospital for four nights to spare him the discomfort of having to travel in to town every day on London's potholed roads to receive the rest of his treatments.

The private ward was on one of the top floors of the hospital and I was eager to see it as I knew it would have an amazing view.

'Don't get too excited,' said Graham as the lift ascended. 'It's actually rather shabby up there.' Sure enough, I was shocked by the small room with scuffed walls we were directed into: it screamed seedy motorway motel, not private medi-spa. Granted, the views of leafy London were amazing, but the room didn't even have an Ikea print on the wall. Even Travelodges had those.

'Let's get a selfie of us and the view,' I said to Graham. As we took the photo, a young doctor walked into the room.

'Hello,' he said. 'I just need to ask you a few questions and then you can settle yourselves in. Firstly, if you brought any pain-relief medication in with you, I need you to hand it over.'

'There is no way my husband is surrendering his Oramorph,' I told him. 'The last time he stayed here overnight it took your nurses seventeen minutes to respond to his call for help. That's *totally* unacceptable.'

In the face of my fierce resistance, the doctor backed down, and reluctantly agreed to let Graham keep his pain meds, but when the head nurse arrived, she immediately informed us that this went against hospital policy. I changed the subject.

'My husband is having violent seizures,' I told the doctor, eyeing the unpadded headboard of the battered-looking bed. 'Who's going to check that he doesn't injure his head in the night?'

'Oh, I suppose you can pay a healthcare assistant to sit in his room overnight,' he said, 'although they would probably be

A BAG-OF-MARBLES BRAIN

asleep when your husband was awake.' Even though the Ministry of Defence would be footing the bill, it was galling to hear that the British taxpayer would be paying thousands of pounds for a healthcare assistant to have a nap.

I could feel my temper starting to flare up and went into full 'lioness protecting her cubs' mode: 'I'm starting to think my husband would be better off being cared for by me, at home, since you're not even familiar with your own pain-relief policy,' I said. 'In fact, he received *appalling* care the last time he was here.'

I looked over to Graham, who was making a throat-cutting gesture with his hand, but by now there was no stopping me. 'That time the doctors here didn't even give him a brain scan. His brain is now *riddled* with brain tumours and they failed to spot that. He could have had a seizure while driving and *killed* people – or himself. I have absolutely *no* faith in *any* of you!'

'I'm sorry, ma'am,' said the doctor sheepishly, looking down at his shoes like a naughty schoolboy, thereby destroying any remaining shred of respect I had for him.

'Should we leave, Graham?' I asked. He nodded. And so, my cheeks flushed with fury, I rushed round the room collecting our belongings and then we headed for the exit, followed in quick succession by the head nurse, the doctor and the finance officer who'd hurtled out of her office wanting to discuss refunding the hefty fee we'd already paid.

'Talk to our lawyers about the payment!' I called out as we stepped into the lift.

'I'm sorry if I caused a scene,' I said to Graham as we descended to the ground floor. 'At home I can give you Oramorph in seconds whenever you need it, and our headboard is padded so you won't hurt your head. I didn't trust those bozos one little bit.'

STILL RUNNING AFTER ALL THESE TEARS

Graham chuckled. 'Their faces were a picture when we stormed out. I bet they're gutted as they've just lost £10,000.'

'My goodness, does it really cost so much to stay in that shitty little room?' I gasped. 'You could stay at The Ritz for that.'

'Actually, I checked, and you can stay in an *executive suite* at The Ritz for less than that,' Graham laughed, 'but sadly I don't think the Ministry of Defence would reimburse us.'

'Sadly not. I quite fancy staying at The Ritz,' I said. 'By the way, why were you signalling me to be quiet?'

'It was a bit embarrassing for me,' said Graham. 'The doctor you were ranting at was the one who'd given me the finger-touching test the last time I was here.'

'He's lucky I didn't know that at the time,' I laughed, 'or I'd have given that Fucker an even greater piece of my mind. Or even the finger!'

'I think he got the message,' said Graham, smiling.

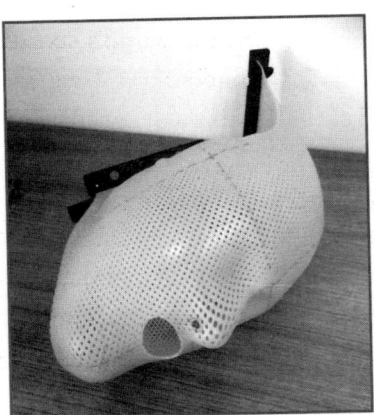

Graham's Voldemort radiotherapy mask

Chapter 12
The longest day

♪♪ Mood music: *Hopelessly Devoted to You* by Olivia Newton-John
Because we both were

'How on earth does the UK, the world's sixth biggest economy, have roads like this?' I wondered as I zig-zagged around the family-pizza-sized craters with the heartbreaking knowledge that each time I drove through one, Graham would cry out in pain and clutch his right side where a large tumour was gnawing away at his rib. This was precisely why we'd wanted Graham to stay in the hospital but The Fuckers had made that impossible.

Graham emerged from his sixth and final whole-brain radiotherapy session holding a gruesome-looking blue plastic mask that resembled the creepy goalie hockey mask worn by serial killer Jason Voorhees in the *Friday the 13th* films.

'My nurse gave me my mask as a souvenir,' he said cheerily. 'Apparently another cancer patient grew flowers in hers.'

I shuddered. 'There's no way I'm planting petunias in this,' I thought, stowing it in my tote bag as we made our way from the radiotherapy department to the ward where Graham would receive his first dose of epirubicin, a new chemo drug. The nurse tasked with administering the ruby-red concoction informed us that this type of chemo was so toxic that it was 'like taking a scouring pad to the inside of your veins'. Charming. In fact, it was so lethal, she told us, that she had to administer it to Graham personally via a syringe rather than a drip: that way, if there were severe side effects, she'd be able to instantly stop the infusion. The nurse had just inserted the needle – in a cubicle the size of a toilet – when Graham's nurse, whom by now I'd nicknamed Nurse Ratched after the passive-aggressive character in *One Flew Over the Cuckoo's Nest*, appeared. She proceeded to greet Graham and once again ignore me. There could be no mistake that the snub was, as it had been when I'd first met her, deliberate.

Incensed, the minute she left, I texted my friend Sarah and told her what had happened.

'Graham's nurse sounds like a nightmare,' she texted back. 'How dare she treat you like that. Doesn't she understand how much pressure you're under? It's not her job to make you feel worse!'

'I'll ask to speak to her as it worked when I was bullied by a fashionista at *Cosmo*!' I texted back.

'Yes, an LJ charm offensive sounds like a good plan,' wrote Sarah, unaware that I was sorely tempted to go for the 'nuclear option' and let rip with all my grievances.

'Ha, ha, more like a rage offensive!' I replied. 'But you're right – rapport works better than torture, according to a radio programme I listened to last night.'

'We need to talk,' I texted Nurse Ratched, who'd given us her mobile number as she was our main point of contact with Dr Yes.

'Alone, or with Graham?'

'Alone,' I shot back. She reappeared and led me to an empty room. I could feel the fury bubbling up inside me but I remained calm and quietly spelled out all my concerns.

Nurse Ratched gave some implausible explanations that, had I been in Armageddon Mode, I wouldn't have let her get away with, but I knew she held a lot of sway in the hospital, so performing nothing short of a miracle, I held my tongue.

THE LONGEST DAY

However, when Graham and I returned home, my rage erupted like an Icelandic volcano, tearing through my body with a ferocity I'd never felt before. My temples throbbed, my face flushed bright red. The lump in my throat made it hard to swallow, let alone breathe. My anger was so intense that I truly thought I was going to become Croydon's first documented case of spontaneous human combustion. That I'd burst into flames and, when the fire brigade came to investigate, they'd discover a smouldering pile of ash and bones surrounded by unscathed furniture. Strange as it may sound, I actually feared for my life as I'd never felt this way before. I simply couldn't go on feeling like this.

And then it hit me: the only thing I thought might, just might help, was going for a run. Four years earlier, shortly after Graham had been diagnosed, a very loud voice in my head had proclaimed, in the middle of the night, as if through a megaphone: 'RUNNING WILL BE YOUR SALVATION'. I knew those words to be true, but often couldn't muster up the energy to do the one thing that was guaranteed to make me feel better. Instead, I'd scoff down too much chocolate and swig buckets of wine. Running always felt like slogging through superglue, but that day I forced myself to walk to Addiscombe Recreation Ground, a small, trapezoid-shaped park near our home, before breaking into a run. The first section was slightly uphill, but I pushed onwards, ignoring my body begging me to stop already. 'I think I can, I know I can,' I chanted to myself as I passed the tennis courts. A squirrel scampered up the side of a tree to my right, bringing our beloved little Pecan to mind. I choked back a tear. When I reached the top of the path and turned left, I was grateful that I was now on the flat, which would allow me to catch my breath. The leafy canopy above me threw down little patches of sunlight where the leaves weren't dense enough to block out the sun. Another sharp left and I was running downhill, savouring the way gravity was sharing the load and giving me the chance to process the rudeness of that nurse. What type of person didn't greet a woman who'd just been told her husband didn't have long to live? How fucking dare she show no remorse about all the balls she and the other Fuckers had dropped? Quite frankly, there was only one word for the way Graham's care was being handled, and that word was 'shitshow'. Now my anger made more sense to me. Of course Nurse Ratched's behaviour wasn't bloody okay. I felt my rage being replaced by a deep sense of compassion for myself and what we'd gone through over the past four years. And step by step, bit by breathless bit, the anger started to subside. Round and round that park I waddled, dreading the uphill section but knowing that the flat and downhill bits were just around the next corner. I don't know how many laps I ran, but what I do know is that afterwards an entirely different woman walked through our front door than the one who'd left. That run was like cutting off the napalm supply to a flamethrower, it really was.

The next day I urged Graham to come for a walk with me as it was a gloriously sunny summer's day. The minute we stepped outside it was apparent Graham was a changed man: he had to hold on to a neighbour's wall for fear of falling over and at times was tottering like a frail geriatric. On the consent form we'd been told the side effects of whole-brain radiotherapy were minimal, the most serious of which seemed to be 'tiredness'. Tiredness? Really? The treatment was intended to relieve Graham's symptoms, but as far as I could tell it had medically lobotomised and hobbled him. I was so worried about how unsteady Graham was on his feet that, leaving him sitting on a low wall, I rushed back inside our house to fetch a pair of walking poles and a cycling helmet, so that if he did fall over he wouldn't sustain a head injury. Slowly

THE LONGEST DAY

and painfully we made our way to the end of our road and back. Even now, Graham's sense of humour didn't desert us.

'I must look like a right plonker dressed up like this,' he said. 'Our neighbours must be thinking I'm training for a trek to the North Pole.'

Six days after his radiotherapy ended – and showing little improvement in his walking – Graham experienced what he'd later describe as 'the worst day of my life'. At 4.30am he had another massive seizure, by far the worst he'd ever had, that paralysed his entire left-hand side. Suspecting a stroke, I dialled 999 and not long afterwards, two paramedics arrived and blue-lighted us to a nearby hospital. On arrival, I was asked to remain in the waiting room while Graham was taken off for a brain scan. An hour later, a young doctor with kind brown eyes informed me that Graham hadn't had a stroke and that the seizure had been caused by a swelling around a brain tumour that steroids and anti-seizure meds could hopefully prevent in future. I was allowed in to see Graham, who was very relieved to see me, and we sat chatting for several hours before he was suddenly told he was going to be moved.

'Say goodbye to your husband,' the porter said. 'Visitors aren't allowed on this ward due to Covid rules.' I looked on helplessly as Graham was wheeled away, realising too late that I was in possession of his mobile phone, so he had no way of contacting me. Several hours and much pleading later I managed to gain access to the ward where I found Graham, visibly distressed, sitting all alone in a wheelchair in a private room, like a tiny shivering bird on a telephone wire.

STILL RUNNING AFTER ALL THESE TEARS

'This is the worst day of my life,' said Graham quietly as I helped him pee, noticing with alarm that his leg was shaking uncontrollably.

Several hours later, in the mid-afternoon, an elderly oncologist arrived.

'Your husband has to be able to walk upstairs to your bedroom unaided before I can discharge him,' he said.

'That's ridiculous,' I replied. 'If we have to wait for that, he'll be here for two weeks!'

After a long discussion the oncologist reluctantly agreed to let Graham go home. Four hours later, I was told he'd 'forgotten' to sign Graham's discharge notes so we'd have to remain even longer while this was sorted out. We waited, and waited. Assuming that transport home had been arranged, I went to enquire when the ambulance would arrive.

'Perhaps in the next three hours,' said the nurse in charge.

'*Another three hours*? We've already been here for twelve! Can I arrange a private ambulance?' I asked in desperation.

'I'm afraid not,' said the nurse. 'Perhaps you can book an Uber?'

By chance I bumped into the young doctor who'd cared for Graham when he'd first arrived early that morning. His eyes were bloodshot and he looked utterly exhausted.

'I need your help,' I told him tearfully. 'The ambulance still hasn't come so I'm going to arrange an Uber but I need Graham's discharge notes. I'll also need a porter to help me get him into the car as he still seems to be paralysed and I'm not strong enough to lift him.'

The doctor promised to help, and a little while later, a full 13 hours after Graham was admitted, the discharge summary was printed out.

THE LONGEST DAY

When the Uber arrived, a porter came to assist me. Together we grabbed Graham under both armpits and heaved him bodily onto the back seat of the Uber where he writhed in agony. I then rushed round to the other rear door and, using both arms, including my 'bouncy castle' injured one, hauled Graham further into the car and into a seated position, all the while reassuring him that he'd soon be home.

'You two are so good together,' said the porter as he helped me put on Graham's seatbelt. 'I wish you well for the future.'

As we were driven home through the pot-holed streets, Graham groaned quietly with each jolt while I made frantic calls to my neighbours. At first, no one picked up as it was so late, but eventually two of them returned my calls and agreed to help me carry Graham upstairs. A collapsible garden chair was the only way we could think of to lift him. Even though Graham weighed just 63kg, it was an immense struggle to manoeuvre him up our steep stairs. At one point I thought a neighbour was going to fall backward and so I grabbed his bottom and pushed against it to stop that from happening.

'Oooh, Matron,' he joked. 'I haven't had a woman do that to me in a *very* long time!'

'It's your lucky day,' I laughed.

By about 10pm, Graham was safely back in our bed. The worst day of his life, and one of the longest and worst of mine, was finally over.

Cutting Graham's hair

Chapter 13
Hanging up my carer hat

♪♪ **Mood music:** *My Eyes Adored You* **by Frankie Valli**
The song that captured our enduring love

Hospice. The word that had so terrified Graham 17 months before was now suddenly – and painfully – relevant. In the three days since Graham had been discharged from hospital, he'd been screaming in agony so loudly during the night that on several occasions I'd feared our neighbours would call the police. The hospice doctor we'd consulted had convinced us that the only way they'd be able to bring his excruciating pain under control would be for him to be admitted as an inpatient so that they could try out new pain-relief options and immediately treat any side effects resulting from them.

'It's time you stopped being Graham's carer and became his wife again,' she told me.

On the morning Graham was due to be transferred to the hospice, he asked me to shave his head since the whole-brain radiotherapy had done what the chemo hadn't: made a lot of his hair fall out.

'I don't want to resemble a hirsute Gollum,' he told me. 'And I only want you to shave my head, not my beard, as I don't want to look like a cancer victim.'

It was a surprisingly tender moment as I sat Graham up in bed, wrapped his shoulders in a lime-green towel and began to remove the hair everyone thought he'd dyed as it was still so dark despite his salt-and-pepper beard.

STILL RUNNING AFTER ALL THESE TEARS

The triple-lubricated Gillette razor glided smoothly over Graham's scalp and, just as his beard (in my eyes at least) had aged him ten years, his baldness aged him another ten. For the first time since his diagnosis, he looked really ill.

When two burly, 60-something paramedics arrived to transfer him to the hospice, Graham suddenly enquired whether he could ask them a question.

'Sure, mate,' said one of the paramedics, a chubby, elderly man who looked like the sort of jovial uncle who'd offer you a Werther's Original sweet.

Carefully fingering his bald head, Graham asked: 'What does my hair look like? It feels long but Lisa was supposed to have shaved it.'

The paramedic burst out laughing. 'I thought your question would be more profound, mate, and that you were going to ask me and George an existential question there. Honestly, you look just like us!' he said, pointing to their bald heads.

Graham chuckled, and I walked over to stroke his head. To my surprise, he was right – I *had* missed a bit. The razor was brought out again and I gave Graham another thorough shave, to relieve him of that worry, before the ambulancemen took him away.

I followed the ambulance in our car, and was relieved to find parking in a side street. Having washed my hands for the UK-government-recommended two rounds of *Happy Birthday* in the trough that had been installed for this purpose under the entrance awning, I signed in and was given directions to Graham's room. He'd already been helped into the hospital bed by the time I arrived, and I was pleased to see he'd been given

HANGING UP MY CARER HAT

a room with expansive windows overlooking a courtyard and garden. My first task was to fill in a one-page profile about Graham that would help the staff understand the patient they were caring for. As Graham had fallen asleep, I sat by his bedside and filled it in on his behalf. Under 'What people appreciate about me' I put 'My sense of humour, integrity, intelligence and kind and caring nature (I made tea for my wife and took it upstairs even when I could barely walk to show my support for her).' Under 'What is important to me' I'd written 'Being pain free; acknowledgement of the severity of the pain I'm in – at times it's like holding my hand in a flame and so I can't wait ages for medication to be administered; getting back my walking and sitting skills.' Under 'How to support me' I wrote 'Please supply me with Oramorph and a urinal as soon as I need one as I've been ignored in other hospitals; please avoid touching my right ribcage as I have an agonising tumour there.' At the bottom of the piece of paper I drew a sketch of Graham's head – a little round circle depicting him with a beard, spectacles and only five hairs on his head.

Next up was a two-hour solo interview with one of the hospice doctors that was punctuated by tears. I poured out my heart to her, telling her what immense pain Graham was in and how we no longer trusted healthcare professionals after the horrendous experiences we'd had. She expressed sympathy for our ordeal, assured me that they'd do their best to manage Graham's pain, and then went on to explain the concept of 'total pain', something I'd never heard of before.

'Pain isn't just physical,' she told me. 'When someone has a terminal illness, their suffering can also be caused by spiritual, emotional and social factors. Graham may be scared of death, for example, or have issues he needs to resolve with loved ones.

STILL RUNNING AFTER ALL THESE TEARS

When someone's experiencing total pain, even a pinprick can feel like being stabbed.'

I told her that Graham had told me many times he wasn't afraid of death and, as far as I knew, was completely at peace with everyone he held dear. What I didn't realise then, and wish I'd known, was that death itself is actually never something to be feared, it's *dying* that should worry us far more.

By the end of the interview, I was clutching a fistful of wet tissues, but I reckoned it was worth it as I felt the hospice now had the full picture. Surely they wouldn't make the same mistakes everyone else had made? Now that Graham was in the hands of experts, I hoped I could hang up my metaphorical stethoscope and put on my wedding ring again, as the other hospice doctor had suggested.

While I was out of the room, Graham had undergone a similar interview with a different doctor and I was touched to see that his answer to the question 'What is important to you right now?' read: '1. Pain 2. Mobility 3. Lisa.'

That evening, Graham was served roasted-vegetable lasagne, seasonal vegetables, fresh fruit salad and a Big 5 smoothie.

'Goodness me,' he said as he eyed all the nourishing foodstuffs crammed onto his tray, 'I can't believe I'm going on a health kick, starting today.' I laughed, too, amazed that they'd managed to pack so much nutrition into a single meal. Satisfied that he'd be well looked after, I took my leave, detouring past a 24-hour Tesco store to pick up a bottle of whisky so I could have a nip while watching *Below Deck*. This would be the first night in ages that I wasn't on 'pee duty', and I wanted to make sure I slept like a log.

HANGING UP MY CARER HAT

By the time I arrived back the next day, feeling less tired after not having had to help Graham urinate throughout the night, he'd already had breakfast. I had a chat to the head nurse, and mentioned how concerned I was that Graham hadn't had a bowel movement for six days.

'Can't you give him a suppository?' I asked, knowing from personal experience how awful it can feel when you're blocked up.

'I don't think it'll do much good,' she said.

'Surely it's worth a try,' I persisted, wondering why the staff weren't more worried about this.

'I bet this is your dream job,' said Graham apologetically as the nurse inserted the tampon-shaped suppository. Fifteen minutes later he'd done a cowpat-sized poo that astonished the care assistants when I summoned them to help me clean him up. I fetched my imaginary stethoscope: my job as medical director was clearly not yet over.

Just after lunch we had a visitor: a doctor with prematurely greying hair pulled into a low ponytail.

'I'm Doctor Elaine. How are you today, Graham?' she slowly whispered, like an undertaker giving seating directions in a crematorium. I could almost hear a tinny-sounding electric organ playing in the background. Why was she talking in that weird Doctor Death voice?

'I'm worried, Graham,' she continued.

'About what?' Graham asked, alarmed.

'Your health,' she replied. Graham cast a fearful glance at me. With those two words she'd dealt our positivity a hammer blow. I was livid. I'd informed both of the other doctors that we'd taken the decision to remain hopeful and not discuss how long Graham had left to live. Were those lengthy conversations really just another massive waste of breath? Graham had a fucking PhD, for fuck's sake. English was his first language. *Of course* he knew that being admitted to a hospice – and having a brain riddled with brain tumours – meant he was in a bad way, so why the hell did she have to state the obvious?

'I don't think you're going to be well enough to have chemo on Friday,' she continued.

'Let's just wait and see,' I said, attempting to reassure Graham. 'That reminds me, I wanted to let you know that I'll be giving a talk at the RunFestRun festival on Friday, so I won't be around to help transport Graham up to the hospital if the chemo goes ahead.'

'Will there be another event next year?'

'I assume so.'

'If I were you, I'd cancel your appearance,' she said. 'You can always attend next year.'

Doctor Death stood up to leave and I followed her out into the corridor. I couldn't let the 'mood grenade' she'd dropped go unchallenged.

'I've made it *very* clear to everyone here that Graham and I live in hope not fear,' I said, my voice trembling with the effort not to shout. 'I told you that we cope with this horrible illness by remaining optimistic.'

The doctor shifted uncomfortably from foot to foot.

'Why *exactly* did you think it necessary to tell Graham you were worried about him?' I continued. 'You're taking away his hope.'

Doctor Death inclined her head to one side, giving me the full 'sympathy head tilt'.

'Do you want me to *lie* to Graham?' she challenged me.

I thought for a moment. 'Yes,' I said slowly. 'He wants to live in hope till the very end, and I can't see any point in you saying things like that.'

HANGING UP MY CARER HAT

'In that case, do *you* want to be lied to?'

Again I hesitated. 'No,' I replied. 'I think I'm strong enough to deal with whatever you need to tell me, but Graham isn't at this point. And one final thing, please don't tell him you're cancelling the chemo – just say it's been postponed.'

When I returned to Graham's room, I could see the damage Doctor Death had wreaked: he was looking extremely pale and his previously upbeat mood was now flatlining.

'If I don't get that chemo, I'm a dead man,' he said sorrowfully.

'Graham, don't talk like that,' I said. 'The chemo's just been postponed until you're stronger. They haven't cancelled it.'

A couple of years later I read a remarkable book called *Grief Works* by the psychotherapist Julia Samuel, who supported the stance I took with Doctor Death. 'I strongly disagree with medics and therapists who insist that their patients need to be forced to face reality when they're in denial,' she wrote. 'My belief is that it isn't our job to march around in hobnail boots in someone else's consciousness, breaking down their important defence mechanisms, as if we can be absolutely certain about what's best for them.' Thank you, Julia, thank you *so* much.

In his heart-warming book *Being Mortal*, the American surgeon Atul Gawande quotes Sarah Creed, a hospice nurse who says the following about patients admitted to a hospice: 'Ninety-nine per cent understand they're dying, but one hundred per cent hope they're not.' Sarah goes on to say that when admitting a patient she avoids saying 'I'm so sorry', but instead says 'I'm the hospice nurse, and here's what I have to offer you to make your life better. And I know we don't have a lot of time to waste.'

Henry Marsh, the renowned neurosurgeon and author of *And Finally*, also backed up my view when he himself was diagnosed with advanced prostate cancer. 'Hope is all-important,' he said

STILL RUNNING AFTER ALL THESE TEARS

in a *Guardian* webinar I attended. 'We can cope with almost everything if we hope we will live longer. You must never lie to patients but also not deprive them of hope.'

As a hypnobirthing teacher and trained doula (birth companion), I've been privileged to attend five births, and recall seeing posters stuck to the hospital walls reminding medical staff of the vital importance of skin-to-skin contact for newborns. Perhaps it's time hospices and hospitals considered installing posters for the terminally ill, too, to remind caregivers that the dying should never be deprived of hope. The message I'd like to see printed on them? 'To live in hope is to make room for joy.'

I left the hospice just after dinnertime that day because I'd booked in a hypnotherapy session with a truly lovely fertility client, Justine, who was about to undergo another round of IVF. We'd been working together for close on a year and she'd decided to have one last attempt. I'd been delighted at her decision as something inside me just wouldn't give up on the idea that she was destined to become a mother and, I later found out, her husband had felt the same. I simply couldn't desert her in her hour of need when we'd come this far.

'Are you sure you're okay to go ahead with the session?' said Justine, looking concerned, when I connected with her on Skype. I usually wouldn't dream of telling my clients what was going on in my private life, but we'd known each other for so long that she could immediately tell I wasn't myself.

'Justine, this may sound really strange, but right now working with you is *exactly* what I need,' I told her. 'I feel so powerless at the moment, but knowing I can do something to help you makes me feel strong.' We went ahead with the session as planned and, although I was exhausted when I started, by the end I felt energised. Justine, too, said she felt a renewed sense of hope.

Just before going to bed, I checked the emails on my phone and was overjoyed to receive a message from another hypnotherapy client letting me know that she was pregnant – with twins! It was the third such message I'd received since Graham had been admitted to the hospice.

'I think the Universe is trying to tell me something,' I smiled as I reached to switch off my bedside light, not knowing that before long, Justine would indeed be cradling a newborn in her arms. Her baby's name? Hope.

Graham smiles at me from his hospice bed

Chapter 14
Unbearable pain and a visit from a poltergeist

♪♪ **Mood music: *Poltergeist* by Banks**
The song about 'noisy ghosts'

'Whaaaaaat?' screamed my brain when, having arrived early to help feed Graham breakfast, a hospice nurse informed me that he'd had two anxiety attacks in the night.

'We had to sedate him because he was really anxious and suffering from a lot of total pain,' she said.

'He's never suffered from anxiety before,' I told her, 'not even when he was first diagnosed, so that doesn't make sense.'

My mind was racing – I felt sick at this news. There was no way that Graham was in total pain. Why would he suddenly be afraid of death or remember some unfinished business? This was a man who'd been questioned by the Iranian secret police in Shiraz for two hours without showing any signs of fear. A man who'd braved the burning barricades in Bolivia during the 2003 Gas War and not once believed we'd be killed, despite the fact that nearly 60 locals lost their lives. Graham just didn't *do* anxiety.

'It may have been because his call buzzer was placed in his left hand,' the nurse continued casually. My mind could not compute what I was hearing: it felt as if a vortex had opened up under my feet and was sucking me under. Graham wasn't experiencing 'total pain', he was experiencing *Actual Physical Pain*, and couldn't summon anyone to administer pain relief because the call button had been placed in his *paralysed* hand

STILL RUNNING AFTER ALL THESE TEARS

and the nurses' station was at the far end of the corridor from his room. I was horrified. And I felt a huge wave of guilt at having left him alone and defenceless. There was no way I was ever going to do that again.

'Please can you bring me several changes of clothes, my toiletry bag, my facecloth, my travel mug and a bottle of red wine,' I texted a friend. Despite the fact there wasn't a shower in Graham's room, I made the decision to move into the hospice, resolving to wash myself in his hand basin whenever I needed to.

I rushed to the nurses' station to raise my concerns.

'Please can you come back later,' I was told, 'we're in the middle of a handover.'

Back in Graham's room, now on high alert, I observed how long it took for Graham to receive his Oramorph, which had been confiscated on arrival. We'd press the buzzer and often wait for up to 20 minutes before a staff member would arrive. After being told he needed pain relief, they'd amble down to the medicine safe to fetch his medication with the same sense of urgency as if they'd been asked to clean up a spill in the supermarket pickle aisle. I never once saw any of them hurry. I wanted to insert a rocket up their arses.

'Why don't you hold your hand in a flame for up to 30 minutes and see how you like it?' I thought angrily when I realised that this was how long Graham was often having to wait before the morphine actually kicked in. Back home, I had free access to Oramorph and could administer it to him in seconds.

That afternoon, Graham's family came to see him, and so he was hoisted into a wheelchair and taken out to the garden. It was not a good visit as Graham was in considerable pain.

'I don't want any fucking tea, Ma,' he said to his mum, the

UNBEARABLE PAIN AND A VISIT FROM A POLTERGEIST

first time in 35 years that I'd heard him swear at her.

We cut the visit short. Back inside I alerted the staff that Graham was ready to go back to bed and needed them to operate the hoist. We waited. And waited.

'We're just helping another patient and then we'll be with you straight away,' said a nurse when I went to enquire what was taking them so long.

More time passed, and when Graham told me he needed to do a poo, I told him to go ahead as he was wearing incontinence pants and I believed the nurses were only minutes away. For another 20 minutes I did what I could to distract him from the pain and the indignity of sitting in his own excrement, but I could see from his face that he was in torment.

'Please, Lisa, I beg of you. Please go and fetch those nurses. I am in so much pain,' he cried.

I again went to fetch help. This time I was told they were busy taking dinner orders. A full hour after we'd got back to his room, two staff members pitched up, hoisted him back into bed and helped get him clean. I was close to tears.

That evening, after dinner, I chatted to Graham while sipping Malbec from my travel mug. Sadly, by now, he was too ill to join me. I told him that one of the Marie Curie nurses who'd been assigned to care for him had mentioned something called 'hospice at home', in which terminally ill patients were cared for by district nurses and carers in their own homes.

'I'd much rather be at home than here,' said Graham.

'Me too,' I replied. 'There are ridiculously long delays in fetching your Oramorph, and what happened this afternoon was just horrendous.' It's evidence of how sleep deprived and exhausted I was that I didn't for a second think to question why the experimental pain meds that had been promised hadn't been administered, despite them being the main reason we'd agreed to having him admitted.

'I really do want to go home,' said Graham.

'Well that's settled then, I'll arrange it tomorrow,' I reassured him.

Before getting ready for bed, I had second thoughts about our decision. Would I be able to cope with nursing Graham myself? I'd done so before, but had found it exhausting, especially with my injured arm. In my sleep-deprived, highly charged emotional state, I didn't trust myself to think rationally. Calls to Sarah and Nadia, two of my most level-headed friends, confirmed it was the right thing to do.

'You managed at home before,' said Sarah.

'Do whatever Graham wants,' said Nadia.

With my mind made up, I went back to Graham's room and used the remote control of the recliner next to his bed to lower the backrest and raise up the footrest so that I could sleep in a more or less horizontal position.

'This is almost as good as travelling Business Class,' I joked with Graham, who'd 'turned left' several times when travelling for work, whereas I'd always gone cattle class. I slept fitfully but just after midnight was jolted awake by an agonising cramp in my calf. I'd never experienced pain like it; in fact it was so bad it felt as if I'd been knifed.

'Oh shit, oh shit, what can I do?' I wailed, almost crazy with pain as I struggled to rise to my feet and hobble over to the wall to stretch out my leg. Within 20 seconds the pain subsided and, after checking that Graham was still comfortable, I was able to resume sleeping in the chair, despite the loud ticking of the oversized wall clock installed above the door. All I could think, as I lost consciousness, was how horrible it must have been for the many

UNBEARABLE PAIN AND A VISIT FROM A POLTERGEIST

patients who'd died in that room hearing, and seeing, their lives, quite literally, ticking away.

Two hours later my eyes shot open. The swing-arm lamp over Graham's bed was switching itself on and off and I felt the backrest of the recliner slowly straightening up and pushing my body into a seated position.

'Poltergeist!' I thought as my chest contracted with fear, watching the flashing light with an almost morbid fascination. I sat frozen to the spot, uncertain of what to do. And then I felt something hard poking into my thigh. Looking down I discovered the recliner's remote control wedged down the side of its seat.

'That would explain it!' I thought with a huge sigh of relief. But the light that had started flashing on and off of its own accord at precisely the same time? I knew Graham would beg to differ, but that was most certainly the work of the entity that had gate-crashed our first date.

Poltergeist and calf agony aside, it was a peaceful night and Graham needed only a single morphine top-up, proving my theory that he'd felt too unsafe to sleep the night before because he couldn't request pain relief when he needed it. That morning, I did something I never, ever thought I'd do: I signed a Do Not Resuscitate (DNR) order on Graham's behalf. Before I'd have thought that only people who were psychopaths would agree to medics making no attempt to resuscitate their loved ones if they collapsed, but a bleak statistic in the hospice brochure changed my mind: 'In people with very serious, advanced illnesses (for example, advanced cancer or severe heart or lung disease), only about one person in 100 who receives CPR will recover enough to leave hospital,' it said. None of the TV shows told you that statistic. CPR is always portrayed as being heroic, the most obvious thing to do. In *Dear Life*, palliative medicine specialist Dr Rachel Clarke asserts that modern CPR was never intended to be performed on patients who're dying from an irreversible condition, describing it with horrific candour as 'violent, bone-crunching work' in which 'a dead body is essentially assaulted by a team of doctors who hope to achieve its resurrection'. She goes on to say that 'the prolonged lack of oxygen during cardiac "downtime" risks leaving patients alive yet permanently brain-damaged, inhabiting a twilight world in which they have been stripped of their former personality for good. Some people, including me, regard this prospect for themselves as a fate worse than death.' If you truly love someone, I realised, it simply wasn't fair to prolong their suffering just so you could spend a few more hours or days with them. Especially if they'd be in pain.

I also informed the head nurse that Graham wanted to go home.

'It's certainly possible,' she said, 'but as today's Thursday, and it's a bank holiday weekend, we won't be able to arrange for a hospital bed to be delivered to your house until next week.'

'You're buying a lot of tea,' smiled the woman serving me in the canteen that afternoon. 'It's not all for me,' I grinned back. 'It's for my husband's colleagues. Back home I have about twenty mugs a day, so you can imagine how hard it is for me having to wait for the nurses to offer me some.'

'I totally sympathise,' she said. 'I'm addicted to the stuff, too.

UNBEARABLE PAIN AND A VISIT FROM A POLTERGEIST

You see my insulated mug next to the sink? I've told my family that I want my ashes kept in it when I die!'

'What a great idea,' I laughed, before placing the six paper cups in a cardboard cup holder and taking them outside where Graham, who'd been wheeled out in his bed, was waiting in the sunshine. I could tell his colleagues were taken aback by his gaunt appearance and shaved head as he'd been working full-time only weeks before.

'I need to pee urgently, Lisa,' Graham said.

'Look away everyone, look away!' I said with mock gaiety as I retrieved Graham's portable urinal where I'd hidden it under the bedsheets and helped him use it.

'This adjustable hospital bed is a godsend,' I told them. 'I entered a race three weeks ago and slipped off one of the inflatable obstacles, tearing some of the tendons in my shoulder. Ever since, Graham's called it my "bouncy castle arm". It hurt like hell when I had to haul him into an upright position when he needed to pee at home, but now this bed does most of the work.'

As I related this story, I caught Graham rolling his eyes as if to say, 'Only Lisa would do something like that!' I'm still not sure whether he meant enter an obstacle race when I was desperately unfit, fall off one of the inflatables – or finish the race despite having a suspected fractured arm.

After that afternoon's wonderful visit, I fed Graham the scallop risotto that Sanober, the Indian wife of Graham's close friend and colleague Michael, had lovingly made for him.

'Food is what Indian people do to show their love in situations like this,' Michael told me. I didn't know it then, but that was to be the last meal Graham would ever eat.

STILL RUNNING AFTER ALL THESE TEARS

That night I prayed Graham would get some rest, but it was not to be. At 1am he awoke with agonising full-body cramps – every muscle in his body was clenching uncontrollably. This wasn't his usual excruciating pain, it was the worst it had ever been. I had an inkling of what he was going through as I'd experienced the same agony in my calf the night before. I summoned the nurses and he was given his usual dose of Oramorph, to no effect.

'This isn't cancer pain,' I told the nurses, 'this is muscle-cramp pain. What Graham needs is a muscle relaxant.'

'Oramorph, he needs Oramorph,' one of the nurses kept robotically repeating.

'Please give him a muscle relaxant,' I begged.

After the nurses had left the room, I held Graham's claw-like, cramping hand tightly. I thought of the painting I'd seen in the hospice corridor that morning. It depicted the agony of Christ's crucifixion, the Romans' favoured method of execution as it involved a long, slow death and maximised fear and suffering.

'I can't go on like this,' Graham groaned. 'I want to die. You wouldn't treat an animal this way. I want to go home.'

'Oh my God,' I thought. 'Graham's being tortured to death in a hospice and there's nothing I can do to help him.'

'How bad is the pain, Graham?'

'Errrrrr, seven out of ten.'

'And how high did it go tonight?'

'When I woke up, easily an eight or nine.'

'Nine? And tell me about the cramping. It started at one o'clock, and you only got some kind of relief by two o'clock. And it's now four o'clock, and you've been in pain for absolute ages.'

UNBEARABLE PAIN AND A VISIT FROM A POLTERGEIST

'Arghhh!'

'What do you want right now?'

'No pain. No pain at all. None whatsoever.'

'What do you want for your funeral, my love?' I asked him.

'I want it to be a very simple affair. Arghhh,' he groaned. 'We don't want a big event. I can't cope with that, even if I won't be there for it.'

'Yes,' I cried, 'because *I* can't cope. I can't be at something like that with my heart broken in front of everyone, I just *can't*. Also you need to say where you want your ashes scattered. I will always keep some of them because you'll always be in my heart.'

'Because you and me will be soulmates then.'

'Yes, of course. We're *already* soulmates. So what do you want, Graham?'

'I want you to keep some ashes and the rest to be scattered in Hermanus.'

'Really, by that bench? That's *my* choice for *my* ashes!'

'Aaaaaaah!'

'And where do you want to be right now? At home or here?'

'Home.'

'Why do you want to be at home?'

'So I have no pain. Please end my pain.'

The nurses soon afterwards returned and told me they'd finally obtained permission from a senior doctor, whom they'd had to wake up at home in the early hours, to administer the sedative midazolam. Within minutes of receiving it, Graham was sound asleep.

STILL RUNNING AFTER ALL THESE TEARS

If ever evidence was needed that assisted dying should be legalised in the UK, that night's horrific events was it. Graham screaming in agony and pleading for his pain to end has been seared into my soul and causes me intense distress to this very day. After breakfast, I fired off an urgent message to Nurse Ratched, requesting that she ask Dr Yes to phone the hospice and help make the case for taking Graham home as soon as possible. I somehow had it in my head that I could be prosecuted if I insisted on having Graham discharged when he was so unwell, even though the head nurse hadn't shown any resistance to the idea.

'Is there anything you can do to fast-track Graham's discharge as the experimental pain meds have not materialised?' I texted. 'Graham was in severe pain for THREE HOURS last night before they gave him the muscle relaxant he needed. He's suicidal from the pain and the delays in getting pain relief in an understaffed environment.'

There was no reply to my text message, so I went ahead and arranged a private ambulance.

'I'll be taking Graham home this afternoon at 2pm,' I went back and told the staff, not caring if I was interrupting a handover, and also thinking that I'd nurse Graham on the floor of our living room on my knees if the hospital bed didn't arrive in time.

A week later, I got a response from Nurse Ratched: 'Hi Lisa, sorry I have not been in touch. How is Graham doing now that he is home?' By that time Graham had been dead for two days.

The painting of Ludlow that hung over our bed

Luke and Anthony at Graham's bedside

The market scene painting we bought in Vietnam

Chapter 15
No place like home

♪♪ Mood music: *A Thousand Years* by Christina Perri
The song that explains how true love transcends time

'Graham's going to be spending his final days in an art gallery,' I thought to myself as I looked with new eyes at the bedroom Graham and I had painted dark grey only six months before. Above the hospital bed that the hospice had arranged to be installed was a colourful original painting of a market scene that we'd unearthed in a dusty souvenir shop in Hanoi while backpacking in Vietnam; above our king-size bed was one of the first original artworks we'd ever bought together – *Midday Carillon* – depicting a higgledy-piggledy Ludlow town square full of scattering pigeons and people blocking their ears as the eighteenth-century market hall's bells noisily struck noon.

The hospice had pulled out all the stops to make Graham as comfortable as possible at home: they'd rapidly put a care system in place that meant district nurses and carers would be visiting Graham several times a day, all at no cost to us. I was incredibly grateful for this support as I knew that it would have taken me ages to organise it, and quite frankly, I wouldn't have known where to start.

I'd only just settled Graham when our dear friends Sarah and Anthony and their 15-year-old son Luke arrived. They'd skipped attending RunFestRun and come to offer us moral support. I immediately dispatched Anthony to fetch the paracetamol Graham would need in the coming days.

STILL RUNNING AFTER ALL THESE TEARS

'I can't understand why they can't give Graham a stash of the bloody things,' I told him. 'He's getting through eight tablets a day and you can only buy thirty-two at a time. I used to feel like a bloody drug dealer going from the corner shop to the pharmacy to the supermarket topping up our supplies.'

When I popped back upstairs to check on Graham, Luke was sitting upright on our bed, resting his back against our headboard.

'Graham, can I ask you a question?' I heard him say, running his hand through his curly mop of dark hair.

'Sure,' said Graham weakly.

'I've often wondered this: are you a spy?'

'No, Luke, I'm not,' said Graham, smiling.

'Come on, you can tell me,' said Luke. 'I won't tell anyone.'

'I'm not a spy, Luke. And if I told you, I'd have to shred you.'

This was my cue to tell one of my favourite Graham stories: the time he very nearly *did* become a spy. Bored in his job at the time, he'd completed the recruitment test MI6 had published online and heard nothing more for quite some time. When the invite to attend an interview finally came, he was on a solo cycling-and-camping trip in France. I'd had to access his Hotmail to find out some insurance information and had spotted the email, which said he had just 24 hours to respond.

After a comedy hour of trying to use my French-Intensive-dropout language skills to ask the campsite manager to get *'monsieur a la Angleterre dans le gris voiture'* to phone me – and a frantic call trying to contact my French-speaking cousin whose son was too afraid to wake her from her nap – I hit upon the idea of putting my request through Google Translate. Another call to the bemused campsite manager and, when I'd pretty much given up all hope of speaking to him, Graham phoned.

NO PLACE LIKE HOME

'I'm not cutting short my trip – I just got here,' he said. 'I'll just say I didn't get the email.'

'Graham,' I said in my sternest Judy Dench M voice, 'if *anyone* can tell whether you've opened an email or not, it would be MI6. I *strongly* suggest you come home.'

After attending the interview, Graham found out it was a boring desk job where he wouldn't be doing intelligence analysis – and definitely not any 007-esque roof-top scaling and information gathering. Instead, he'd merely be collating 'spy stuff' from the real spies, so he decided that it was an 'Oh no!' rather than a 00 and that he didn't want the job after all. Luke loved this story, as did Graham.

'That's the closest I ever got to becoming a spy,' said Graham. 'Although by some weird coincidence, my computer user ID at the Ministry of Defence was GW007!'

Painting Graham's toenails was his sister's idea. Her two young daughters had first varnished his nails one Christmas decades ago when they'd been gifted manicure kits as pre-teens.

'Please, please can we paint your toenails, Uncle G?' they'd begged him, tugging off his shoes and socks.

'Oh, go on then,' Graham had said, much to their delight.

A month later, Graham went on a Foreign Office work trip with a gruff Scottish sergeant major. During a stopover in Dubai Airport, Graham changed his socks.

'Holy shite, Graham!' the sergeant major had exclaimed, looking in horror at Graham's shocking-pink nails. 'I cannae believe my eyes!'

'What?'

STILL RUNNING AFTER ALL THESE TEARS

'Your toenails!' the sergeant major had spluttered, obviously taken aback that Graham was so laidback about revealing this secret side of himself.

'Oh them,' said Graham casually, resuming tying his laces. 'My nieces painted them.'

Graham hadn't found it necessary to offer any further explanation and was quite happy for his colleague to believe whatever he wanted to believe. When retelling this story, Graham often bolted on the tale of how the officer tasked with conducting his security vetting for the Ministry of Defence had once asked Graham's boss at the jewellery store where he was employed part-time whether Graham was in the habit of wearing women's clothing to work.

'My boss told the officer he'd never seen me in a dress,' Graham would laugh. 'Just as well that he couldn't see my bra and suspenders under my suit!'

Now, with Graham safely home, we knew painting his toenails was something he'd find amusing and would lift his spirits. It certainly did ours, and those of some of his carers and nurses: others, I'm certain, like the sergeant major, were probably rather taken aback.

Sparkly toenails aside, the day after Graham came home he lost the ability to swallow his paracetamol and morphine tablets, so he was issued with a syringe driver, a small, battery-powered pump that delivers a steady trickle of morphine through a small tube directly into the bloodstream.

'If he's already on a driver, it's very bad, very bad,' said Morine, Graham's Ugandan carer, with a frown as she and I made Graham's bed. I didn't reply, somehow holding onto the hope that this setback was only temporary.

The district nurses, who arrived twice a day to check Graham's syringe driver, were wonderful, and when I discovered the head nurse, Nurse Makho, was Zimbabwean, I told her about our memorable trip to her country after a torn calf muscle scuppered my chances of qualifying for the 2012 Comrades Marathon.

'On the day I was supposed to be running Comrades, Graham and I had dinner at the Victoria Falls Safari Lodge,' I told her. 'We could hear hyenas gnawing through the bones of a carcass they'd found while an a cappella group serenaded us with *Shosholoza*, a song we always sing at the start of Comrades. Even though I was gutted not to be running, I couldn't imagine a lovelier way to spend Comrades Day.'

'I know *Shosholoza*,' said Nurse Makho. 'Shall we sing it to Graham?'

'I know it, too,' said Morine. 'My son-in-law is Zimbabwean.'

And with that, all three of us broke into song, singing the tune originally sung by Zimbabwean migrant workers as they travelled by steam train to South Africa to work in the mines. Graham smiled at us, and squeezed my hand to let me know he was enjoying our impromptu concert. Traditionally a song of hope and encouragement, it was the perfect anthem to sing to Graham as he continued on what would be his final journey.

Just two days after we'd managed to get Graham home from the hospice, I yet again found myself having to go into battle on his behalf. Until then I'd been profoundly grateful for the devoted care he'd received from the district nurses but I was in for a shock. It was a Sunday, and most of Graham's family had come round for a visit, giving me the chance to have a shower and get dressed as I'd been so busy caring for Graham, I hadn't had a chance to do that.

STILL RUNNING AFTER ALL THESE TEARS

'Graham's been frowning ever since we got here,' said his mother to me anxiously 30 minutes into their five-hour visit. 'I'm worried that he's been lying on the syringe-driver's tubing and that the morphine hasn't been getting through.'

'I'll speak to the district nurses about this when they come round this evening,' I reassured her. 'But in the meantime, let's reposition Graham and tape the tubing onto his mattress so that he can't lie on it.'

At the conclusion of the family visit, Graham's mother once again expressed concern that Graham had seemed to be in pain the entire afternoon.

'That's awful – he's never been in continual pain that long before so I'll definitely let tonight's nurses know,' I promised her. It's incredible to me now, looking back, that I didn't think to ask Graham whether or not he was in pain, but I was so exhausted and sleep deprived by that point that I just thought I'd mention it to the district nurses when they next visited as I couldn't do much for him in that respect without their help.

Later that evening, 90 minutes behind schedule, a district nurse I'd never met before arrived, accompanied by a care assistant. I was midway through giving Graham a bed bath, but explained our concerns while continuing to wash him. Without going through the usual driver-checking routine, which involved reading out and recording how much liquid morphine and battery charge remained, the nurse unexpectedly announced: 'Your husband's not in pain so we're leaving.' She then disappeared downstairs. I was stunned. They had made absolutely no attempt to communicate with Graham: not a single question was directed at him to check whether he was in pain or not. And there had been no attempt to reassure me that the driver had been working correctly either. Though Graham was, at times, unable to speak, he'd often been able to communicate by smiling, or blinking 'yes' or 'no'. I carried on tending to Graham and then the reality of what had just happened hit me: they were going to leave Graham, whom I was now convinced had been in pain for over *nine hours*, to continue to suffer yet more agony throughout the entire night. I knew I couldn't let that happen.

Leaving Graham half naked on the bed upstairs, I flew downstairs to find the two women filling in paperwork in our dining room.

'Stop!' I screamed, holding up my white barrier cream-covered right hand. 'My husband's in pain and you've done NOTHING to help him!'

The nurse looked at me coldly. 'I didn't come here to be shouted at by you. Do you want me to leave or to do my job?'

Shocked by her hostile tone, I shot back defiantly: 'I want you to leave.' Which she immediately did.

'Oh my God,' I thought, instantly regretting my rash decision. Fearing the consequences of my knee-jerk reaction, I hastily reached for my phone to call the out-of-hours nurses.

A little while later, a different district nurse arrived and, thankfully, swiftly administered a much-needed morphine injection after asking Graham to blink if he was in pain, which he duly did. Within minutes, Graham, who'd been grimacing and frowning for hours now, was finally pain-free and fast asleep.

'I wanted to say how much I admired the resilience you've shown over the past few years as you've battled your illness. I have very fond memories of the work we've done together on Pakistan over the years.' As Graham's friend and colleague Michael read out this handwritten letter from Sir Philip Barton, the head of the Foreign Office, my heart swelled with pride. I was amazed he'd found the time to write to Graham in the aftermath of the Taliban takeover of Afghanistan, and immensely grateful that Graham got to hear his kind words while he was alive, rather than me receiving them in a condolence card. Exactly 20 years before, Graham had been the research analyst responsible for Afghanistan when 9/11 happened. He'd been inundated with requests for information and analysis, and had spent a week sleeping on the floor of his office in Whitehall. Throughout Michael's visit, Graham was unable to speak, so Michael and I chatted among ourselves, sharing funny stories we knew Graham would appreciate.

'Do you remember the time you adopted a donkey, Michael?' I asked. He nodded.

'Graham and I discovered it was the same donkey another friend of ours had adopted. We thought it so funny that this poster-boy donkey probably had tens of thousands of adoptive parents who all thought they were the only special humans in his life.'

Graham raised his head. 'Donk Dean!' he exclaimed.

'Yes, Graham!' I said. 'That was indeed the donkey's name. I can't believe you remembered it.'

The hospice booklet had informed me that dying patients could often hear – and understand – everything that people around them said. This was proof, and I was immensely proud of the way I'd kept all the conversations within earshot of Graham upbeat and hopeful.

That afternoon Nurse Ade, one of the district nurses who'd been particularly supportive, took me to one side.

'I can see you need to sleep,' she said. 'Why don't you get a Marie Curie nurse to look after your husband tonight?'

NO PLACE LIKE HOME

I initially resisted the idea as I didn't want yet another stranger in my house and by now didn't trust anyone to care for Graham beside myself, but eventually she persuaded me. Before she left, Nurse Ade gripped both of my hands and said with great conviction: 'It's going to be hard after your husband goes, but you are strong. You will be alive.'

Ade's words both inspired and encouraged me. How did she know that I secretly thought I couldn't live without Graham? I wondered, recalling our suicide-pact conversation.

When the Marie Curie nurse turned up, she quietly installed herself in an armchair in the office next to our bedroom, leaving the door ajar so that she'd be able to respond instantly should Graham cry out in pain during the night. After kissing Graham goodnight in his hospital bed, I lay down wearily in our double bed, on the side Graham always used to sleep on, and fell asleep immediately. I didn't wake up once. Nor, I don't think, did Graham. I never had the chance to thank the nurse whom, I assumed, stayed up all night and regularly checked on Graham, though I never heard her come into our room, because she soundlessly let herself out first thing in the morning. But I credit her for gifting me a day where both Graham and I were on top form: like a flickering candle that burns more brightly just before it splutters out, Graham seemed to rally and was even able to say a few words at times throughout the day, during which I phoned friends and family so that they could say goodbye. By now I knew Graham didn't have long to live, and thought it important that everyone got their chance to bid him farewell. The call that reduced Nurse Ade to tears, causing her to leave the room, was the one I made to my dad as I cradled Graham in my arms.

On speaker phone, my dad, who rarely spoke from the heart, said: 'I just want to tell you, Graham, that I very much appreciated

STILL RUNNING AFTER ALL THESE TEARS

the way you took such good care of Lisa from a very young age, both when you were in South Africa and later when you lived in London. I know you supported her when you were travelling and when she was writing her books. I'm also eternally grateful to you for running all those endless marathons with her – so that I didn't have to!'

Just before he went to sleep, and after returning the kiss on the lips I'd given him, Graham whispered to me: 'Never forget me.'

'Graham, my love,' I said, 'we've known each other since I was a teenager and we've grown up together. I could *never* forget you – you're part of my very being.'

His last-ever words to me were almost unbearably poignant: 'I will miss you.'

The family mementoes that gave me courage on the day Graham died

Saskia and baby Runa visit Graham

The crane-patterned shirt I chose for Graham

The PolarNight 10K medal Graham was cremated with

Chapter 16
Till death us do part

♪♪ **Mood music:** *Goodbye My Lover* **by James Blunt**
The song that captures the grief of saying goodbye to my soulmate and best friend

Sadly, Graham never did experience the radical remission we so fervently hoped he would. He didn't live to 85 either, which was the age he wanted to die at, and which he scratched into the condensation on the shower door with his forefinger every day post-diagnosis to make this desire known to the Universe. Instead, the numbers were reversed. Always slightly rebellious, he lived longer and died faster than many people expected.

When we awoke on the day that would be his last, Graham hadn't eaten or drunk anything for several days but I nonetheless dipped a pink foam swab stick into my tea and gently wiped it across his lips so that he could share what I was drinking. He could no longer speak, but when I smiled at him, he smiled, and when I kissed him, he kissed me back. Having once volunteered for the brain-cancer charity Brainstrust, I knew how fortunate we were that the brain tumours hadn't altered Graham's personality or behaviour.

'The problem with brain tumours is that they can make your loved one violent or aggressive – and they may not even recognise you,' I remember the charity's founder telling us during our training. 'What that means is that sometimes you're left caring for someone you still love but actually don't like very much.' I counted myself lucky that Graham was still my Graham, the man I'd liked and loved for 35 years, until the very end.

STILL RUNNING AFTER ALL THESE TEARS

I knew, that day, that I needed the help of my female ancestors, so I spritzed myself and the room with Arpège, my mother's favourite jasmine-scented perfume. I also found a tablecloth I'd inherited from Oumie, my maternal grandmother, the most loving woman I'd ever met, and placed that on a low table near our bedroom window. As the actor Greg Wise wrote in *Not That Kind of Love*, the heartbreakingly beautiful book he co-wrote with his sister Clare, whom he nursed until her death aged 51 from breast cancer: '… we truly are all propped up by those who have gone before – the living held up by the dead.' At the foot of Graham's bed, I hung the personalised blanket depicting photos from his childhood that his niece Grace had got specially printed as a gift for him. To honour his Ghanaian birthplace, I covered Graham's torso with a piece of orange-and-acid-green patterned African fabric. It was entirely fitting, I thought, that Ashanti chiefs who'd died were described as going 'journeying' as they travelled back to the spiritual world of their ancestors. With his love of travel, Graham was going to go journeying, too, but this was one trip I knew I couldn't accompany him on.

When the carers arrived for their morning shift, we washed and changed Graham together, replaced his sheets with new ones and made him comfortable. Once they'd left, I pulled up a footstool next to his bed, gripped his hand and poured out my heart to him. I told him how much I loved him, and how much I admired his courage, quiet dignity and fortitude during his long illness.

'Graham, my love, you did everything you could to stay alive for as long as you possibly could but now it's time for you to go,' I told him. 'I love you, and I always will, but I give you permission to die, because losing you will be an easier pain to bear than watching you suffer.'

TILL DEATH US DO PART

At lunchtime, Graham's colleague Saskia arrived with her four-month-old baby Runa. Graham had described her as his protégé, as he'd been so impressed by her that he'd hired her before she even graduated. A petite woman with a pixie cut and a mischievous laugh, I could see why Graham and Saskia got on so well, not just because they had similar research interests but because they shared the same sense of humour. By this time Graham's breathing was already laboured and noisy, something that's known as the 'death rattle'. Saskia seemed unfazed by it, however, and sat on a chair next to Graham's bed with her baby on one knee, and one of the fancy hipster sandwiches she'd brought from Hoxton balanced on the other.

'Tell me about Runa's birth,' I said. 'I was absolutely delighted to hear you did hypnobirthing as, I'm sure Graham told you, I'm a hypnobirthing teacher.'

'I'm not sure Graham wants to hear my birth story,' she said, laughing and casting a glance over at him.

'Oh no, go right ahead – he's used to it. In fact, when I returned from my training, I insisted the poor man watch an hour-long DVD showing eight hypnobirths. I'd been incredibly excited to discover that birth doesn't have to be full of screaming like you see on *One Born Every Minute*.'

'Well, if you're sure he won't mind...' said Saskia, taking a bite of her sandwich.

'Do carry on, I absolutely love good birth stories,' I said, taking a bite of mine.

'It was a beautiful spring day, the day Runa was born, so my partner Matt and I went for a walk in the park to see the blossoms.

STILL RUNNING AFTER ALL THESE TEARS

I was feeling really calm but then all of a sudden, I threw up outside a café, rather startling a passerby.'

'Oh no!' I said, laughing. 'I hope Graham can hear you, because for some unknown reason he would find that terribly funny.'

Saskia went on to explain how she'd used hypnobirthing breathing to stay in control throughout her baby's birth.

'Active labour was fast and intense,' she told me, 'and suddenly Runa was here and I pulled her up onto my chest. It was just such a beautiful experience.'

'Oh, I'm so glad you had such a fantastic birth,' I replied. 'Being relaxed can make all the difference.' It occurred to me how poignant it was to be discussing the start of Runa's life just as Graham was nearing the end of his.

Saskia placed Runa on our double bed and she promptly snuggled into the duvet and fell asleep while her mum went on to describe some of her work travels with Graham.

'I'll always remember sitting at the top of the Margalla Hills with Graham looking out over Islamabad,' she told me. 'It's surprisingly leafy for a city of over a million people.'

'Graham told me about that view, too,' I said. 'I hope to visit Pakistan someday and see all the places he knew and loved.'

'Did he tell you about his first trip to Pakistan?' she asked.

'I'm not sure, what happened?'

'Well he and a very senior colleague were supposed to meet a top military person and apparently Graham made a strong first impression... by walking straight into a glass door! I think he'd forgotten to put in his contact lenses that day.'

'I love that, and it's not a story I've ever heard before,' I laughed. 'Did you hear about the time he went to Japan with three of his colleagues and they ordered several rounds of sake in a restaurant?'

'No, I don't think they told me this one.'

'Well, Graham wasn't unduly affected by the sake but his boss wasn't familiar with how potent it can be. When he got up to go to the loo, he lost his balance and crashed through the paper screens surrounding their table. Apparently the Japanese diners seated nearby were utterly disgusted by this "sake lout" behaviour!'

I wiped a tear from my eye as I pictured the scene, and when I looked over to Graham, I thought he was smiling.

Saskia continued reminiscing, this time about how Graham, much to the frustration of the higher-ups, often refused to toe the line at work.

'He sometimes behaved like the naughty boy you wish you'd been friends with at school,' she told me. 'I don't know what his school reports said, but I wouldn't be surprised if he was the cheekiest kid in the class.' Saskia was right. She probably hadn't heard how Graham had been demoted from his house captainship at boarding school for selling the beer he'd brewed in a disused flat to the junior boys for 50p a mug, but she'd imagined his schoolboy self perfectly.

I noticed that Graham's face had turned a weird yellow colour and rushed to his side just as a district nurse was preparing to insert a catheter. For quite some time his breathing had been punctuated by long pauses when he seemed to hold his breath. I lowered my head to Graham's chest, and he let out a long sigh, followed by an even longer pause. And then he exhaled once more, a very tiny puff of air as if he was trying to stop a feather landing on his lips. That was the moment breath became air. He never breathed again. I was silent for a few moments and then I looked up at the nurse: 'I think my husband's just died. Please can you check and let me know as I don't want to call his mother and tell her he's dead if he's not.'

The nurse shook her head. 'Only a doctor can do that,' she told me.

I put my head against his chest once more. There was no sound. Wordlessly I walked to the window and pushed it open to allow Graham's soul to fly free, a death-day tradition I'd been taught by a hospice nurse I'd met while running the Chicago Marathon.

The next eight hours were a vortex of thoughts, emotions and images. I know I called Graham's mother, though I have no recollection of what was said. My friend Rose phoned, letting me know that she and her partner Mark were about to arrive at East Croydon station en route to visiting us.

'Graham's just died,' I told her. 'But come anyway.'

I recall seeing Saskia pacing around our garden while talking on her phone, no doubt notifying Graham's colleagues about his death. People arriving, though I don't know what I said to them. Walking downstairs and being surprised to find everyone congregated in my kitchen eating what was left of the sandwiches Saskia had brought. Going back up to Graham and holding his hand, and finding it was still warm. Speaking to Graham and telling him I loved him, and that I was glad his suffering was finally over. A female doctor coming round and pronouncing Graham dead. Breaking the news to so many people that I went hoarse. A neighbour saying, 'I believe you get to choose the people you want to be around you when you die.' Graham's mother offering to stay overnight so I wouldn't have to spend my first night without him on my own.

The following morning I woke up beside my mother-in-law in the bed I'd shared with Graham for 27 years. Graham lay in his own bed at the foot of ours. I went downstairs and made his mother and I mugs of tea. Through the soul-crushing sadness, it made my heart sing to think that the three of us had woken up in the same room. Except, of course, in reality, only two of us had woken up that day, but my brain couldn't really compute that. All I could think about, and took enormous comfort from, was the fact that Graham had spent his last night in his beloved home with the first and last women who'd ever loved him.

I wanted to take my time saying goodbye to Graham, and I also wanted to wash his body one last time, so I asked the undertakers to collect him in the late afternoon. After running some warm water into a bowl, I tenderly wiped Graham's skin, which looked so fragile now, like medieval parchment. In the middle of his chest, I noticed the small blue pinprick tattoo that had been used to line up the radiotherapy beams correctly during his first radiotherapy sessions. It looked like something a sniper would have aimed at if he wanted to be sure of a kill. Graham had joked, when it was first done, that he'd finally succumbed to peer pressure and got inked at the age of 56.

'I'll be getting LOVE and HATE tattooed on my knuckles next,' he'd said, 'and then, perhaps, a spiderweb on my neck and face.'

The skin on his hands looked wrinkled and old – he'd always remarked that he had an old man's hands, even in his 20s – but his belly and thighs were surprisingly smooth, like a teenager's. The words of a war poem by Laurence Binyon that Graham was fond of reciting to me came to mind: 'They shall grow not old, as we that are left grow old / Age shall not weary them, nor the years condemn.' It came as a shock to realise Graham would never grow old. I'd never see him with white hair or a stoop. He wouldn't be celebrating our 50th wedding anniversary in a mint-green suit while I wore a Cinderella-style ballgown, as we'd often fantasised after he'd been diagnosed. Instead, I'd be facing old age without him.

It took me some time to decide how to dress Graham. After much deliberation, I selected one of the six new shirts he'd bought at TK Maxx in typical-Graham defiance at his diagnosis. The one I chose was a beautiful deep blue, adorned with snowy white clouds and majestic pink-and-white cranes, birds in Japanese mythology that are thought to be messengers of the gods and that are revered as symbols of good fortune and enduring relationships. I completed the outfit with a pair of khaki chinos and a black woollen waistcoat with a Nehru collar he'd bought on a work trip to Afghanistan. My mum had been cremated with one of her running medals, and so I now wanted to give this same honour to Graham. It felt important to acknowledge that, after four long years of never giving up, Graham had now crossed his final finish line. The medal I eventually picked out for him was the one he'd been awarded after the PolarNight 10K in Tromsø, the race we'd combined with a trip to see the Northern Lights for our 29th wedding anniversary. The beautiful medal – embossed with the timeless heavenly spectacle whose other-worldly beauty had brought us both to tears – perfectly symbolised our long and happy marriage.

When the undertakers arrived a short while later, I took them up to our bedroom.

'I want my husband to have one more look at the sun and the sky when he leaves our house, so I don't want you zipping him up in a body bag,' I told them.

'We're afraid we can't allow that as seeing a dead body could upset your neighbours,' one replied. I dug my heels in, and after a

TILL DEATH US DO PART

while it was agreed that Graham would be placed into the body bag, but that the top would be unzipped when we reached the ambulance.

After Graham had been transferred from the hospital bed to the stretcher, the next hurdle was getting him downstairs, which involved a 90-degree change in direction in the narrow hallway at the top of our stairs. The undertakers shuffled forward, and then shuffled backward again, trying to figure out what to do.

'Why don't you stand my husband up on his feet?' I suggested.

As they hoisted Graham into a vertical position and easily made the turn, it flashed through my mind that the thing Graham had most wanted to do while in the hospice was stand up.

'Oh my love,' I smiled to myself. 'I'm so glad your final wish came true.'

When we got to the ambulance, having passed the small group of neighbours I'd invited to come and say their final farewells, Graham was slid feet first into the back and the body bag was unzipped as promised. When I touched his face one last time, standing on the road outside the house that had been our much-loved home for 27 years, Graham's eyes were partially open so I knew he could see the sun, the blue sky arching over him and the canary yellow fez I'd been wearing on the day we first met. To this day I don't know how I managed to find it, but I wanted his last memory of me to be of the teenage girl who'd adored him from the very minute she first laid eyes on him.

Raccoon balloons dressed as Graham and his dad Reg

After my 54th birthday run

Commemorating Graham's cremation with Sarah

Our quirky crow painting by Alan Wallis

The Champagne labels I designed for Graham's colleagues

Chapter 17
A celebration, a cremation and a crow

♪♪ **Mood music: *The Carnival Is Over* by The Seekers**
The song Graham wanted his loved ones to remember him by

The first thing Graham did the week after he died was break our gas fire – or at least that's what I accused his mischievous spirit self of doing. It was only the first week of September but there was already a nip in the air and now he was out of the way in the afterlife he knew I couldn't be trusted not to put the heating on. I'd always told our boiler engineer that if he read about a homicide in Capri Road, it would involve a fight over Graham once again turning the heating off the minute my back was turned. Body temperature-wise, Graham was always Saudi Arabia in summer whereas I was more Wales in winter.

I'm surprised Graham's spirit hadn't drunk his small Champagne collection in the cupboard under the stairs, too, as he always said he didn't trust me around his booze either. Many years ago, while he'd been posted to Bahrain by the Ministry of Defence, I'd discovered a stash of five large, half-gallon bottles of Jim Beam bourbon wrapped in tracksuit bottoms at the top of his wardrobe. Sick with worry that he was a closet – quite literally – alcoholic, I'd called and confronted him.

'Yes, they're mine,' he said. 'I know what you're like once you get your little chums around and I wasn't sure you wouldn't polish it off!'

STILL RUNNING AFTER ALL THESE TEARS

I thought he'd approve of what I was now intending to do with some of his Champagne: give it as gifts to his family, friends and colleagues with personalised labels I'd designed stuck on the front, with a line on the back that read: 'Best drunk when drunk, or when you want to share a few happy memories of Graham'. I didn't want them to cry over Graham's death but rather get a little tipsy celebrating his life. As the journalist Julie Burchill wrote so touchingly: 'Tears are sometimes an inappropriate response to death. When a life has been lived completely honestly, completely successfully, or just completely, the correct response to death's perfect punctuation mark is a smile.'

As Graham didn't want a funeral, and neither did I, I was free to host a series of small get-togethers to commemorate his life in a way I found not only bearable but celebratory. I'm overjoyed that my goodbyes to him involved balloons, whisky and incontinent crows rather than faux-sad-faced undertakers parading solemnly down our road in front of a hearse.

The main event was a family affair that can be summed up as 'raccoons and balloons'. Raccoons were Graham's all-time favourite small furry animal – in fact, his colleagues had once adopted one for him at Northumberland Zoo – so I ordered a dozen raccoon-shaped helium balloons to decorate his mum's living room with. I dressed one of them in a floral shirt Graham had loved and another in his father's 1970s bomber jacket to represent his late dad. I also ordered a personalised giant helium balloon showing Graham wearing a python round his neck at a voodoo temple in Benin captioned with the words 'LOVE YOU GRAHAM'. Three words that summed up how I felt. 'Love you',

A CELEBRATION, A CREMATION AND A CROW

present tense, because I always would. Every time I looked at that balloon, I cried.

The day was spent sharing all our favourite memories of Graham – the way, as a shy toddler, he'd twirled his fringe with one hand and sucked his thumb with the other; the way he'd stubbornly studied for a PhD in philosophy, disregarding his father's warning that 'there's no money in it'; the way he'd allowed his nieces to put his hair into pigtails at one of his birthday parties. A highlight was a display of funny photos of him. The best one depicted the time we'd visited his sister who was having building work done and so had a blue Portaloo positioned on her driveway. Graham had rung the doorbell and then raced over to the toilet so that, on opening her front door, his sister would be greeted by the sight of her grimacing brother perched on the loo, his trousers round his ankles, pretending to do a number two.

Just as everyone was getting into their cars to go home, one of the raccoon balloons broke away from his 11 brothers and escaped from the house, soaring high into the air above the rooftops. To me, that rogue balloon symbolised Graham's anti-authoritarian, mischievous streak. 'I'm never *knowingly* naughty,' he'd say, referencing the John Lewis slogan, after yet another misdemeanour such as scoffing the last slice of cheesecake before I could get a look in, knowing full well that that was *exactly* what he was.

I celebrated my 54th birthday, the first in 35 years without Graham in my life, in Colchester with Sarah and Anthony. One of my birthday gifts from them was a heart-shaped ceramic plaque embossed with the words 'There are friends, there are family, and there are friends who become family'.

'I've talked to my three boys,' said Sarah as she brought me a mug of tea in bed the way Graham would have done, 'and we've agreed to adopt you!'

After breakfasting on pancakes, whipped up specially in my honour, I went on a solo run along Bluebottle Grove Dyke, a series of steep-sided banks and ditches. The path was overhung by trees and underfoot, colossal, moss-covered sinewy roots plunged into the dark soil. Sarah had told me that the dyke was a late Iron Age defensive ditch, and that she liked to imagine Roman soldiers marching along this path after they conquered Colchester: I could almost hear the sound of their sandalled feet crushing the withered autumn leaves underfoot as I ran. I was literally running 'through leaves', like Vita loved doing, and so, after I'd spent some time reflecting on what it meant to be unexpectedly facing the future alone, I deliberately turned my thoughts to all the things Graham and I had loved doing together. Braaiing fresh sardines on our BBQ on sunny Saturday afternoons; calling each other to come and admire Pecan's dancing; hate-watching *Antiques Roadshow*, which we dubbed *Old People TV,* despite regarding ourselves as *way* too young to do so; giving each other sweat-soaked hugs at the finish lines of multiple marathons and admiring the salt streaks on each other's running kit; littering the end of our emails to each other with 'FAs', which stood for 'fondness attacks'; buying incredibly cute, playful things such as Obobo, a tiny cloth-rabbit ornament dressed in an orange Japanese kimono, and a plant pot featuring a smiling squirrel, despite Graham's otherwise very grown-up, minimalist design aesthetic; trying to score in *University Challenge*, and always concluding, with much indignation, that it was impossible to conjure up the answers

A CELEBRATION, A CREMATION AND A CROW

when we barely understood the fiendishly difficult questions; squabbling over who got more chips at Ozzies, our local chippy in Addiscombe; Graham dancing to his self-written *Tesco Song* ('I'm going to T, E, S, C, O'), complete with Village People *YMCA*-like arm actions, every time he went to the supermarket; talking to each other using our own special words only he and I understood or found funny; toasting the setting sun with cava in our garden on the longest day of the year; telling the same story of how we met, to each other, over and over again. I also reminded myself of what my father had said after my mother's untimely death at the age of 68: 'We should celebrate the time we did have with her, rather than grieve the time we won't get to spend with her.' Repeatedly telling myself how unbelievably lucky I'd been to have had a happy 35-year relationship with the love of my life – whereas some people never got to experience even a minute of such deep love their entire lives – helped me to swerve my thoughts away from how much my life had been hollowed out by my loss. The sweaty selfie I took afterwards showed a red-faced, red-eyed woman with tears in her eyes, but nonetheless, she was beaming.

The day after my birthday, after a breakfast of pastries and freshly brewed Peruvian coffee, Sarah drove me out to Mersea Island on the Essex coast so that we could hold a ceremony by the sea while Graham was being cremated. I'd chosen a direct cremation – where there's no formal funeral ceremony – which had also been what David Bowie, Graham's favourite singer, had chosen for himself. In the preceding three weeks, tributes had poured in from Graham's Foreign Office colleagues around the world, including

STILL RUNNING AFTER ALL THESE TEARS

several ambassadors. They assured me that Graham was going to be missed on all four corners of the earth, from Tunisia to Madagascar to Iran to Ghana, his birthplace, where a candle was lit in his honour, something that I think would have surprised but delighted him. All of the emails and sympathy cards spoke of his keen intellect and encyclopaedic knowledge of Pakistan, but what I was most touched by was the way colleagues spoke of his kindness: how he'd made them feel welcome in the rather intimidating corridors of power, and always reassured them that he, too, had found joining the Foreign Office daunting. The most touching message I received was from his close friend Michael, relating that Graham had once said to him, while walking to Victoria Station through St James's Park: 'Lisa is the best and most consistent thing in my life.'

When we pulled up in the car park at 8.10am, my dad video-called me from South Africa, so all three of us walked out to a bench overlooking the gently lapping waters of the Colne estuary together. Having lost my mum, Dad knew exactly how difficult Graham's cremation day would be.

'It's just so sad,' he told me, 'to have your loved one handed back to you in a little box.'

At the exact time of the cremation, Sarah and I lit some tea lights and then, while holding up a photo of Graham, poured whisky on the ground, a form of libation traditional to Ghana. A gaggle of Canadian geese honked hauntingly in the distance, as if playing *The Last Post*. The man I'd loved since childhood was gone, but I loved the way he'd chosen to stay on this earth, at least bodily, until after my birthday. Other than for my first marathon, when Graham had been temporarily working abroad and had forgotten what day the race was on, and my 50th birthday, he'd never missed an important event.

A CELEBRATION, A CREMATION AND A CROW

'Please try to give me a sign that you're fine after you've died, if you can,' I had said to Graham a few days before he died. I deliberately didn't specify what the sign should be as the one I'd received from my late mother – the one that had changed the course of my life – was rather unusual and not at all in keeping with her values. Mum wasn't interested in manicures, money or materialism as she believed it's what's on the inside that counts, so it took me by surprise that the sign she chose to give me took the form of cash. Time and time again, when I was going through a rough patch – and often during particularly gruelling marathons – I'd glimpse the glint of an abandoned 20p or dropped penny and take courage from the inexplicable knowledge that my mum was watching over me.

The most significant example of my mother's guidance came the year after her death when I was debating whether to resign from my job as a sub-editor on the magazine where I'd worked for over a decade. I joked that when I came to work I checked my brain in at reception, spent the day on autopilot, and then collected it on my way out. It was definitely time to leave, but I was terrified as I'd be giving up a regular income and final-salary pension. Finally, I believe, my mother lost patience and made the choice for me. The way she communicated this was nothing short of spectacular. My commute into London involved transiting through Victoria Station, and one day, as I hurried towards the Tube station, the strong scent of Lush bath bombs in my nostrils, I saw an unmistakeable sign. A sign so large it could probably have been seen from outer space (or at least from a helicopter). I can't remember what was being

STILL RUNNING AFTER ALL THESE TEARS

advertised – possibly a bank that could make your money grow exponentially – but as far as the eye could see, across the entire concourse, huge posters depicting over-sized coins had been affixed to the floor. I strode over the cash carpet with joy in my heart: my mum had given me the permission I needed to quit the job I'd grown out of and chase after my dreams. Soon after that I resigned, and within months I'd gained my first hypnotherapy clients, landed a publishing deal with Simon & Schuster (who published Nelson Mandela and my favourite writer John Irving, for crying out loud) and been head-hunted to work on *Women's Running* magazine, a job that saw me flying all over the world to report on foreign marathons. And all thanks to an unlikely okay from above.

Graham's sign, when it came, was a little more muted, but nonetheless very unexpected and beautiful. A month after his death, I was washing up a mug at his mother's house when I looked out of her kitchen window and saw a crow on the low wall outside. It was staring at me quizzically, its head tilted to one side. Until that point, despite completing dozens of trail marathons and going on countless camping trips and walks, I'd never seen a crow in real life, which is surprising, considering that apparently there are as many as two million carrion crows in the UK. Graham and I even had a large painting of a crow in our dining room, but I truthfully had never seen a live one. Now there was one perched a few feet away from me. And what's more, there was a squirrel, a dead ringer for our beloved Pecan, sinuously bounding across the lawn behind it.

'Hello, Graham,' I said, my heart filled with the deepest joy. 'How are you?' The crow nodded, waggled a short way along the wall, wiggling its hips like a catwalk model, and then departed in a flash of bluey-black. I'd found my sign, and excitedly messaged

A CELEBRATION, A CREMATION AND A CROW

friends and family about it. One of the replies I received was from my sister Loren.

'I found you an online article all about the amazing qualities of crows,' she wrote. 'They're highly intelligent, handy at DIY, take a bird's-eye view of situations, and mate for life!'

I couldn't wait to read the article as my sister's description fitted Graham perfectly. 'While the crow may not have the exotic flair of the flamingo,' Kristen M Stanton wrote in her UniGuide blog, 'underneath the onyx depths of those shiny black feathers is a bird brain beyond compare. One of the keys to crows' survival is that, like raccoons, they're omnivores and will eat anything.' What were the chances of an article containing not only Graham's spirit animal the crow, but his favourite small furry animal and my own spirit animal, the flamingo? I was covered in goosebumps. Not only that, but the article seemed to be offering me life advice from Graham beyond the grave: 'If a crow crosses your path, it could be a sign that you have the ability to handle yourself in any situation – even if you don't always feel that way.' He must have known that, having supported me my entire adult life, I was dreading dealing with our finances, the housework and selling our house without him. For pity's sake, I'd never once, in all my life, put air in our car's tyres or taken our car for an MOT. 'It's easy to get emotional when we face challenges in life. The crow reminds us to step back, cock our heads, and look at the challenge from a different perspective.' This summed up Graham's approach to life word for word: he'd always advised me to analyse situations rationally and not just react to them emotionally.

Ever since, every sighting of a crow has felt as if Graham has reached out from the Other Side and stroked my face. It's been a chance to chuckle, to talk to him, to celebrate him and to remember him and, on one memorable occasion, to tell him off. I

STILL RUNNING AFTER ALL THESE TEARS

was doing the South Norwood parkrun a couple of months after he died, revelling in the chance to spend time outdoors after weeks tethered to my laptop doing 'sadmin', the tedious paperwork following a bereavement. I was last, as usual, so no one was there to witness the crow I sighted near the finish.

'Hello, my love,' I panted, delighted at this unexpected visit and knowing that Graham would be really proud of me for participating. The crow flapped its wings a few times, then shot skywards before swiftly circling back. And then, what do you know, it shat on my head.

'Holy shitbiscuits, Graham, was that strictly necessary?' I blurted out. 'I already knew you were here – you really didn't need to poop on my head.'

The seated Buddha I gifted Graham

Glenn Badham's *Solitaire*, the painting that saved our marriage

Rainbow over Worthing

My Pecan-inspired doorknocker

My medals on display in my new kitchen

Enjoying my beautiful seaside balcony

Chapter 18
Where did my mojo go?

♪♪ **Mood music: *A Whiter Shade of Pale* by Procol Harum**
The song at the start of our favourite film, Withnail and I

I read somewhere that 40 per cent of Swedish women who'd lost a spouse found the pre-loss stage more stressful than the post-loss stage, and much to my surprise, this was true for me. Although I missed Graham desperately, I was released from the anxious thoughts that had plagued me night and day throughout his illness: were we doing enough to give him the best chance of living longer? Was there anything else we could try? Was there another book I could read? Would a miracle cure be found in time? Would Graham die gasping for breath? It was a relief, I realised, to no longer be living in the shadow of death. While I found myself compulsively talking about Graham to friends and family as I notified them of his passing – so much so, in fact, that I went hoarse – I shed surprisingly few tears. After almost four long years of pre-grieving his death, it was almost as if I didn't have any more to shed.

'Life right now is like a box of cornflakes; you need to let things settle down before taking big decisions,' said my Uncle Ian shortly after Graham's death. I knew this was wise advice: all the experts advise against making major changes such as jacking in your job or moving house soon after a bereavement because you're not in your right mind, you're really not, no matter how expected a death is. And yet, one week to the day after Graham died, I entered a top-floor flat overlooking the ocean in Worthing and

STILL RUNNING AFTER ALL THESE TEARS

knew I'd found my Forever Home. The passageway leading into it was unusually wide and, as I walked down it, I could sense Graham beside me, smiling approvingly as I spotted the glossy grey kitchen units that were identical to the ones he'd installed in our Croydon home. Not only that, but there was a cross-legged wooden Buddha seated in the en-suite window that looked almost exactly like the one I'd given Graham 25 years before. The one that we used to joke – along with *Solitaire*, a painting by Glenn Badham of a man reading a philosophy book – was responsible for keeping us together as we couldn't bear the thought of fighting for 'custody' over them if we were to go our separate ways. What's more, the open-air balcony overlooked the promenade, where Worthing parkrun was held: I could trot down to the start in 20 minutes and then would be able to sit out on a patio chair and enjoy a post-run coffee gazing at the pier and, in the distance, the Isle of Wight. I've only experienced love at first sight twice in my life, and this was the second time. I duly put in an offer that was accepted, and three months later, moved in.

Before I could enjoy my new flat, however, I first had to fix three things: the dodgy 37-year-old boiler which, when it roared into life, sounded like it was going to burn my flat down; the kitchen floor, that despite having being laid at about the same time as the eggs in my fridge, had to be replaced almost the minute I moved in as several of the tiles had already cracked, and my Japanese toilet. My flat's original owner, who was mad-keen on gadgets, had been delighted to show the latter off: 'It cost well over a thousand pounds,' he'd boasted while showing me around. 'Look, if you kick the side of it, the heated seat rises automatically. It also has a sprinkler system. And hot air to dry you off afterwards.' Peering down into its pebble-dashed interior (the seller had apparently never thought of using toilet cleaner),

WHERE DID MY MOJO GO?

and suppressing a small heave, I'd feigned being impressed. Having used the loo for a few days, however, I soon realised that although it could sing, dance and hum *God Save the Queen*, it stubbornly refused to flush, sometimes even *after* I'd tipped a bucket of water into it. And so, with toes bruised from kicking it in frustration – and not because I wanted to see it magically raise its bloody heated seat – I bid the toilet, and £600, a fond farewell and got a new, English, one, that didn't come with any newfangled features.

Despite being a DIY virgin, I did everything I could myself: affixing my Pecan-inspired door knocker to my front door, hanging paintings, installing fire alarms (though I did nearly blind myself when the drill bit buckled) and even detecting and fixing a leak in my shower after one plumber told me it would involve the demolition of my entire en suite. My mantra became 'What would Graham do?' No, he would not spend a fortune ripping up an entire bathroom without doing a preliminary investigation himself. A mug of water thrown at my shower screen proved the leak wasn't coming from under the shower but from a damaged screen seal: a £50 job not a £5,000 one. Just call me Inspector Clouseau.

My proudest accomplishment was when I – armed only with a drill, a screwdriver, a long curtain rod, two footstools and a pile of towels – managed to hang my 180-plus medal collection in my kitchen. All by myself. Graham had insisted on displaying my running medals in our study back in Croydon, so I knew he wouldn't approve if they returned to their old home in a box under my bed.

STILL RUNNING AFTER ALL THESE TEARS

'Keep busy, my lovey – it saved me after Mommy died,' was the advice my dad gave me after Graham's death. 'Doing my law degree gave me something else to focus on – I can't imagine how I'd have coped without it.' Having my house move, renovations, probate and other 'sadmin' to occupy myself with definitely distracted me from my grief, though looking back I wish I'd also carved out more time to grieve. The one thing I made sure I made time for, however, was writing thank-you letters to the women who'd cared for him in his final days: his carers and the amazing district nurses, whom I gave a coffee machine to in order to show how truly grateful I was for their kindness. They hadn't just cared for Graham, they'd literally 'loved him to death', and the compassion they'd shown to me, too, had been a lifeline during the darkest days and nights of my entire life. I also steeled myself to sit down and write letters of complaint to all of the caregivers who'd let us down, as I knew my anger at the way we'd been treated would only subside if I managed to get my thoughts down on paper. It was truly horrendous reliving all the horrible things I'd witnessed, but I was convinced that if I didn't do this, I'd spend the rest of my life having 'and another thing...' imaginary arguments with them, which would drive me bat-shit bonkers. No one should have suffered the way Graham – and I – did, and I ardently hoped that by pointing out where they'd gone wrong, they'd reflect on their actions and never again subject their patients to similar treatment.

The hospice was the first to respond, and to my great relief, they promised to make their staff aware of my concerns and implement several of my suggestions, including letting patients know they had the right to die at home if they so wished and allowing patients to self-administer pain medication. The hospital where Graham had his stroke assessment also sent an email full of no fewer than nine 'sorries', two 'apologies' and a four-point

WHERE DID MY MOJO GO?

action plan about how they could do better. The response to my other complaints was far less satisfactory, but I took comfort in the fact that I'd had the courage to stand up for what I believed in.

My New Year's resolution the year after Graham died was to run two spring marathons in his honour, so I duly entered one in Paris and one in Brighton. Paris was a bit of a stretch as it had a strict time limit, but the cut-off for Brighton was very generous so I knew I'd probably be able to finish it, come what may. Or so I hoped. Before, whenever I started running regularly, I quickly made progress – even my 'jellybot' as Graham fondly called it, usually firmed up after only a fortnight of training – but now I was getting worse with each run, not better. I seemed to be just about okay running 2km along the flat-and-fume-free Worthing promenade to my nightly hot yoga class in the centre of town, but on the way back, I had to keep bargaining with myself: 'You can walk to the end of the road, Lisa, then you simply *have* to run. All right, you don't have to run quite yet, start when you get to the church. Okay, the car park. No, the seafront. Okay, you don't feel like it today, just walk the rest of the way home.' I wasn't sure whether it was the result of the Covid booster shot I'd had a few weeks before that had made me incredibly achy and fatigued, or whether I'd actually caught Covid and not realised it, but eventually I found I couldn't even force myself to run between two lampposts. What the hell was going on?

And then, one day in late February, it happened – admittedly after I'd spent a lot of time in the hot yoga tent trying to touch my toes when I couldn't keep up with the super-fast yoga flow sequences the rest of the class were doing. My back spasmed so

STILL RUNNING AFTER ALL THESE TEARS

badly that I could barely move. I was bent over double like a boomerang.

When I went to see my osteopath – I had to catch a taxi there as I could no longer drive – she dropped a bombshell: 'I'm not going to tell you to stop running altogether as I know it means so much to you, but you're going to have to take a break from it for quite some time. There's no way you can run those two marathons.' And just like that, my running mojo left not only the building, but my life.

Going for a run together

My sister Loren with Dad

On the sofa at Southport

Dad loved medals too

Dad tucking into his favourite meal – eggs and bacon

Dad wearing ear defenders to protect his ears against the deafening sound of his smoothie being made

Chapter 19
Forget me not

🎵 Mood music: *Mama Tembu's Wedding* by Margaret Singana with Ipi'n Tombia
The (only) song my dad could play on the guitar

'People metabolise grief in different ways,' I once read somewhere, and in my case, after Graham died, I considered moving to the South Pole for a year to run a post office. Yes, really. Looking back, contemplating spending time with a handful of strangers and thousands of penguins – in total darkness for six months of the year, with limited internet and nowhere to run, literally – was just more evidence of how much I'd been unhinged by grief.

I was also experiencing unnerving physical symptoms – six months after Graham's death I woke up with agonising chest pains at 2am. 'I'm sure it's indigestion,' I reassured myself. 'There's no way it's a heart attack unless I get pins and needles down one of my arms.' The pain got worse... and then I felt a tingling sensation in my left arm. 'Oh God no!' I thought. I lay there, frozen in fear, not knowing what to do. I couldn't face another medical emergency so soon after all the ones I'd endured with Graham – the very thought of spending any more time in a hospital made me feel sick to my stomach. And so I didn't call an ambulance but simply turned over and waited for the pain to subside, which it eventually did.

When I told my friend Sarah about the incident the following day, she was furious. 'You could have died!' she spluttered. 'That was very irresponsible. I want you to go to your GP right this

STILL RUNNING AFTER ALL THESE TEARS

very minute. If it wasn't a heart attack, it might be Broken Heart Syndrome, which some people experience after traumatic events. The symptoms are apparently very similar.'

Shocked into action, I duly went for an ECG and later a stress echocardiogram, which thankfully proved normal.

Three months later, having completed my renovations and sorted out my financial affairs, I flew to South Africa to see my dad, who was living in Southport, a village a two-hour drive south of Durban. Now 83, it was obvious Dad's health had declined a lot since my sister Loren and her husband had emigrated to Portugal five months earlier. They'd previously lived three doors down from him, and I suspected that without the daily interaction with them, he'd become depressed. No longer preparing his own meals or working on his Master's thesis in Environmental Law, he was now spending most of his time slumped on the sofa watching a never-ending diet of cricket and rugby on TV. The only time he seemed to take any interest in what was on the screen was when *Doodsondes* aka *Forbidden Apple*, a Turkish soap opera incongruously dubbed into Afrikaans, was on. Set in high-society Istanbul and featuring a cast of pouting and posing, scheming supermodels, it had us both hooked.

Although for the two weeks I was there Dad knocked on my door at 8am sharp every day to take me out for a run around the grounds of his residential complex, each 'run' was in fact mostly a walk, and he was incredibly unsteady on his feet. The irony wasn't lost on me that, now that my dad had finally, after all these years, slowed down enough to be able to run with me, he could no longer really run. By now, having ceased running for two months due to my strained back, I was grateful for the chance to gradually resume it again.

FORGET ME NOT

Most worrying, though, was the way Dad kept forgetting everyday words, and the frustration it was causing us both.

'I need the whatshisname, my lovey. You know, the whatshisname. Ag man, Leecy, you know what I mean,' he'd say, which prompted a five-minute guessing game as to what he actually wanted. Matters weren't helped by the fact that I, too, was suffering from memory loss, which is common after a bereavement. As had happened when my mother died very unexpectedly, so-called 'grief brain' meant I couldn't remember the names of commonplace objects, sometimes struggled to formulate sentences and forgot the names of close friends. Though I very much wanted to talk to my dad about Graham's death – he'd been very fond of his son-in-law and had loved discussing world affairs with him – his language difficulties made this impossible.

Loren and I spent dozens of hours on WhatsApp discussing what to do about Dad. An added complication was that our dad had atrial fibrillation, an abnormal heart rhythm that causes your heart to beat irregularly and often too fast, and that makes you five times more likely to have a stroke. He also had suspected prostate cancer but his urologist had advised using the 'watchful waiting' approach as Dad wasn't experiencing any symptoms. This would enable him to avoid treatment which came with numerous unpleasant side effects, such as urinary incontinence and bowel problems. We were convinced Dad would wither away within days of being admitted to a care home so we couldn't entertain that option. Eventually we decided to leave things as they were but ask Dad's current carer, Dumiso – who until that point had been living off-site but coming in daily to shop, cook and clean for him – to move into our father's spare bedroom to be on hand in case Dad needed him in the night. With a heavy heart I flew back to the UK.

STILL RUNNING AFTER ALL THESE TEARS

I was appalled by what greeted me when I returned to South Africa three months later for what I thought would be a two-month visit. I was informed that Dad, a lifelong runner who'd run every day since he was a schoolboy, had not only stopped running due to agonising pain in his legs, but had now started becoming agitated and trying to go for runs at 2am. When he was later diagnosed with dementia, I found out that this is a classic sign of 'sundowning', a state of confusion that occurs in the evenings and that's common in people with the condition. Not only that, but he was eating the same two dinners – takeaway fish and chips, and greasy spaghetti Bolognese – every day because he claimed they were the only food that had any taste. There and then I took the decision not to return to the UK but to stay to care for Dad until he died. Fortunately, I could continue working remotely by writing articles in the evenings and seeing my hypnotherapy clients online.

And so began one of the most stressful periods of my life. Dad's house needed a spring clean, so I blitzed it from top to toe, going down on my hands and knees to scrub the kitchen floor from beige back to white. I made Dad his favourite bacon and eggs, spent hours batch-cooking hearty stews and even attempted the 'chuck-it-all-in' oxtail recipe my father was famous for. Having peeled dozens of carrots and onions, and after simmering the bony meat for a good five hours just to make sure it really was as melt in the mouth as Dad's version, I triumphantly served it to him for dinner.

'This is utterly, utterly tasteless,' Dad remarked, battering my ego as effectively as if he'd taken a club to it. Little did I know at this point that he wasn't being rude: I later learned that people with dementia often start to dislike foods they've always liked and enjoy flavours they've never fancied before. They also crave sugary foods: cue Dad's sudden love of chocolate, especially Lindt Lindor truffles, which I'd never seen him eat my entire life.

The most alarming thing of all, however, was Dad's lack of balance. He almost toppled over every time he went to the loo, so I took to escorting him there, knowing a broken hip often spells the end for the elderly.

'Why are you following me to the toilet, Leecy?' Dad said indignantly when I sprang up to help him the minute he rose from the sofa.

I explained I was only coming along to make sure he didn't fall.

'But I won't fall,' Dad said, half stumbling down the passage.

When we reached the bathroom, I insisted he touch the toilet bowl with both knees as I'd realised he wasn't getting nearly close enough and so was peeing on his socks.

'Where's my privacy?' he grumbled bitterly.

'Dad, once you're positioned properly, I'll leave you to pee in peace,' I told him, before exiting the room but peeping round the doorway to make sure I could catch him if he fell. Despite my best efforts, my dad nonetheless collapsed twice, completely unexpectedly, on the same day, when I took my eyes off him for a few seconds.

My dad's deteriorating health wasn't the only worry I had to contend with – the worsening state of South Africa's infrastructure, caused by maintenance problems, sabotage and corruption, was equally concerning. Water cuts were a frequent occurrence, and load-shedding – when the electricity supply is cut to ease pressure on the failing grid – left us without power for up to three hours, several times a day. On one occasion, there was no electricity for

STILL RUNNING AFTER ALL THESE TEARS

three days and nights, meaning all my precious batch-cooked food was at risk of defrosting and would have had to be thrown away. The only way I could save it was to drive to a neighbouring town to buy bags of ice. On the third night without power, I headed for bed at 6pm when it grew dark but simply couldn't go to sleep at such a 'baby bedtime'. Bored witless, with no book or TV to distract me, I lay on my back and studied a tourist map of KwaZulu-Natal for an hour by torchlight before once again trying to fall asleep.

Another thing that made living in South Africa so challenging was the security situation. Despite being surrounded by an electric fence, our complex's WhatsApp group was full of scary messages about homes that had been burgled.

'Will the person who left a ladder outside no 44 please take it inside immediately as it could be used in a burglary,' wrote one resident.

'I'm the owner of 44 and that was the ladder used to break into my house last night,' Number 44 replied.

'Number 44, isn't that the fourth break-in you've had since moving here? You need to do something about your security,' wrote another.

I lived alone in my sister's bungalow and despite the burglar bars, panic buttons and electric fence, I never felt safe. As they say in South Africa, it's a country where the law-abiding citizens live behind bars and the criminals roam free. At least twice a week my burglar alarm would go off, which necessitated a nerve-wracking, heart-thumping, ten-minute stumble around the house, usually in inky darkness because of load-shedding, to check whether anyone had broken in, or whether the alarm had been accidentally activated by a cat. Having armed security guards roaming the garden by torchlight did nothing to calm my nerves as I often wasn't sure whether they were armed robbers. On three separate occasions, I forgot to reset the alarm after it had gone off, realising to my horror in the morning that I'd left myself vulnerable to attack for many hours.

With my body flooded with adrenaline day and night, and my grief over Graham still weighing heavily in my heart, I knew the only thing that would help me feel better – besides voice-noting my friends and chatting to my cousin Anna, who happily was on maternity leave and so could take my calls whenever I was free to make them – was to run. Since injuring my back six months before, I'd barely run at all, but now that I was fully recovered, there was no excuse not to make a comeback. For safety reasons, my only option was to do so inside the complex, a very short route mostly comprised of hills. One was so steep that I had to zig-zag up it while walking, and rest halfway to stop myself passing out. The only flat section was a tennis-court-sized car park, which I often ran laps around when I couldn't face the inclines.

And then there were the frogs; and the deadly snakes that came to feed on them. KwaZulu-Natal is notorious for its poisonous serpents whose venom can kill you in hours: mambas, adders, puff adders and cobras all lurked in its sub-tropical undergrowth. Every morning, among the frogs lying like miniature maple leaves where they'd been squashed into the tarmac by passing cars, there would be a handful of newly decapitated snakes, killed by the gardeners in the course of their duties. Talk about running scared.

The final hazard was the neighbours. I'd barely break into a sweat before one would pop out of their house and ask after my father: I'd give a Dad Update, run 100m, and then stop and repeat the news to the next. Through his hitherto daily runs, regular as clockwork, I realised my dad had made many friends in the complex and that they were all as concerned about him as I was. I persevered, however, not realising at the time that running not only releases feel-good chemicals such as endorphins and serotonin, but endocannabinoids, a substance similar to cannabis. No wonder it made me happy! So even though my daily runs were incredibly short and more stop than start, more walk than waddle, they had a profound impact on my mood, got me outside and helped me feel less isolated. I'm not sure how I'd have survived my Southport sojourn without them.

Not only was Dad becoming increasingly unsteady on his feet, but he began to find it difficult to command them to walk.

'Come on, Daddy,' I'd urge him. 'Walk towards me.'

'I am!' he'd say, his feet rooted to the spot. Sometimes it took me an exhausting 15 minutes to get him from the living room to the bathroom, just ten or so metres away. After Dumiso told us he was exhausted from waking up in the night to keep an eye on our dad, my sister and I realised Dumiso could no longer cope on his own and took the decision to hire additional full-time professional carers. The care agency insisted on sending us carers who were on duty for 48-hour shifts. They were supposed to sleep in an armchair in Dad's room, soothe him and accompany him to the loo during the night, and then follow him wherever he went during the day to ensure he didn't fall. When I queried how they could do their job while chronically sleep-deprived, Petronella, the agency's owner, sent me a link about 1.5-hour sleep cycles that she said proved they could manage. I was deeply reluctant to put the carers through this ordeal, but I had no option: with no public transport available, it was difficult for the carers to reach us, so it supposedly made sense for them to have longer shifts. But of course, it didn't.

FORGET ME NOT

Day by day, Dad's health deteriorated.

'Your father is really confused now,' Blessing, one of the carers, told me. 'He's been hitting the TV roughly and doesn't listen to me when I tell him to stop. He's asking me who the people are who have big sticks in their hands and want to hit each other. I told him they were playing cricket, but he didn't seem to understand me.'

I, too, had noticed disturbing signs. One day I caught my dad talking to a pillar on his patio that he had mistaken for a person. Another time he became upset when lying in bed and looking at his feet.

'There's something in the bed with me,' he said fearfully, wriggling his toes.

'Dad, those are your feet,' I pointed out.

'Don't be ridiculous, I don't have red feet,' he retorted crossly.

'You do when you're wearing red socks,' I laughed, giving him a hug.

A visit to a GP confirmed my dad had dementia, as we'd suspected for quite some time, although the diagnosis was made without testing his cognitive abilities – the doctor based his assessment only on what I told him.

'You have a very bumpy road ahead,' he said. 'Soon your dad won't even recognise you.'

I was hugely relieved that my father had been seated outside when I was given this latest life shock. It seemed so cruelly, desperately unfair: Dad had followed almost all of the 'dementia-prevention rules' his entire life by running regularly, never smoking, staying slim, having a healthy, low-sugar diet and eating omega 3-rich pilchards every day. He'd even recently given up drinking his beloved beer, for goodness' sake, and swapped it for alcohol-free. Yet here we were. I felt numb.

Dad looking like a Ferrari driver

Armchair exercises in the common room

Dining out in style

Fun and (ball) games at the care home

Chapter 20
Flying by the seat of our pants

♪♪ Mood music: *Jerusalema* by Master KG featuring Nomcebo Zikode
The song that welcomed Dad into his care home

When, despite having round-the-clock care from up to three people at a time, our dad had another fall, in which he injured his head, my sister Loren and I realised with heavy hearts that the situation wasn't sustainable. Dad's picture-perfect Facebook World, as Loren called it, the one in which we'd pretended that he could still live independently and do whatever he pleased, was crashing down around our ears. A life-threatening fall now felt inevitable, so we reluctantly began researching care-home options. Loren, who was still in Portugal, spent several days looking into care facilities there, in the UK, in South Africa and even Chiang Mai in Thailand, which was renowned for its person-centred dementia-care resorts. An expat hypnotherapy client of mine living in Bangkok, however, warned me of the dangers of the 'burning season', when local farmers cleared their fields for planting by burning leftover vegetation. The resulting smoke caused severe air pollution and health issues such as respiratory and cardiovascular problems. We were also aware of how challenging the 24-hour journey to get Dad to Thailand would be.

I, on the other hand, dashed off emails to everyone I knew in South Africa asking whether they could recommend any care homes. Some of the suggestions were, quite frankly, upsetting.

STILL RUNNING AFTER ALL THESE TEARS

There was no way we were going to let Dad live in a four-bed dorm with a tiny locker for his belongings and only curtains for privacy. It would be like sending him to a low-budget boarding school. One care-home chain, however, looked promising, and in a meant-to-be coincidence, Loren and I came across it at the same time. It had a spectacular setting overlooking magnificent mountains and was a short drive from several beaches. What's more, it was situated in Cape Town, which I knew really well, having lived there for almost seven years, and where both the electricity and security situation were far better than in KwaZulu-Natal. We agreed this was clearly the best option and immediately set about planning how to get Dad there: his condition was deteriorating by the day, and I was concerned that if we waited any longer, he wouldn't be well enough to fly.

We didn't dare tell Dad about the plan. Instead, with all the 'need to know' secrecy of a CIA Special Ops mission, I planned to clandestinely pack his suitcases the night before and then announce that I was taking him on holiday to Cape Town on the morning of our trip. Having witnessed his reluctance to attend medical appointments, which we dubbed 'medical safaris' to make light of his deep dislike of them, we were convinced this was the best course of action. I knew that if I told Dad in advance, he'd suddenly feign a terrible stomach ache or say he was 'feeling lousy', and that I'd spend the entire flight worrying about whether he really was too sick to fly.

The day before we were due to leave, I was dismayed when Dad began peeing all over the house, the first time he'd done so during the day.

'Dad, why are you doing this now?' I sobbed as I mopped up the puddles of urine in the passage outside his bedroom.

Worried that the airplane might be turned back mid-flight

FLYING BY THE SEAT OF OUR PANTS

if my dad began urinating in the aisle, I booked an emergency appointment with his GP, who advised me to withhold my dad's diuretic medication and keep him dehydrated until we reached our destination.

'And I'm going to prescribe some beta blockers,' said the sympathetic doctor. 'They're not for your dad, but for you! They'll help reduce some of your anxiety.'

I've flown in aircraft with broken seatbelts before, and ones where the seats were like flimsy, rusting garden chairs that had been nailed in place. I've even experienced turbulence so terrible that I thought the cabin crew were going to be crushed to death by the levitating food trolleys. But none of those flights was as tense as this one. Despite what you read about the Mile High Club, sky toilets definitely aren't made for two, and I shuddered to think how I'd manoeuvre my dad into one before the urge to go overtook him.

Once onboard, I gripped my dad's hand firmly the entire journey, sick with fear as I imagined urine drenching nearby passengers while I fumbled to help him use the pee bottle that, camouflaged by a floral scarf, I was clutching on my lap. The beta blockers lay forgotten in my hand luggage.

'Only two hours to go,' I kept repeating to myself. 'Only an hour and fifty-five minutes to go.' Just then the man seated next to Dad struck up a conversation, something I usually dread during flights. On this occasion, however, I was deeply grateful for the distraction. It turned out he was a keen triathlete, so after he'd shared a few tri tales, I regaled him with how repeating a mantra of 'noodles and beer' had got me through the Olympic-distance London Triathlon when the murky water of the Royal Victoria Docks, the colour of Coca-Cola, had tempted me to abandon the event after only a few seconds.

STILL RUNNING AFTER ALL THESE TEARS

'She's run more than a hundred marathons, you know,' whispered Dad, much to the man's astonishment. He looked at me quizzically for affirmation. I nodded, amazed that my dad had remembered.

In the event, Dad was a dream travel companion and waited patiently until we were in the terminal before needing the loo. A pre-booked taxi whisked us off to the care home and, with the minimum of fuss, Dad was installed in his room, a bright and airy space with a view of a well-maintained garden. I joined Dad for dinner that night in the spacious dining room where he was served a beautifully presented meal that would have done any hotel restaurant proud. I was mightily relieved to see him eat his dinner without asking me any uncomfortable questions: the lie about us being on holiday seemed to be holding up. As I guiltily snuck off that first night, en route to the Airbnb I'd rented just a kilometre down the road, I felt like an anxious parent who'd dropped their toddler off at nursery for the first time. How on earth would Dad survive living in an institution? At home, everything had centred on him: a picky eater, he'd now have to eat unfamiliar food with people he'd never met before, be cared for by strangers, and learn to live in a room no bigger than his former kitchen.

I needn't have worried. When I returned the next day, I found Dad in the common room dressed in his favourite red jacket and baseball cap, looking for all the world like a Ferrari driver. A bemused smile played across his face as he observed the carers and nurses performing a very energetic version of the pandemic gospel hit *Jerusalema* in which they showed off their signature moves by slapping their thighs and heels and roaring with laughter.

After the impressive display, we were invited to take a turn on the dance floor and I asked my dad if he'd like to join in.

'No, I just don't feel like it,' he said.

FLYING BY THE SEAT OF OUR PANTS

I let the matter drop, careful not to be too bossy on his first day in alien surroundings. A few seconds later, he changed his mind.

'Do you want to dance, Leecy?'

'Sure,' I said, helping him to his feet and leading him in a slow waltz, the first time I'd ever danced with my dad. Graham and I had decided not to have any dancing at our wedding reception, which meant Dad and I hadn't even had the traditional dad-daughter swish around the dance floor. By the time the tea trolley arrived, pushed by the Food Ambassador – a glamorous Xhosa woman wearing blood-red lipstick and a beautifully braided bun – I knew my dad was going to be happy there. That conclusion was confirmed when a small sausage dog, whom I discovered went by the name of Lucy Van Heerden, casually trotted by and proceeded to hoover up some muffin crumbs a resident had dropped.

'Since when do dogs have surnames?' I chuckled.

'Beats me,' Dad grinned back.

'I'm in such a bloody state – a mental state – I feel lousy,' Dad said to me a few days after arriving at the care home. He had good days when he was calm and content, and not-so-good days when he'd keep peppering his sentences with 'whatshisnames' and not recognise the corridor he lived on.

'Are you serious? Is it *definitely* down here?' he'd ask when I pointed out where we needed to go. When we reached his room, his face would light up and he'd exclaim, 'It's a miracle! This really *is* my room! How did we get here?'

'You have a *very* clever daughter, Dad,' I'd tease him. 'And besides, it's easy to tell which room is yours because there's a photo of you on the door!' Pointing to a smiling portrait of my dad that had been affixed there, I'd always say, 'Who's that handsome bugger?'

Every time, Dad would get right up close to the picture and almost coyly proclaim: 'Me!'

While my father's memory wasn't as bad as the gentleman who made the same observation each time I sat down at the dining table where Dad ate his meals – 'That's the largest wristwatch I've ever seen. What's the name of it? Skagen? Never heard of it' – I could see he needed a thorough professional assessment as his previous dementia diagnosis had been made without him even being present in the room. I consulted the head nurse, who recommended a local GP, Dr Shannon Odell, a palliative medicine specialist. The moment she walked into my dad's room, dressed in a white broderie anglaise dress and carrying a heavy black doctor's bag, I knew I liked her, and Dad did, too. Sitting on the edge of his bed, she began a gentle questioning.

'What day of the week is it today, Dr Jackson?' Dad wasn't sure.

'That's not really a fair question,' I laughed. 'Even *I* don't often know what day of the week it is.'

'What season is it right now?' Again, Dad couldn't answer, hazarding 'Winter?' when it was, in fact, summer.

'Can you draw me a clock-face, please?'

Dad took the GP's pen and hesitantly sketched a distorted Dalí-esque melting watch.

'I'd like you to read the words on this page,' said Dr Odell, holding up her clipboard, 'and then do what the words say.' My dad squinted at the piece of paper.

'Close... your... eyes,' he said slowly, before squeezing his eyes shut for a moment and then opening one of them so that he could take a sneaky peek at the doctor. He obviously found this style of interrogation rather amusing.

FLYING BY THE SEAT OF OUR PANTS

'Very good. And now I want you to construct a sentence with a noun and an active verb.'

What the heck, I'd studied English literature at university for three years and *I* wasn't entirely sure what Dad was being asked. I'd forgotten, however, that Dad, too, had studied English literature, at the age of 68, when he'd done his law degree, so this didn't faze him. Smiling sweetly at the doctor, he said softly, 'Doctor, please close your eyes!'

The GP and I hooted with laughter.

'In all the years I've been a doctor, I've never had a patient say that to me!' she said, packing up her bag.

Out in the corridor I took Dr Odell aside and explained that we hadn't told my dad about his suspected dementia, or his suspected prostate cancer, as we knew he'd find the news devastating. I also told her about Graham's horrendous experience in the hospice and my fervent wish for my father to be spared that fate.

'Making sure that my dad is not in pain is my number one priority,' I told her. 'I haven't discussed end-of-life care with him but I do know that he supported my uncle's decision not to have chemotherapy or disfiguring facial surgery when he developed mouth cancer, so quality of life, rather than quantity of life, is what matters to him.'

'I'm so glad you shared that with me,' Dr Odell said. 'Don't worry, pain relief is my main priority, too. We're definitely on the same page.'

I'm not sure whether it was as a result of the memantine dementia drug Dr Odell prescribed but shortly after he began taking it, my dad's speech and ability to walk improved dramatically. But what was most interesting to me was that he began to reveal a great sense of humour. Now in my eyes, my dad was many things – highly intelligent, athletic and generous to a fault – but the one label I would never have attached to him was a GSOH. On a visit to London, 20 years before, for example, he'd kept almost somersaulting over the barriers in the Tube stations because he'd inserted his ticket into the incorrect slot, thereby opening the barrier to his left. I'd howled with laughter at this, but he never once saw the funny side and kept repeating the error every time we used public transport.

'What's so funny?' he'd grumble as yet another commuter got free entry to the Tube.

Now, however, he relished playing tricks on me. A particular favourite was to sit in the communal lounge in the morning and pretend not to recognise me. I'd bounce into the room, eager to embrace him, only to find him staring right through me, as if he had no clue who I was. Every time he did this, the words 'Oh no, it's the dementia!' would flit through my mind and, as my face is an open book, my dismay would be plain for all to see.

'Dad? It's me, Leecy.'

No answer, just a blank stare.

'Dad, how are you, Dad?' Still nothing. And then he'd suddenly reach out both arms to me and let out a huge laugh before drawing me closer for a hug.

There are several other father-daughter moments that stick in my mind from our almost daily drives. Over time our relationship became more and more loving and reminded me of what I'd once shared with Graham: I gave Dad's leg affectionate squeezes after changing gears and asked him the kind of questions Graham and I used to entertain ourselves with when we became bored on our numerous road trips.

FLYING BY THE SEAT OF OUR PANTS

'How much do you love me, Dad?' I asked.

'A hundred per cent. No, a hundred and twenty per cent,' he replied.

'Do you like having me around?'

'I LOVE having you around!'

'What do you like most about me?'

'Your delicious personality.'

'What exactly do you mean by that?' I asked, deeply touched by this compliment.

'Well, you know, you're just so... vibrant!'

Sharing a joke...   ... and lamb chops

Dad making himself at home in my tiny house

Bowled over by carpet bowls

Joy on Christmas Day

Ordering Chimpanzee pizza

Chapter 21
Care-home comforts

♫ **Mood music: *Welcome to Cape Town* by David Kramer**
The care home's joyful anthem

I never imagined spending most of my time in a care home at the age of 55, but when my dad moved to Cape Town 15 weeks after Graham died, that's what happened. I'd felt really guilty lying to my dad that he'd be staying in a hotel, but I needn't have worried. While the dementia had stripped him of much of his memory and independence, it was also merciful, and allowed him to live in happy ignorance. He never once questioned why there was a beautiful woman in a headscarf called Catherine – who looked uncannily like the one Johannes Vermeer had painted in *Girl with a Pearl Earring* – sitting beside his bed at night. Or why some of the 'hotel' staff wore nurses' uniforms. Or why we had to sign out when we went for day trips. He just calmly accepted that he had a comfy bed and a loving daughter and left it at that. Later I would learn that these little white lies we tell our loved ones with dementia are known as 'fiblets', and that there's really no need to feel guilty about using them as they spare them incalculable pain and distress.

I had confirmation we'd done the right thing one day when, as we walked to a viewpoint in the care-home grounds, I asked Dad if he was happy there.

'I love it here. In fact, I'm thinking of moving in here for a few weeks – with you! My feeling is… you should move in here, too.'

STILL RUNNING AFTER ALL THESE TEARS

'I've already booked you two more weeks,' I told him, 'but I can't stay here as I have my own tiny house down the road.'

'Are you serious, Leecy?' Dad said excitedly. 'Thanks, my lovey!'

That's not to say my dad was always happy. At times his stubbornness emerged, sometimes when I was least expecting it. For example, when Dad saw the inside of my pocket-sized rental, he was as smitten by it as I was. It was either that, or the lamb chops I cooked him, which he absolutely adored.

'I want to stay here from now on,' he informed me.

'I'm afraid you can't, Dad, because you wouldn't be able to get up the stairs to the bedroom.'

'Says who? I can.'

'Dad, you know you can't. You can barely get down the stairs to come in here.'

'Well then I'll just flake out on the floor somewhere,' he told me, sucking the lamb fat from his fingers.

'I really want you to stay here, Dad, but it's just not possible right now.'

'I'll sleep here – on the floor – because I *love* you.'

Oh how that broke my heart. Dad didn't ask for much – only my company, the occasional lamb chop, and now this. The one wish I couldn't grant him was what he wanted most: never to be parted from me.

Having witnessed the joy on my dad's face during his fitness classes, where they did seated exercises to music, I resolved to do them with him every morning. Another resolution was to fit in a daily run beforehand as, for the first time while back in South

CARE-HOME COMFORTS

Africa, I'd spotted runners – even female ones – out training on their own.

The care home was close to the Two Oceans Marathon route, frequently voted 'the most breathtaking course in the world', and I was determined to make up for the months of living under virtual house arrest in KwaZulu-Natal, where I could only run inside my dad's compound. The route from my tiny house to the care home along a sandy track was only a kilometre long, but it had soul-stirring views of the faraway Atlantic, rocky crags and mountain slopes clothed in rows of green grapevines. On either side of me, protea bushes poked out above the long yellow grass, which often hid families of guinea fowl who'd scoot through the veld at tremendous speed like miniature Usain Bolts, their legs moving so fast they turned into a blur. Thankfully I never encountered the porcupines several road signs warned of. Even though these fortified rodents only run at about 6mph, they've been known to kill leopards and lions so I didn't fancy trying to outstrip them. Nor did I want to turn up at the care home with a pincushion bum.

Although it felt great to be running 'free range' again after my 'battery chicken' experiences in Southport, security was never far from my mind. The multi-coloured ribbons fluttering from the fence enclosing nearby Tokai Forest made sure of that. I'd seen them several times when taking my dad for ice cream at Constantia Uitsig Wine Estate, and at first had thought they were pretty decorations. The truth was far darker. They were a memorial to a 16-year-old girl who was brutally raped, murdered and robbed while out running in the forest in 2016. The teen had wanted to fit in a quick 30-minute run while her mum waited for her in a parked car nearby. Her naked and bound body was found, face down in the sand, under some fynbos bushes, and her stolen iPhone was later sold by her attacker for R200 (less than £2). Every time I went for my run up to the care home, I wondered whether I was being supremely foolish, but it was the only time I could run as I needed to spend the rest of the day with my dad. I knew my daily run was keeping me sane, but was it also endangering my life?

Although I was tempted to run in Table Mountain National Park, a short distance down the road, I never did. Just as well, as in 2023, when I was back in the UK, three runners were mugged there at knife and gunpoint during the Ultra Trail Cape Town 100-mile race, despite numerous marshals dotted along the course. Never again would I take for granted the freedom to run when and where I chose: in the UK I'd sometimes go for a run at 9pm at night, something that was unthinkable in South Africa. My stay was turning into a lesson in gratitude for all the things I often didn't appreciate enough in the UK: water, electricity, security, and the freedom to run.

One day, for reasons unknown, Dad decided he didn't want to attend the exercise classes any more, despite extolling the virtues of staying fit on an almost daily basis.

'I feel lousy, my lovey,' he said, reclining on his bed with his arms crossed behind his head, looking for all the world like a Roman emperor waiting to be fed grapes.

'What's wrong, Dad?' My heart contracted with fear as it always did when he mentioned a health issue, his suspected prostate cancer diagnosis always at the forefront of my mind.

'I just don't know. Anyway, I don't think the exercise class is operating today.'

CARE-HOME COMFORTS

'How would you know that, Dad?' I asked, by now fully aware that this was a ploy. 'You're just being a lazybones!'

At that point Melinda du Toit, the occupational therapist, popped her head round the door.

'We're about to start the class, Dr Jackson; will you be joining us?'

Dad looked bashful and a small smile flitted across his face.

'But this bed is so pleasant and comfortable…' he muttered as Melinda and his carer Catherine helped him to his feet. Minutes later he was seated in a chair performing the actions to the *Hokey Cokey*. I have to confess that after only two verses I was pooped, and willing the tea trolley to arrive. Dad, however, took it all in his stride. A lifetime of running will do that for you.

One of the most avid exercise-class attendees was 90-year-old Mildred, a former physiotherapist. Mildred was the most animated hand-jiver, putting to shame the West End cast of *Grease* whom I'd seen perform *Born to Hand Jive* live. Making a hitchhiker's thumbs-up sign with both hands, she'd fling her arms back over her shoulders so energetically that I marvelled that they remained attached to her wrists. Aquiline-nosed, and with a voice that sounded just like the Queen's, Mildred kept Melinda on her toes from the vantage of her wheelchair.

'You've left out the bottom exercises,' she called out, pointing to her lap.

'Yes, Mildred, you're right, I have,' smiled Melinda. 'Okay everyone, we're now going to tighten our bottoms, yes even the gentlemen.' My dad dutifully did his pelvic-floor exercises, by this point also no doubt praying for the arrival of his tea.

Another resident I nicknamed Naughty Norman threw himself into the activities with gusto – literally. During every song he'd completely ignore Melinda's instructions and instead throw his

STILL RUNNING AFTER ALL THESE TEARS

arms and legs in the air simultaneously, executing a seated jumping jack. His delight at his performance – and the amusement it gave the rest of us – was a joy to behold.

Another new activity my father took pleasure in was carpet bowls. A white ball would be placed on the floor in the centre of the communal lounge and then we'd all be invited to roll coloured plastic balls towards it, with those who came closest scoring points. My dad and I were fiercely competitive, and I did my utmost to hit the target, but my balls either stopped well short of it or annoyingly rolled underneath one of the armchairs. He, on the other hand, was really rather good.

'Dr Jackson, you have one thousand one hundred points. Congratulations, you've come third,' proclaimed Melinda after one of the games. Dad pushed himself up onto his feet, grinning as he shook Melinda's outstretched hand. But then he looked confused.

'Where's my prize?' he said quizzically, rubbing his thumb and forefinger together. 'I thought you said I'd won one thousand one hundred rand?'

All the carers burst out laughing as I explained to Dad that we'd been playing for fun, not hard cash.

The carers usually helped my father make his weekly menu choices, but one morning I thought I'd help out by doing it myself.

'What would you like to eat this week, Dad?' I asked him, looking at the daunting list of three-course breakfasts, lunches, dinners and snacks.

'I don't know because I haven't eaten it yet,' he shrugged.

CARE-HOME COMFORTS

We ticked off a few meal options and then came to Tuesday's dessert.

'Would you like tiramisu or fruit salad for pudding, Dad?'

'*Terrorist soup?*'

'Not terrorist soup, Dad, *tiramisu*!' I spluttered.

'What on earth is that?'

'It's a kind of Italian dessert made from biscuits, coffee and liqueur.'

'I've never heard of it. Fruit salad, I think.'

Getting Dad to choose meals was one thing, getting him to eat them was a different ballgame entirely. Having lost control of pretty much everything else, this was one area of his life where he still held on to some.

'I can see from here that this lunch is nothing to write home about,' he proclaimed even before his food was set down in front of him. 'In fact,' his voice dropped dramatically to a stage whisper, 'this is all utterly *shit*!'

'We won't tell the poor chef!' I chortled, my mouth watering at the artfully presented quiche and salad he'd just been served.

Towards the end of the meal, he mustered the courage to show more resistance: 'Don't make me eat any more, Leecy, I'm serious. I've vomited five times today.'

I glanced at his carer in horror, but she shook her head with a smile. No, Dad hadn't been sick. Not even once.

'But Dad,' I persisted, 'you need the protein. If you don't eat it, your muscles will waste away and you'll end up in a wheelchair.'

'No I won't. And besides, since when did you become the Protein Professor?'

I even resorted to blackmail, once, when his weight had dropped perilously low.

STILL RUNNING AFTER ALL THESE TEARS

'If I refuse to take you to my tiny house because you didn't eat your dinner, how will you feel?' I threatened him.

'That's your loss,' he shot back.

'But Dad, you *need* to eat. If you caught a stomach bug right now, you wouldn't have any weight to lose and you could easily die,' I implored him.

'I don't care. I like being thin,' he said. 'When I go running, I don't want to carry extra weight around with me.'

'But Dad, you're not running at the moment. Please, Daddy, just have one more bite.'

'You can "please Daddy" me all you like, I am *not* eating another *molecule*.'

'But Dad, I've tasted your food, and it's really not so bad.'

'It's not so good, either,' he replied glumly.

One afternoon I took my dad to a restaurant in an attempt to make up for the 'vomit-inducing' food in the care home. He was always a T-bone man – 'Rare! Baked potato! No onion rings!' is probably his most memorable catchphrase. So when my schoolfriend Liz came to visit I thought it would be a great idea to treat us all to a steak in a treehouse restaurant nestled in a grove of milkwood trees overlooking Noordhoek Beach.

While Liz and I chatted away, Dad pocketed a few toothpicks (he was obsessed with them, and nabbed a few whenever he could), donned his glasses and began a thorough examination of the extensive menu. When the waiter arrived, Dad ordered an Appletiser, a beverage I'd introduced him to a couple of weeks earlier.

'Appletiser is unbelievably delicious,' he informed us excitedly. 'Have you tasted Appletiser before? I've been meaning to ask you, Leecy, what exactly *is* Appletiser?'

I explained it was carbonated apple juice.

CARE-HOME COMFORTS

'Yes, but how exactly do the bubbles get into the juice?' Dad pondered out loud. Even with dementia, he was continually curious about the world.

A few minutes later, I was deep in conversation when Dad suddenly looked up and proclaimed: 'They have chimpanzee on the menu.' A sorrowful look passed between me and Liz as we wordlessly acknowledged yet more evidence of his cognitive decline. Only nine months previously he'd been working on his Master's thesis, and now he was making bizarre comments.

'I'm sure that's not true, Dad,' I said nervously. 'Where does it say that on the menu?'

'Here,' said Dad, pointing to page four.

I flipped open my own menu and hastily scanned the laminated pages. What in the world had made Dad think the restaurant served bush meat? Even though some South African restaurants do serve crocodile kebabs and warthog loin, I was pretty sure this wasn't one of them. All I could see was the usual fare: steaks, pasta and pizza. And then I spotted it. There was indeed chimpanzee on the menu: Chimpanzee Pizza! A foul-sounding culinary abomination topped with avocado and pineapple.

Liz and I were still laughing when Dad made another unexpected announcement: 'There's porcupine on the menu, too,' he said solemnly. This time I wasn't going to dismiss his claim as quickly as I'd done before, and scoured the rest of the menu. Sure enough, Dad was right about that, too: the wine list featured a 'crisp Sauvignon Blanc with delicious blackcurrant notes and a zippy finish'. Its name? Porcupine Ridge.

With my chubby-cheeked baby sister Loren

Loren, right, often looked like a ragamuffin

My sister's Chihuahua-themed 40th birthday

Loren runs the Rome Marathon

Two flamingos conquer Comrades

Chapter 22
Oh sister, where art thou?

♪♪ Mood music: *Scatterlings of Africa*
by Johnny Clegg & Savuka
The song that reminds me how much my sister Loren loved Johnny

My sister Loren and I were formed in the same belly, under the same loving heart. We were incredibly similar, but also very different. I was closer to her than anyone else on earth besides Graham, but I was also often at loggerheads with her. Like Virginia Woolf, Loren was diagnosed with bipolar disorder at the age of 48, just before Graham was told he had mesothelioma. The symptoms of bipolar, when it's unmanaged, include extreme changes in mood so her diagnosis finally helped me understand why she could flip from being my loving little sister, whom our family fondly called Lollipop, or Lolly for short, to, at times, raging at me relentlessly for no discernible reason.

Loren was a brilliant construction lawyer renowned for her razor-sharp intellect and dedication to her job, who went on to attract some of the most prestigious clients her law firm ever acquired. One of my favourite stories, as told to me by Angie, her best friend and former personal assistant, was the time she commandeered a car in order to submit some legal documents before a very tight deadline. Unable to locate the vehicle that was supposed to be waiting for her, Loren had run up to a man seated in his car at a set of traffic lights and jumped into his passenger seat, instructing Angie to hop in the back.

STILL RUNNING AFTER ALL THESE TEARS

'Take us to Transnet on Smith Street,' Loren ordered the terrified man.

'Are you hijacking me?' he asked.

'No,' said Loren. 'I just have to get to Transnet in the next few minutes. Step on it!'

Once they'd reached their destination, with no time to sign in at reception, Loren distracted the security guards while Angie was tasked with crawling under the turnstiles clutching the precious documents, managing to submit them with seconds to spare.

'Loren was fearless,' Angie told me. 'For her, nothing was impossible.'

Born two years and two weeks apart, my chubby-cheeked little sister and I were inseparable – and insufferable – as children. We played together constantly – and fought incessantly.

'What did you do that for, Lolly?' screamed the ten-year-old me as I chased Loren through our house after she'd punched me in the arm for no reason.

'Oh, I was just a bit bored,' she'd giggle, acknowledging that she was merely looking for a bit of excitement and knowing she could outrun me anytime. One year we agreed to gift our mum a day of her daughters not fighting. We managed to get to 10am before we threw in the towel and conceded we needed to find Mum a different Mother's Day present.

Besides fighting, we shared many other interests. Dressed in our favourite outfits – mine a girly daffodil-yellow dress and Loren's a ragamuffin ensemble of orange T-shirt and purple leggings layered with brown shorts – we spent hours playing 'My friend, my friend'. This was a game in which we pretended to be best friends

OH SISTER, WHERE ART THOU?

who both owned adorable 'dogs' crafted from cardboard toilet-roll tubes and lengths of cotton, which we'd drag around behind us like promenading Parisians. Whenever we spotted glowworms in our rockery, believing them to be fairy messengers, we'd write letters to the fairies, tuck them into cracks between the rocks, and then return the next day, breathless with excitement, to see what gifts had been left for us: tiny packets of sweets and, once, a dainty pastel-coloured tea set. We camped out on the flat roof of our house, spending a sleepless night worrying that we'd sleepwalk and plunge to our deaths on the driveway below. We climbed the enormous maple tree in our garden and sent its helicopter seeds spiralling down to earth while writing poetry high among its branches. 'I have a horse / A lovely white / I ride on him / When it is night / I see the stars / I hear the stream / And that is why / I like to dream' is the poem Lolly wrote, aged seven, that I loved so much I memorised it. As little girls, we loved going to the Pretoria Art Museum every week where, in a darkened room hung with Dutch Old Masters, we'd sit on our little folding chairs decorated with zoo animals, doing our French knitting and watching the art historian Kenneth Clark's *Civilisation* series projected onto the gallery's big screen. As teenagers, we always had each other's backs: because our voices were so similar, Loren once lay in my bed pretending to be me when my mother came to check whether I'd returned home from a date, and I once broke up with one of Loren's boyfriends on the phone when she lacked the courage to do so herself.

When I got married, I chose Loren as one of my bridesmaids. She looked stunning in her cream dress sprinkled with flower garlands. During the ceremony, she succumbed to a fit of quivering giggles and, when I caught sight of her shaking shoulders, it nearly caused me to splutter my way through my vows. Like the author Clover Stroud and her circus-owner sister Nell (who died of breast cancer aged just 46), we found exactly the same things funny. Clover wrote in *The Red of My Blood* about the way they'd crease up with laughter at the random phrase PURE NEW WOOL because it was like a secret code between the two of them. Our PURE NEW WOOL equivalent was the word 'poepele' (pronounced 'poop-pel-eh'), which had come about when one of us had mis-spelled the word 'people' in a hastily typed email. In Afrikaans, the word *poephol* (pronounced 'poop-hol') means 'arsehole', both literally and figuratively, so poepele, which sounded very similar, became our private, pejorative word for people we found fist-clenchingly annoying.

'The receptionist at the grotty hotel we're staying at was a real poepele,' Loren once WhatsApped me. 'He wouldn't even lend us a bloody teaspoon, so we dashed to the shops and now have 200 spoons to stir our tea and eat our Haagen-Dazs with!!' Cue hysterics on my part at the follow-up photo of her holding up two fistfuls of plastic teaspoons, a few of which she'd tucked into her hair. On her 53rd birthday, which we didn't know would be her last, Loren posed for another photo hugging the item she proclaimed she loved most in all the world: the little white travel kettle I'd given her 20 years before. A fellow tea addict, I immediately fired a photo back of me embracing our dad's chrome Russell Hobbs kettle while planting kisses on its spout.

We shared the same sense of adventure, too. Loren and her boyfriend Wayne blazed a trail for Graham and I with their backpacking adventures in their early 20s: they lived on pasta, olive oil and garlic for several weeks just so that they could afford tickets to the Uffizi Gallery and other pricey art museums in Florence, and once memorably spent a terrifying night sleeping on the floor of Rome's Termini Station beside homeless people and

OH SISTER, WHERE ART THOU?

drug addicts. Another unusual camping spot was the pavement information booth on Montjuïc Hill that they made their home during the 1992 Barcelona Olympics. It wasn't locked at night and they'd crawl into it with their sleeping bags and backpacks and bed down there before rising at dawn, showering down at the beach and storing their luggage at the railway station during the day. After being gifted tickets by a couple of spectators who'd had to leave early, they'd been lucky enough, in the dying days of apartheid, to witness South Africa's Elana Meyer win silver in the 10,000m and, even more memorably, kiss and do a hand-in-hand victory lap with Derartu Tulu, the first black African woman to win an Olympic gold medal.

A decade later, Loren came on several trips abroad with Graham and me. We all nearly froze to death in our flimsy tent when temperatures in the Grand Canyon plummeted to minus 9°C, and on the same holiday she cajoled us into doing a 17km run at dawn across the Golden Gate Bridge. On another trip, while crossing the border into El Salvador, she nearly got us arrested for bribery when she accidentally handed over her passport stuffed with US$100 bills to an immigration official because she'd withdrawn US$2,000 spending money and it barely fitted into her overflowing bumbag.

Loren was 'the sporty one' in our family and in her 20s she became a Pope-Ellis Ironwoman, a title awarded to athletes in South Africa who, in the same year, have completed the 56-mile Comrades Marathon, the Midmar Mile open-water swimming event and the three-day Dusi Canoe Marathon. The latter, a 120km race, is often described as 'one of the toughest kayak marathons on the planet' as it includes deadly rapids and many miles of exhausting portaging through dense bush. Over the years, Loren accompanied me on five marathons: in New York

STILL RUNNING AFTER ALL THESE TEARS

we wore similar headdresses made from pink feather dusters and stuffed safari-animal toys and she complained bitterly when I dropped and broke the alarm clock we'd been using to pace ourselves after forgetting to pack my sports watch; in Barcelona we both feasted on prawns – and not pasta – at a tapas bar the night before the race; at the wine-and-oyster fuelled Médoc Marathon she plastered herself in so much yellow face paint, butterflies and flower garlands that she could have been mistaken for a fluorescent Caribbean cocktail; in Seville her instruction to 'stop chatting and get moving' got me over the line with a PB of 4h39; and after the Dublin Marathon, she got tipsy and became so friendly with a couple of elderly Irish swingers in a pub that we nearly ended up going home with them for what I feared would be a foursome.

Like me, once she'd discovered something she loved, Loren wanted others to share it, too, and so she frequently urged me to run Comrades. She'd done the race three times – once with almost no training, which had resulted in a near-death experience in the medical tent afterwards. She never doubted I could do it, supporting me all the way and going so far as to enter my first Comrades with me. Before we set off, we posed for photos in Pietermaritzburg, standing on one leg in our matching flappy flamingo hats. Once again her lack of training landed her in the medical tent, although this time, unlike previously, being much older, she was spared the indignity of having an injection in her bottom administered by a medical student she lived with in halls.

Just like our mother, my sister was incredibly brave and caring. She tirelessly researched our mum's breast cancer, accompanied her to oncology appointments and persuaded her, facing vigorous resistance, to start juicing and eating vegetables. When I was too

OH SISTER, WHERE ART THOU?

squeamish to do it, Loren was the one who rinsed the blood from Graham's big toe with Burmese vodka after he'd almost sliced off the top of it after falling into a drainage ditch in Mandalay's unlit streets. And she risked her life to take groceries to Angie when South Africa was gripped by the frenzy of looting and arson that took place while Graham and I were on our last holiday together in Scotland. But it was the care she gave to my 85-year-old grandmother when she was dying of lung cancer that created the deepest impression on me. No intimate-care task was too embarrassing, no kindness too big. Loren was a whirlwind of positivity in the sick room, making Granny laugh and having crafty cigarettes with her behind the carer's back.

'You're the first person I'd want at my deathbed,' I told her when making up after one of our many rows.

Perhaps I should have seen it coming, but I didn't. After Graham had died and I'd moved to Cape Town to care for our dad, I was so caught up in my caring role that I somehow hadn't realised how ill Loren had become. Before Dad relocated to the care home, she'd spent ten days frantically researching all his options and had told me that she'd been so busy that she barely left her house in the Algarve or got any sleep. With hindsight, I could have recognised this as a sign of mania, but because I was so worn out myself, I didn't give it much thought. Every day at the care home I braced myself for a two-hour conversation in which she'd question every decision I took on behalf of our father, and then remind me that while I had had a carefree life in England, and went on marathon-running jaunts around the world, she felt she'd sacrificed her own happiness to care for our parents.

STILL RUNNING AFTER ALL THESE TEARS

After one such exhausting conversation, I told her that if she had anything to say to me, she could do it via email or WhatsApp message, and for a week or so that was our only communication.

The last time I actually spoke to Loren, our father made me speak to her. Not wanting to upset him by telling him about our recent spat, I reluctantly took the handset.

'Did we get bitten by a puppy at a wedding when we were children?' she asked, her voice a flat monotone. I'd only ever heard Loren speak like that once before, and at the time had been so alarmed that I'd contacted her husband afterwards to mention my concerns and ask whether she was taking her bipolar medication.

'Yes, that's the reason we both became terrified of dogs,' I replied.

'But it definitely happened at a wedding?'

'Yes, but I can't remember whether it was you or me who got bitten.'

'Oh,' she said. 'Thanks. I better go. Bye.'

The next day, I received a call from her husband in Portugal.

'Loren's gone missing,' he told me. 'I left her sitting on a bench on a cliff overlooking the sea near our apartment, and when I went out to call her inside some time later, she was gone.' He went on to say that police helicopters and the coastguard were searching for her as it was possible that she'd fallen off the cliff. 'If that's the case, her body will sink and only float to the surface in four or five days' time,' he said.

Denial and magical thinking were the only things that got me through that week. I imagined that Loren was curled up in a ball under a bush and would come home once she was hungry enough. Or had hitchhiked somewhere, as she'd done in Europe in her 20s. Or had hijacked a car. She was incredibly resourceful, and I knew she would have found a way to charm people into giving her lifts or food. Most of the time, I managed to force all thoughts that she had died from my mind, though I shed many tears when Dad wasn't looking. I hadn't told him Loren was missing as I didn't want to worry him unnecessarily.

Four days after her disappearance, I got the call I'd feared.

'They've found Loren's body in the ocean,' said her husband.

Shocked, I couldn't really comprehend what he was saying. Lolly? My naughty little sister? Gone? Dead? No! In that split second I lost my childhood friend and my future deathbed defender. We would never run another marathon together or delight in staying in a grimy youth hostel just so that we could gleefully 'spend more money on wine and museums'. We would never drink tea together as little old ladies, as I'd always imagined we would. Like Clover Stroud and Nell, we had huge blow-ups and sometimes put the phone down on each other, but we also loved each other fiercely as only two people who've known each other since babyhood can. Once again, I felt strangely numb.

It was mostly left up to me to inform family and friends.

'Whatever you do, don't tell your dad,' sobbed my cousin Darian, who'd been very close to my sister. 'My friend Maddy works in a care home and that's the first thing she said to me. People with dementia can't handle news like that because they forget it. Each time someone reminds them, they experience overwhelming shock and grief all over again.'

'I'm so glad you said that as I was already considering not telling Dad,' I wept.

Keeping Loren's death from our father, which I'd dreaded as I'm not a good liar, wasn't the challenge I imagined it would be. Despite the fact that his younger daughter had called him for a chat at the same time every day without fail, Dad only once asked after her.

STILL RUNNING AFTER ALL THESE TEARS

'Where's Loren?' he said, a fortnight after her death.

'She's in Portugal, Dad,' I fibbed, dreading what would come next.

'Oh yeah, of course,' he said. 'I remember you telling me that before.'

After Virginia Woolf filled her pockets with stones and drowned herself in the River Ouse in 1941, her body was found three weeks later, washed up near Southease in East Sussex. Tortured by depression, 59-year-old Virginia's suicide note explained that she couldn't face going through 'another of those terrible times'. Like Leonard, Virginia's husband of almost 30 years, I was plagued by thoughts of whether I could somehow have stopped what happened to Loren, but reminded myself that I was over 5,000 miles away at the time. I had no means of keeping her away from the edge of the cliff or ensuring she took her bipolar medication. I consoled myself, too, that I'd not fought back when she criticised me and had never said anything I'd live to regret. I also knew that I'd fully intended to learn more about bipolar disorder to better understand what my sister was going through and find the best way to help her, but in those overwhelming months, with so much of my energy focused on caring for Graham and our dad, I just wasn't able to find the time to read the books I'd bought. It's heartbreaking that I will never know the truth about how, and why, my little sister died.

The walking stick Virginia Woolf used to get to the river where she drowned is now in the New York Public Library, the very place that my mother, sister and I visited to see the stuffed toys that had inspired AA Milne's *Winnie-the-Pooh* when we ran the

OH SISTER, WHERE ART THOU?

New York City Marathon together. Like Virginia, Loren was a flame who burned too brightly – and whose life was extinguished far too soon.

The bench at the top of the 'borrom' of the hill

Wine farm outing

Enjoying ice cream at Fish Hoek Beach...

... and with my sister Loren's best friend Angie

Spectacular view over Noordhoek Beach

My last ever beer with my beloved dad

Chapter 23
Our father, who art in heaven

🎵 **Mood music: *Lara's Theme* by Maurice Jarre**
The track from *Dr Zhivago* that always made my dad cry

I'm so glad my dad died. No, not *that* he died, but that he died *when* and *in the way* he did. Before the runaway train of bone-cancer pain, which I knew was bearing down on him, hit him, as I knew it would. Because I'd been here before, just 15 months earlier, when that type of pain left Graham begging the hospice staff to put him out of his misery.

My dad's terminal diagnosis came about after he complained of feeling unwell almost three weeks after my sister died.

'I feel lousy,' he said. 'I don't know why. If I did, I'd do something about it. My back hurts. I think I'm suffering from old age.' When Dr Odell, his GP, came to see him, she examined him and asked me to take him for a blood test and scan of his pelvis and legs.

'I'm afraid the news isn't good,' Dr Odell said in a call to me a week later. 'Your father definitely has prostate cancer, and it's spread to his spine and pelvis. I'm sorry to have to tell you that he has weeks or months to live.'

'Oh no,' I thought. 'I'm not ready to face yet another death.'

'I'm going to prescribe regular analgesia,' she continued. 'I promised that your dad wouldn't be in any pain, and I'll make sure of that.'

The doctor rang off and I sat in stunned silence. In a single

STILL RUNNING AFTER ALL THESE TEARS

sentence the course of my life had abruptly changed direction once again. I'd vowed to my sister that I'd be with my dad until the very end, but the end was now a lot closer than I'd thought. I suddenly realised I wouldn't be living in South Africa for five years or more, as I'd envisaged; I'd be going home to Worthing before very long. So mixed in with the shock and deep sadness was a feeling of relief, a feeling I felt incredibly guilty about. At this point I took the difficult decision not to tell my dad about his prognosis, just as I'd shielded him from the news of Loren's death. What was the point of putting him on Death Row if I could make him believe life was business as usual? I didn't want him to spend the time he had left living in fear. Or grieving his daughter.

The dying were her 'most lovable patients' and often became 'a bigger and more generous version of themselves', the palliative-care doctor Kathryn Mannix observed in her wonderful book *With the End in Mind*. She went on to say that they were 'grateful for the tiniest kindness' and had 'reached a phase in their lives when they unconsciously radiate love'. All of this was undoubtedly true of my dad. I never once saw the temper flare-ups that had led to my mother nicknaming him Rumpel (after Rumpelstiltskin, the gnomish fairy-tale character known for his tantrums), and genuinely believe that the final months of his life were some of his happiest. For me, too, the time I spent with him was incredibly healing and precious as I finally received the unconditional approval and love I'd craved from him all my life. When Graham and I had visited him in Pretoria after my mother died, he'd always seemed to be too busy to spend much time with

OUR FATHER, WHO ART IN HEAVEN

us, saying he had to head out to the gym, go for a run, or study for his law degree.

Now, Dad's eyes lit up when he saw me, and he couldn't get enough of my company. Everyone in the care home knew my name, because he was always asking where I was, even though I came to see him straight after breakfast every day and only left after he'd had his dinner.

'Your dad adores you: you can see the way he looks at you – and reaches for you,' said my new friend Tish, a fellow widow, one afternoon when I dropped by her room in the care home for a chat and glass of wine. Dad had been my running inspiration ever since I was a child. Now, one afternoon, hanging on to his carer and me for dear life, he struggled down a really long boardwalk and across the powdery sands at Noordhoek Beach so he could sit on a rock and shout 'Keep going, Leecy' while I ran in big circles round him. I could see the pride in his eyes, and was moved to tears at this show of support.

'There are gems, there are tiny powerful moments, if we just make ourselves available to witness and mark them. They are there, every day, all around us,' wrote Greg Wise in *Not That Kind of Love*. Day by day, keenly aware that each moment was incredibly precious, Dad and I made new memories. Whenever we went on our daily walk to a viewpoint within the care-home grounds, my arm hooked through his in case he took a tumble, I took great care to point out the spiky-leaved cycads. Dad was obsessed with these plants, which looked like pineapple tops, and called them 'living fossils' as they'd been around since the time of the dinosaurs. One of his deepest joys had been tending his extensive collection, protecting them against the leopard moths whose voracious caterpillars could destroy an entire plant if not spotted in time.

'Look, Dad, there's a really unusual cycad,' I'd say, pointing to a squat, blue-green specimen with peculiarly barbed leaves.

'Yes, my lovey, that's an *Encephalartos horridus*,' he'd say, demonstrating his encyclopaedic knowledge that dementia hadn't yet stolen.

'Oh, I love that name. It's so bristly, it really does look horrid!'

We'd walk a little further before stopping in front of a protea bush.

'What do we do when we reach this pincushion protea, Dad?'

'We touch it,' he'd say, gently stroking his fingers over the waxy orange bristles that resembled those on a plastic hairbrush.

'And what do we do when we get to the lavender bush?' I'd ask, crushing a head of fragrant purple flowers between my fingers and bringing them up to his nose.

'Smell it – oh yes, that's lovely, my lovey.'

Eventually we'd reach the lookout and sit down on a bench with views of the craggy Fish Hoek Valley, a deep V-shaped gorge cutting through spectacular mountains that perfectly framed the blue Atlantic. After catching our breath, we'd slowly make our way down the hill.

'I'm tired, Leecy.'

'Let's just walk down to the borrom of this hill and then we can go back,' I encouraged him.

'Borrom? What's borrom?' he teased me, pointing out my sloppy diction.

'Oh Dad, you do make me laugh!' From that day on, 'borrom' became our private joke, and we never once walked to the 'borrom' of that hill without giggling about it.

OUR FATHER, WHO ART IN HEAVEN

Another private joke was to scream 'Whoop! Whoop!' every time we drove over a speed bump on one of our outings. And saying to each other, 'Shall we buy that house?' every time we saw a mansion that took our fancy high up on the slopes above Glencairn and Fish Hoek. Not a day went by that Dad didn't make me smile.

Seeing the world through my father's eyes, and knowing that these were the final few months of his life, made me appreciate everything a lot more.

'Just look at those rocks, Leecy,' Dad would say, pointing to the giant boulders that littered the landscape on the road slicing through Silvermine Nature Reserve. 'How on earth did they get there? What size truck could have carried them all the way up there?'

'I think they've always been there, Dad. I'm sure no one brought them here,' I replied.

'They're amazing,' Dad said, no doubt dimly recalling the forays we'd made together to the Voortrekker Monument in Pretoria when I was a child. Pulling his car over into the veld, in the days before it was illegal, Dad had dug big rocks out of the ground with a spade and his bare hands and had loaded them into his car boot so that he could build a rockery around our swimming pool.

Determined to wring the last drop of joy out of every day and create new memories, we tracked down Dad's cousin Barry Jackson who, I was astonished to find out, had sculpted no fewer than three busts and sculptures of Nelson Mandela on public display in Cape Town, including one outside Parliament and the life-sized one on the balcony of the City Hall commemorating the great man's first public speech after being released from prison. When we met up with him for breakfast at a wine farm, Dad had already eaten, but when Barry's bacon and eggs arrived, he gave in

STILL RUNNING AFTER ALL THESE TEARS

to Dad's beseeching looks and generously shared half of his food with him. That day I gained a new, and now much loved, second cousin.

Other adventures Dad and I went on included a visit to Fish Hoek Beach, where we saw bathers hastily exit the water during an all-sirens-blazing shark alert, and several outings to various sites along the coast to watch windsurfing, yet another of my dad's passions in his younger days, through the wound-down window of our car. We also frequently went out for ice cream, something Dad had never enjoyed before. It was just so satisfying seeing him finally discover the treat I used to fuel a sightseeing trip around Italy.

'I remember a book you and Mommy owned called *Frommer's Europe on $20 a Day*,' I told him, wiping melted ice cream off his chin. 'When Graham and I went to Rome, I loved the gelati so much that I was doing Italy on twenty *ice-creams* a day!'

The Sunday before my dad died, we visited an outdoor pub in Noordhoek called The Toad in the Village.

'Come and have a beer with your daughter,' I told him.

As we sat in companionable silence, occasionally remarking on how good the ice-cold lager was and how glorious the slopes of Chapman's Peak looked as they blushed pink in the rays of the setting sun, we'd never been closer. That would be the last beer – and the final long conversation – I ever had with my beloved dad.

The next day I received a call from the head nurse informing me that Dad had tested positive for Covid. He'd had a cough for the past week, and the disease had been sweeping through the care home for quite some time.

OUR FATHER, WHO ART IN HEAVEN

'It's best that you don't visit him,' she said. 'I think we may have to transfer him to hospital.'

'I'll let you do what you think is best,' I said. 'It's probably wise that I don't come in as I suspect I've caught Covid myself.'

I called Dr Odell to update her, by this time feeling really rough, my body wracked with coughs at regular intervals.

'There's no reason for your dad to go to hospital,' she told me firmly but kindly, 'as we're not going to intubate him if he can't breathe on his own as that would only prolong his suffering and you told me you didn't think he'd want that. And you *have* to be allowed to see him. Just go straight to his room and don't go around hugging all your other care-home friends on the way. Leave it with me: I'll arrange everything with the care home.'

In my state of shock I'd forgotten what we'd discussed previously. I knew my dad would not want to be kept alive artificially as he'd already lost the two things in life he valued most: his ability to run, and his ability to be fully in control of his brilliant mind. And if he lived any longer, I knew the pain from his bone cancer was going to make his life unbearable.

The next day I slept in until late as I felt so ill, and when I arrived at the care home, Dad was dozing with a nasal cannula delivering oxygen draped across his face.

'Leecy, my darling,' he said weakly, briefly opening his eyes. I knew he needed to rest, so didn't stay too long.

When I arrived back on the Wednesday, at about 1.30pm, he was asleep. I was disappointed that I'd missed seeing him eat lunch as I was already missing his company. His carer told me that earlier that day he'd said he wanted to go home. That saddened me deeply but, looking back, I find it comforting to think that perhaps 'going home' had a more spiritual meaning: that he'd meant he was ready to die. I returned to my own sickbed and the following afternoon went back to see him.

'Your dad's blood pressure is very low,' a nurse informed me. 'We're all praying he pulls through.'

I called my cousin Darian back in England, who'd been incredibly supportive of us both.

'It's not looking good,' I told her. 'Dad's blood pressure has fallen dangerously low, so I don't think he'll make it through the night.'

'Oh Leecy, I'm so sorry to hear that,' she said.

Just then, I noticed a change in my dad.

'Hang on a minute, Darry,' I said, 'I think Dad's just stopped breathing.' I rushed over to my dad and gripped his hand, willing him to breathe. His cornflower-blue eyes had opened slightly, and he was staring straight through me. The man I'd looked up to my entire life, and who'd given me two of the greatest gifts it's possible to receive – life and a love of running – was gone.

A whale's tail photographed from my bench

View of the wild Atlantic Ocean from the Hermanus cliff path

The bench in Hermanus where I scattered Graham and Dad's ashes

Loren and I wore matching fascinators at my 40th birthday celebrations

The unforgettable 'golden day' with my family on the beach at De Kelders

Chapter 24
Ashes to ashes

♪♪ Mood music: *Ashes to Ashes* by David Bowie
The cosmic elegy by Graham's favourite singer

'Dad is home now, with Mommy, Loren and Graham. He was dearly loved in this world and will also be in the next. Go well, Dad, our thoughts and love are with you.' Thus ended the message I sent to family and friends on the day of my father's aquamation. When I'd been researching undertakers, I'd discovered this type of water cremation, which uses a heated alkaline solution to break down the body. My father's will stated that he wished to be cremated, but when I discovered that aquamation saves 90 per cent of the energy used in traditional cremations, I knew he'd have opted for it as Dad was a passionate advocate for the environment.

Once I'd collected his ashes, I was left with the dilemma of where to scatter them. As Graham's dying wish had been for me to scatter his ashes in Hermanus, a cliffside town two hours' drive from Cape Town that we'd visited many times since our student days, I believed it would be a fitting place for some of Dad's, too, as my parents had also often holidayed with us there. Hermanus offers the best land-based whale watching in the world, and the awe-inspiring sight of a gargantuan, barnacle-encrusted southern right whale teaching her baby to breach was something Graham and I had often reminisced about.

The only problem was, I first had to get Graham's ashes to South Africa, which proved a lot harder than expected. Asking a funeral company to transport them would have cost twice the price of a return airfare, something Graham, who was always careful with money, would *not* have approved of. I considered using Royal Mail, which allowed only 10g of ashes to be posted, rightly stating that they're irreplaceable and hence no matter what financial compensation they offered, it could never make up for their loss. However, I also suspected I'd never even receive the 10g as the final leg of the journey would have involved the South African postal service, which is practically defunct, due to mail being stolen so often. What's more, a bit of research told me that overseas Christmas cards normally reached their destinations in March and that postal delays of more than six months were not uncommon in South Africa.

My only other option was to ask my friend Mary to courier them to me, even though courier companies expressly forbade sending cremated human remains. I felt extremely guilty doing so, but reasoned that if Royal Mail didn't have an issue with it, there was no valid reason why courier companies should either. My ingenious plan was to disguise Graham's ashes as a craft project by asking Mary to package them with several bottles of glitter along with a birthday card to an imaginary child expressing the wish that she enjoy making a collage with the enclosed 'sand'. During a video call, Mary let herself into my flat in Worthing, where she proceeded to spoon some of Graham's ashes into the two small Tupperware containers she'd bought for the purpose, one for the courier, the second as a back-up should the 'gift' parcel fail to get through. I was really touched by the respectful way she did this, and knew Graham would have appreciated it, too.

So far, so good. The drama started later, when the courier company said the postcode of the privately run postal depot I'd nominated was incorrect. I assured them it wasn't, but suggested

ASHES TO ASHES

sending the parcel to a different branch, this time in Rondebosch, but they refused to sign for it. After recommending yet another branch, and several 'misrouted by courier' messages, the parcel was sent to Fish Hoek, but the store denied having received it.

I was just about to give up hope and try my Plan B, 'Royal Fail' option when my friend Sarah sent me a voice note: 'You can't abandon poor Graham in a random South African courier depot!' she spluttered. She was right, I couldn't, so I drove to Fish Hoek, persuaded the staff to conduct a further search, and lo and behold, they found the parcel!

After sprinkling pinches of Graham's ashes in many of the places dear to our hearts in Cape Town, including the garden of the little flat we'd lived in when we were newlyweds, and the site of our encounter with a poltergeist at our university, I set off on the two-hour trip along the coast to the picturesque town of Hermanus. Here I checked into the clifftop Windsor Hotel, where Graham and I had often escaped for romantic afternoon teas in our dating days. Sarah and Anthony had promised to join me via video call as I scattered the ashes, but the signal cut out almost as soon as I left the hotel, forcing me to go ahead without them. When I reached the half-broken wooden bench where I've always said I want my own ashes scattered someday, I took a few moments to appreciate the soul-stirring waves that had originated as far away as Antarctica and now hurled themselves with great force against the jagged rocks below. Nowhere else I've ever travelled to had touched me quite as much as this ruggedly beautiful place I'd been coming to since I was a teenager. After lighting a handful of tealights and gently scattering the precious ashes in front of the bench, I felt the salt spray mingling with my tears as I told Graham and Dad how much I loved them and that I'd always cherish the many special times we'd shared together. It felt surreal to be scattering their ashes here when I'd always imagined it being my own final resting place. I concluded my ceremony with a few words to my sister Loren, who'd posed with me on this very bench in our matching black fascinators during my 40th birthday celebrations. Oh, how my heart ached for them all. The Canadian writer Margaret Atwood beautifully describes the ritual of scattering ashes as 'a final act of love, a way of letting go and holding on at the same time', and it certainly felt this way to me. I was letting go of another small part of both my husband and my father in this wild and wonderful spot, but holding on to their memory too by creating a new one here, on this cliff, in one of the world's most awe-inspiring settings.

As I strolled tearfully back to my hotel, relieved that I'd managed to fulfil Graham's final wish, I noticed the headquarters of a shark-cage diving company based in Gansbaai, a small fishing town near Hermanus renowned for its great whites. Graham and I had considered doing this heart-pounding activity 13 years before but had chickened out, so I thought I might as well give it a go. It was a decision I would live to regret, but not for the reasons I feared.

Squeezed into a too-tight wetsuit, I was the last of ten people to clamber down the slippery ladder into the stainless-steel shark cage secured to the side of our boat. Chunks of what looked like raw salmon – which the crew had tossed into the sea to entice the sharks to come closer – floated past as our group waited for the maneaters to emerge from the murky depths. Neck-deep in the swell of the Atlantic Ocean, I wrinkled my nose as the smelly fish oil floating on the surface of the water coated the exposed skin on my face. I know you're probably thinking I'm one of the bravest people you've ever heard of, and initially I would have agreed with this assumption, but you'd be wrong. Truth to tell, the experience was about as terrifying as being in a public toilet and finding that it won't flush. Mildly adrenaline stimulating, but not exactly terrifying. Because, for starters, there were no great whites. They'd all been chased off or killed by Port and Starboard, a couple of killer whales so named because their dorsal fins collapsed to the left and right. The bloodthirsty pair had apparently slaughtered record numbers of great whites by ripping out their livers. I believe the orcas ate them with some fava beans and a nice Chianti.

The sharks that were thrashing about a few feet from me were copper sharks, who ranked a measly tenth in worldwide unprovoked human attack stats. Much smaller than great whites, they were also safely behind the cage's solid metal bars, so the only way one of them could take a chunk out of me was if I tried to pet it. We weren't issued with snorkels, so I had to repeatedly push myself underwater in an attempt to see the sharks up close. After dunking myself more times than a chocolate digestive, I finally came eyeball to eyeball with a shark about a foot from my face. The effort of keeping myself down was too much, however, so after only two seconds, I shot to the surface like a rubber duck. Another item ticked off my Bucket List, except I hadn't actually swum with great whites, I'd bobbed about with coppers. I could just imagine Graham having a chortle up on high: there was no way *he'd* have spent mega-bucks on such an expensive day trip without doing plenty of research beforehand. Another life lesson reminding me that perhaps sometimes I needed to 'be more Graham'.

STILL RUNNING AFTER ALL THESE TEARS

Keen to compensate for this underwhelming experience, I resolved to visit De Kelders, a tiny cove backed by a cave, on my drive back to Hermanus, in order to scatter some more ashes there. I'd once spent a gloriously sunny day there with my family during which Graham, Loren and I had fashioned bikini tops out of abalone shells and mermaid wigs out of long strands of shiny green kelp while my parents chatted in the shade of an overhanging cliff, drinking beverages stored in the 'beer fridge' my dad had dug in the wet sand. That day had been one of my 'golden days', one during which time stood still, a memory laced with magic that I'd warmed my heart with many times in the intervening years. Graham and I had made several attempts to revisit that beach over the years but had never managed to find it again. It was as if the place was so idyllic that it only existed in our imagination. This time, however, I had the invaluable assistance of Google Maps.

'Isn't the view beautiful? I've never been here before,' said the slightly built, 30-something man not dissimilar to a young Billy Bob Thornton whom I encountered at the top of the cliff overhanging the beach.

'Yes, it's truly amazing,' I replied.

'Shall I hold your bag while you climb down?'

I eyed the 12ft vertical rock face and reckoned I could use the help.

Safely on the beach, the man and I went to sit on a pile of rocks.

'What are you doing here?' the stranger asked.

'I've come to scatter some of my husband's and my father's ashes, and to honour my mother's and sister's memory, too. We once came here on a day trip as a family,' I told him. 'I'm Lisa, by the way.'

'I'm Fanie Feldman. Nice to meet you. I've also lost a lot of people. First my twin brother, and then my fiancée and baby died in a car crash. My two grandparents also died in the last two years.'

My heart went out to this tragic young man – boy, life could be brutal.

Fanie continued chatting to me: 'I was formerly an international rugby player but now I'm a financial adviser. I used to be a drug user but I'm clean now, have been for ages.'

'Good for you,' I said.

'You see that house up there?' he continued. 'I bought it by selling two bitcoins. I'm also a really good gambler, in fact I'm so good that I've been banned from all the local casinos.'

I should have been on my guard while listening to Fanie as there were a number of discrepancies in his story. Come to think of it, there were more red flags than the climax of *Les Misérables*, but I simply wasn't thinking straight. Grief had switched off my usually reliable radar and I was flying blind. Ordinarily I would have realised that he couldn't possibly have owned a house on the cliff while claiming to never have been to that beach before. And the rugby-playing, bitcoin-dealing, suave gambling persona? Wasn't that a bit too James Bond for a man with filthy fingernails, a septic earlobe, a Mickey Mouse tattoo and a former meth habit?

After chatting for an hour or so, I eventually decided it was time to leave as I wanted to get back to Hermanus before nightfall, so I asked for privacy so that I could scatter the ashes. Fanie walked over to the cave that opened up onto the beach and lit a cigarette while I spent a few moments telling Graham and my family how much I'd loved the time I'd spent with them on that beach. It hit home, then, that I was the sole 'survivor' of that precious day. My parents, sister and husband were all dead. It struck me, too, that I was now an *orphan*. I was no longer protected by the comforting shield of an older generation: I *was* the older generation, and everything, from now on in, was down to me. I could no longer turn to my parents for advice or support. Nor could I rely on Graham. I felt cut adrift, like a tiny rowing boat in the middle of the vast Pacific.

After taking some photos of the ashes I'd scattered on the sand, I stood up before my emotions overwhelmed me.

'Ready to go? I'll carry your bag while you climb up,' Fanie said helpfully. At the top of the cliff, he handed back my bag. 'I thought of committing suicide here once,' he told me.

'You've been through a lot,' I replied. 'But things will get better. Just take one day at a time.'

And then I did something I'd never done to a stranger before: I asked Fanie whether I could give him a hug.

We embraced, and as he pulled away, he said something that made my blood run cold.

'Next time... I'll kiss you!'

I hastily got into my car and drove off, my heart thumping.

Back at my Hermanus hotel, I realised my phone was missing.

'No! No! No!' I cried out loud. 'He can't have!'

He had. Fanie Feldman had stolen not only my phone, but the driver's licence and bank cards tucked into its cover.

A frantic call to the Hermanus police informed me that I needed to go back to Gansbaai to lay a charge, which I did the following day. It was bucketing down on the way there, and the blade of my windscreen wiper suddenly broke off. As I squinted at the road, terrified at the sudden loss of visibility, a huge baboon the size

ASHES TO ASHES

of a small teenager bounded out into the road. I hit the brakes, narrowly missing it.

'Can this get any worse?' I thought. 'If I didn't die from the impact, I would have arrived at the police station with a dead baboon bleeding all over my bonnet.'

'What charge do you want to lay?' said the gruff, bearded Afrikaner tasked with taking my statement. He was the kind of policeman I'd feared as a student when I'd attended anti-apartheid demonstrations. A kind of 'take no prisoners' guy, except that his job was to take prisoners. He remained impassive as I tearfully narrated my story.

'I can give you a full description. I can even tell you his birthday. And his star sign.'

The policeman looked unimpressed.

'I can't explain why I did it – I feel like such a fool – but I even hugged him when I said goodbye,' I blurted out. The policeman shook his head at my stupidity.

'He told me his name was Fanie Feldman, but it's probably not his real name.'

'I *know* Fanie Feldman!' the policeman exclaimed, abruptly looking up from his note-taking.

'You *know* him?'

'Yes, he's a drug addict.'

'No, he's a *former* drug addict.'

'No he's not, he's still using. He came out of jail a month ago. I'm going to get your phone back. I'll tell him he's going straight back to jail if he doesn't hand it over. Wait on that bench over there and I'll go and fetch it.'

Four hours of bum-numbing bench-sitting later, the policeman walked in with my phone.

'You found it!' I cried. 'Thank you, thank you!'

STILL RUNNING AFTER ALL THESE TEARS

But my joy was short lived as my driver's licence and bank cards were missing. I was devastated.

'I've got to get back to Cape Town now,' I said, 'but I have to ask whether I was in danger of being raped? With the cave behind me and the sea in front of me, there was nowhere to run.'

'No, he wouldn't have assaulted you. He's not a bad man, he's just a thief, and drugs got the better of him. And besides, he's gay,' the policeman said.

While driving back to Hermanus, the radio reported that there was still no sign of a 22-year-old German tourist who'd gone missing while hiking in the mountains above the Cape Town suburb of Hout Bay. His personal effects had been recovered and five suspects apprehended, but his body hadn't been found. I shuddered that I could so easily have met with a similar fate. I pride myself on being able to read people. How on earth had my intuition failed me so completely? And then I realised it hadn't. While my phone had been in danger that day, I had not. Fanie had no sexual interest in me whatsoever, and no intention of hurting me, and I'd picked up on that. He wasn't a bad man, only a sad and probably desperate one. And I felt sorry for him.

My Comrades Marathon mentor Nikki Campbell in 2010...

... and in 2023

Frank Lloyd Wright's iconic Fallingwater...

... inspired our 'ancestral home'

Dad built our pool's rockery himself as a home for his beloved cycads

My dad fell in love with The House's granite, glass and wood

Yong yi, Angie and I dress up while packing up Pine Street

Chapter 25
Farewell to all that

♪♪ **Mood music:** *This Is the Time* **by Billy Joel**
The song that makes me yearn for times gone by

'I know this sounds super-dodgy, Nikki,' I wrote, 'but I've been mugged. If I deposit some money in your bank account, would you be able to draw it out for me in cash?' Once again, I had something to thank running for. When my bank told me that the only way for me to access any money was to have it transferred to a South African bank account, I remembered that my Comrades Marathon mentor Nikki Campbell lived in Cape Town and, in that remarkable way that runners form instant bonds that remain intact no matter how much they're stretched by time and distance, she agreed to what could so easily have been a scam.

We decided to combine the cash handover with a run on Noordhoek Beach – the spectacular four-mile stretch of powdery white sand backed by Chapman's Peak where my dad had once watched me train – and met up in a nearby car park. Nikki, a tanned, brunette woman in her early 60s, hadn't changed at all in the 12 years since I'd last seen her. She was shorter than I remembered, though, 'but that's probably because she's just stepped off that pedestal you put her on,' I smiled to myself, recalling how much I'd looked up to her and been grateful for her wise training advice.

We jogged down the tree-shaded road to the beach, past Noordhoek Common, where a group of horse riders were practising showjumping, the air heavy with the smell of manure.

STILL RUNNING AFTER ALL THESE TEARS

'Can we walk for a bit?' Nikki puffed after ten minutes, much to my surprise, and it must be said, relief. This was the first time in my entire running career that someone – other than myself – had needed to walk so soon when running with me.

'When Covid prevented me from doing my twenty-third Comrades, I completely lost my running mojo,' Nikki said, 'and now I just can't seem to get it back. Just call me Nikki Not On!'

I couldn't believe what I was hearing. This was the woman whose passion for Comrades had led her to set up a website where she offered free training plans, advice and virtual bear hugs to thousands of Comrades wannabes like me. I'd never have achieved one of my greatest running dreams without her as my megaphone-wielding, high-kicking, star-jumping one-woman cheer squad. And she had fallen out of love with running, too? It was as unthinkable as Wimbledon suddenly announcing it was going to swap strawberries for watermelon, but nonetheless it was a massive salve for my guilty conscience.

'I know *exactly* how you feel,' I said. 'I've been trying everything I can think of to get back into running regularly, but every time I start, I lose motivation and stop again. Ever since I stopped doing marathons it's been an uphill struggle. I can't remember when I last did even a 5K!' Perhaps mojo loss was more common than I'd thought?

A happiness-inducing technique a runner in the 100 Marathon Club once shared with me came to my rescue during my final weeks in Cape Town. As I packed up my belongings and got ready to leave, I felt lonely and grief-stricken, and became worried that I was at risk of depression. The runner had told

FAREWELL TO ALL THAT

me that she managed her mental health by forcing herself to photograph one thing a day that made her laugh. God knows there wasn't much to laugh about in Cape Town – there was a Dad-shaped hole in my life and the city was blighted by frequent load-shedding, reports of gang wars on the Cape Flats and rampant unemployment – but I did my best, eagerly scouting for ways to lighten my mood. It was like tuning into an unfamiliar channel on the radio: once you'd twiddled your way past the static, the signal came through loud and clear. On day one, a minibus taxi pulled up in front of me at Longbeach Mall, its tattoo-like decals spelling out its name – Cool Runnings – and the legendary catchphrase: 'Any cooler and I'd still be frozen'. The next day, a beaming beggar at some traffic lights held up a hand-lettered cardboard sign: 'My husband had an affair,' it read. 'I need R20 to send his mistress a thank you card.' The woman got R50 from me, plus a grateful smile. Then there were the roadside hoardings advertising The Courier Guy, a local delivery company. 'We would love to handle your package,' they saucily proclaimed. Even the swanky loos in the marble-floored, hideously overpriced mall at the V&A Waterfront were good for a giggle. 'Don't drink the toilet water,' warned the signs above the cisterns. I wondered what foreign tourists made of that.

My all-time funny moment, however, was seeing a store on Fish Hoek's down-at-heel Main Road called the Emergency Happiness Shop. I was intrigued when I spotted it, and imagined myself, in need of a little pick-me-up, walking in and asking for a cup of cheer or a barrel of laughs. But then I realised that what it purveyed was far more mundane: digital cameras, laptops, iPhones and some such. As a technophobe, electronic items provoke clenched-fist frustration rather than joy, but I guess they must be the epitome of bliss for those who worship at the Temple of High Tech.

STILL RUNNING AFTER ALL THESE TEARS

Packing up and selling what I fondly called our 'ancestral home' was my final task in South Africa. We'd moved into our house in Pine Street when I was two years old, so it was the only family home I could remember. After bidding farewell to my dad's carers and friends in the care home, I undertook a ten-day, 1,500km road trip from Cape Town to Pretoria, my first without Graham, one that was punctuated by a hair-raising puncture in the middle of nowhere and frequent bouts of weeping as I struggled to get to grips with my losses. I visited places I'd always dreamed of going to – the tiny village of Matjiesfontein with its Victorian-era, much-haunted hotel; The Owl House in Nieu-Bethesda, where a lonely spinster had filled her house and garden with fantastical statues made from concrete and glittering ground glass – but without Graham there to share them with, everything felt flat. Like food without salt. Or tea without milk.

As I neared Pretoria, I mentally psyched myself up for what was to come. I knew that emptying out our house was going to be like washing and dressing the body of a loved one for burial. My sister had already tried to do it – and couldn't.

'You don't know what it's like,' Loren had told me tearfully. 'You walk into a room determined to do a clear-out and then you find Mommy's bible, or a string of pearls or cameo brooch that belonged to Oumie, and you cry so much that you can't do anything.' I knew that everything I remembered would still be there, frozen in time: my grandmother Oumie's piano, on which I'd done my music practice aged eight, hunched under a tablecloth with my mother to shield us from the ferocious early morning sun; the kiaat wood bed I'd slept in since I was a toddler; the

FAREWELL TO ALL THAT

riempie chairs my maternal grandfather, Oupie, had so carefully restrung with strips of oxhide.

The place truly was like a Museum of Family Memories, and when I arrived and walked into the garage for the first time, I howled when I spotted two little yellow plastic watering cans, side by side, on my father's workbench. Why wasn't Loren here with me? We would have cried together, of course, but we would also have snort-laughed as we relived all our childhood antics and celebrated our departed loved ones with each heirloom we touched.

To fully understand 'The House', as we all referred to it, you need to be aware of its blue-blood history. The brainchild of Vivian Sydney Rees-Poole, an architect who worked with Sir Herbert Baker on the Union Buildings (Pretoria's equivalent of The White House), it was surprisingly modern for a house built in 1943. Flat-roofed and constructed from blocks of multi-coloured granite, it was inspired by Frank Lloyd Wright's iconic Fallingwater – the house that hovers over a waterfall – which graced the cover of *Time* magazine in 1938. My father fell in love with The House's clean lines, hardwood finishes and gleaming parquet floors aged 30 and, when he couldn't quite afford it, resorted to borrowing money from the owners to buy it. He spent the next 50 years renovating it, driving my mother crazy in the process, as he had the habit of eagerly starting a project, and then only finishing it *decades* later. In a fit of enthusiasm, he once stripped the kitchen of all its dated tiles when I was eight, and eventually replaced them with stylish Italian ones a decade-and-a-half later after I got married.

The House was far more than a building with four walls and a roof; it was a member of the family, as much cherished as it was a source of shame. Like an aristocratic grandfather who

STILL RUNNING AFTER ALL THESE TEARS

insists on going about embarrassing his offspring by wearing ripped corduroys and a scruffy shirt covered in spilled soup, it had a perfect pedigree but always seemed to be in a state of dishevelment.

'Your bathroom is the only room in your house that's nice,' a teenage Sunday school acquaintance once concluded, disdainfully surveying the damp-infested walls and half-finished redecoration projects undertaken at different times by my perfectionist dad, who refused to allow anyone other than himself to carry out any of the work. This from a girl who lived in a hideously ugly bungalow and whose main form of entertainment, at least when I went round, was picking blood-engorged ticks off her dogs.

Dad's most notorious renovation was our guest toilet. He removed the door, but never got round to rehanging it. The loo was hidden round a corner, so its lack of privacy didn't bother any of us in the least… until we had a family reunion. Then, Loren and I watched in intense amusement as several guests went to find the missing door and, having discovered it propped up against a wall in our passage, where it had stood for the past five years, backed into the loo clutching it.

'What is *wrong* with these people?' we giggled uncontrollably, oblivious to the fact that a doorless loo wasn't, well, normal. Many years later, I heard that other guests resorted to driving to a nearby petrol station to use its facilities, so horrified were they by our bathroom arrangements.

Knowing that getting rid of a lifetime's worth of memorabilia would feel like 10,000 mini bereavements, and unable to face doing it alone, I asked my sister's friend Angie if she'd help me.

FAREWELL TO ALL THAT

Further reinforcements arrived in the form of my sister-in-law Yong yi, who flew out from Taiwan where she lived with my brother and my niece. One of her tasks, as she had a mobile phone that took much better photos than mine, was to photograph all the items we were going to get rid of to lessen the emotional impact of their loss.

For two weeks, barely stopping to eat, we systematically went from room to room, carefully photographing items, wrapping them in newspaper and boxing them up. My parents' running medals, Loren's school reports, babyhood toys: every item ripped a Band-Aid off my heart. Thank goodness for my two helpers, who cheerfully submitted to my maniacal, grief-fuelled work ethic. I was determined to leave The House in pristine condition so, wet rags at the ready, we cleaned every single surface, light fixture and picture rail, our fingers wrinkled like prunes from being in contact with soapy water for so long. I cried softly as I wiped out several years' worth of dust from a kitchen cabinet: I remembered lying stretched out on one of its wood-shaving-covered shelves, aged three, as my dad hand-built it. Yong yi and I kept vowing to go out for a run, as I was keen to show her the 2km circuit I'd been nagged into doing on a daily basis by my father as a teenager (the one I sometimes pretended I'd done by hiding between two cars with a book for 15 minutes and then sprinting up our long driveway in order to look suitably sweaty when I arrived back), but we simply didn't have time.

We were working to a tight deadline because the Universe had sent us Neil and Carolyn, the wonderful couple who bought The House. When they came round for a viewing, they stayed for several hours, during which time I discovered that, like my dad, they were enamoured by The House's unique architecture and hardwood fittings and, like Graham and my mum, they had

STILL RUNNING AFTER ALL THESE TEARS

a keen interest in history. Like Graham and me, they'd also both lost their appetites when they first fell in love. By the time they left, with assurances that they'd send me renovation updates, I knew my departed parents would wholeheartedly approve of the new custodians of House Jackson, as they promised to call it, which made my task significantly easier emotionally.

While in Pretoria, in lieu of a funeral, I took Piet, one of my dad's colleagues, and Yvonne, Dad's cousin's wife, out to lunch. Piet spoke of how my dad had been an amazing mentor at the Atomic Energy Corporation, and Yvonne, a woman with a ready laugh and formidable energy, praised his kindness when Nigel, her husband of 58 years, died.

'Your dad was the most lovely, gentle man,' Yvonne told me over an organic salad in Jackson's, her family's buzzing eatery and wholefood store, where she still worked full time as a bookkeeper at the age of 78. 'When Nigel passed away, your dad often called me to check I was okay, and he was really supportive of both of my sons when they were grieving, too.' If she'd said this about my mother, it wouldn't in the least have surprised me, but to hear this about my dad, who'd always avoided emotional conversations when I was growing up, truly warmed my heart.

'God sent you to your dad, and you gave him all your love and the best of everything in the last days of his life,' were her kind words to me when she bade me farewell.

On the day before we went our separate ways, The Wet Rag Brigade gathered together one last time under a gigantic Cuban palm tree to scatter some of my parents' ashes in the rockery surrounding our swimming pool that my dad had built with his

FAREWELL TO ALL THAT

own hands, finally reuniting them in death at the beloved house they'd called home.

'We have honoured The House,' said Yong yi with some satisfaction at the conclusion of our little ceremony. Indeed we had.

My chameleon before it lost its head

The battered groyne at Climping Beach

Creating my pebble cairn was an act of remembrance

At the start of my celebratory run

Chapter 26
Living with living losses

🎵 **Mood music:** *Everybody Hurts* by R.E.M.
The song that captures the agony of letting go

It came as a huge shock that my greatest grief hadn't been for Graham. I'd expected to feel as though I was living in one of Hieronymus Bosch's horrendous paintings of Hell, in which torturing demons crucify, impale and hacksaw sinners in half - as if I'd had all four limbs ripped off and my heart and entrails wrenched out of me. Instead, I found myself at unexpected moments sobbing very quiet tears, gasping for air in tiny sips like a guinea pig with asthma. Yes, there were a few times when I let out long, bellowing howls like stags in rut, but generally my grief for Graham was snack sized. Manageable. Bearable.

No one was more surprised than I was. My worst fear in the entire world had come to pass and yet, as Nurse Ade had predicted, I was alive. Why didn't I have to be picked up off the floor and tranquilised like so many other bereaved people I'd read about? Why didn't I cry all day with a short break for lunch, like one widow I'd met? Why hadn't I experienced the 'paroxysms of despair and yearning and longing and of daily, nightly longing to die' that Queen Victoria described after the death of Albert, her husband of 21 years? Or the 'waves, paroxysms, sudden apprehensions that weaken the knees and blind the eyes and obliterate the dailiness of life' that the American writer Joan Didion wrote about in *The Year of Magical Thinking* after losing her husband John, whom she'd been married to for almost 40 years? And then it came to me: Graham and I had grieved his death *together*. In a final act of kindness, he'd cried with and supported me during the four years prior to his passing. If I could have cried him back to life, I would have, but I couldn't, so I did what I knew he wanted me to do – which was to try to get on with the business of living.

But while Graham's death didn't break me, what happened afterwards very nearly did. One day, seven months after he'd died, and a month before I flew to South Africa for the first of my two visits, I was so overcome with anguish that I started imagining hurling myself off my balcony: I didn't actually want to die, I just wanted an end to the pain. What prevented me from doing so was knowing Graham would be disgusted that I'd considered discarding the thing he most valued – life – carelessly, like a single-use plastic bottle. Thankfully, I had the good sense to contact my dad. I sobbed great big snotty sobs down the phone as my bewildered father listened to my outpouring.

'Dad, I can't take this pain any more,' I cried, taking a gulp of whisky though it was only 10am. 'This is just so, so hard.'

If you haven't heard your 50-something daughter cry since she was a child, how do you find the words to offer her comfort? And yet Dad did. I can't recall exactly what he said, but he phoned me every two hours that dark day, seeking reassurance that I'd be okay.

What drove me to this state of desperation? It was because a family member was rude to me. The woman who'd stood up to the world's most eminent medics was now someone who could be tipped over the edge, almost literally as I now lived on the sixth floor, by an insensitive comment. I found that terrifying. Graham's death, and the harrowing experiences that preceded it, had left me feeling flayed: as if I no longer had any skin or defence against the outside world. I didn't know it then, but what I was experiencing is common after a bereavement: brain imaging has shown that grief

LIVING WITH LIVING LOSSES

deactivates the parts of the brain that control emotional regulation and rational thought and sends the parts that switch on the fear response into overdrive. I'd only been on the receiving end of a thoughtless, unkind remark, but my brain had reacted as if my life was in terrible danger from a homicidal maniac.

However, my meltdown wasn't just an over-reaction to a single upsetting incident, it was also an outpouring of grief over the 'living losses' that Graham and I had experienced since he was diagnosed with cancer. The friends who'd unexpectedly shown us that spending time with Graham was most definitely not a priority, even as he lay dying. We'd both invested enormous amounts of time and energy into nurturing our relationships and yet, when we needed them most, some people had rushed to our side while others, quite frankly, had behaved as if cancer was contagious and had fled. When I asked a former colleague I'd known for almost two decades, for example, to cover two of my shifts at *The Official Ferrari Magazine* so that I could go away for a long weekend with Graham in case he didn't survive surgery, she refused, even though she was free on those days. Another friend, whom I'd invited over for a cup of tea after Graham was brought home from the hospice, declined, saying simply that she didn't feel like it. The most upsetting example, however, was a close friend of Graham's who promised to visit him the day before he died. When I went downstairs to let him in, his wife was standing at our front door with a bottle of gin in one hand and a tube of Pringles in the other.

'Where's your husband?' I said, craning my neck to see where he was.

'He's not coming in,' she said, quickly pressing the gifts into my hands before turning on her heels and rushing back to their car. It was left up to me to go back upstairs and explain to Graham that the visit he'd long anticipated wouldn't be happening after all.

STILL RUNNING AFTER ALL THESE TEARS

What I found strangely consoling, however, was that this is an all-too-common experience. At one of the Grief Works webinars I attended, hosted by the psychotherapist Julia Samuel, the question 'How do I let go of anger towards people who've let me down?' got twice as many votes as any other topic that attendees wanted to discuss. The British-Swazi actor Richard E Grant – the star of *Withnail and I*, our favourite film – who lost Joan, his beloved wife of almost 35 years to lung cancer the same month Graham died, reported that people he'd known for years had crossed the road rather than talk to him after her death.

'Whether they think you're going to fall apart and you're an emotional wreck, I don't know,' he said. 'But I will never speak to them again.'

A fellow runner confided in me that before she developed terminal cancer, she and her best friend had spoken every day but when she was diagnosed, her friend emailed her a list of Bach Flower Remedies… and then didn't contact her for six months.

Twenty months after Graham died, I continued to experience flashes of intense emotional distress. After much reflection, I came to the shocking realisation that I'd cried about 95 per cent of my tears over 'living losses' and over certain people in my life who were a continual source of pain due to their lack of kindness, and barely five per cent over Graham. If I was ever to find the peace I yearned for, I had to follow the advice of Tish, the elderly widow I'd befriended in my father's care home, who'd said: 'Don't give these people permission to keep hurting you.'

Peace, all I wanted was peace. Peace, what did peace mean to me? It meant freedom from asking myself 'What did Graham and I do

LIVING WITH LIVING LOSSES

wrong?' and 'Why am I being treated like this now that Graham's gone?' It meant forcibly peeling away the claws of anxiety that embedded their long talons in my heart. I knew, too, that if I didn't find my way back to peace, I was in grave danger of falling seriously ill. On the Holmes and Rahe Stress Scale, which rates 43 common life events according to how stressful they are, I'd scored 362: anything over 300 meant you had an 80 per cent chance of experiencing a major health breakdown in the next two years. After all I'd been through, I wasn't prepared to scoff down that particular crap crêpe. The time for building bridges, I realised sorrowfully, was over: it was now time to, very regretfully, burn some.

The Universe seemed to agree that this was the best course of action: 'Stop pressing rewind on the things that need to be deleted from your life,' read a quote that dropped into my inbox as part of a Heart Leap Substack post by Suzy Walker, who'd left her editorship of *Psychologies* magazine and moved from London to Northumberland to live a more simple, creative life.

A fortuitous book recommendation helped me navigate what I knew would be a painful process: Elizabeth Day's *Friendaholic*. In it, Elizabeth speaks with heart-wrenching honesty of ending a friendship after no longer feeling safe in it because she didn't know when next her friend might say 'something uncharitable', mirroring what I'd experienced when I'd had my meltdown. She also wrote about the sense of *shame* that accompanied this rift, in contrast to break-ups with romantic partners, which are seen as far more socially acceptable. Shame was a dominant emotion for me, too. Had Graham and I really been such bad judges of character? Such failures as friends? But then a paragraph in *Friendaholic* jumped out at me in which Elizabeth wrote that the end of a friendship doesn't mean that relationship wasn't valuable – or that you're not a good friend – only that it no longer

STILL RUNNING AFTER ALL THESE TEARS

has a place in your life. With that one paragraph, Elizabeth Day absolved us.

She also reassured me that in people over 50, research has shown that having more than four or five close relationships can actually be disadvantageous, and can negatively impact your mental health. By clinging on to relationships with people who didn't support, comfort, love, appreciate or value me, I realised, I wasn't being a true friend… to myself.

Even after I'd ended all the relationships that had been causing me pain, I kept experiencing moments when my body would be flooded with sickening, righteous rage. Alone in my flat, I'd find myself shouting at the people who'd let Graham and me down. After one such angry outburst, as I rose from the toilet, a ceramic chameleon ornament crashed to the floor of its own volition, decapitating itself. When I tried to stick the chameleon's head back on, it wouldn't attach, and I ended up with glued-together fingers, as if I was permanently giving a *Star Trek* Vulcan salute. I concluded this was yet another 'poltergeist moment'. And, come to think of it, it hadn't been the first in my new flat: I'd returned from my first solo camping trip only to find that one of our paintings – the portrait of a giant crow no less – had fallen off the wall, the only one of all those I'd hung up to do so. Yes, it was high time I researched the phenomenon that had haunted me since my university days.

Turns out poltergeists aren't the spirits or ghosts I thought they were, despite their name meaning 'noisy ghost' in German. According to The Paranormal Society, they're 'mass forms of energy that a living person is unknowingly controlling' that can

LIVING WITH LIVING LOSSES

cause mysterious noises, lights to turn on and off and chairs and other objects to move around by themselves. And interestingly, their activities often centre on someone who's under an extreme amount of stress.

'I am *not* prepared to flat-share with a poltergeist,' I declared firmly, resolving to release this negative energy – and its toxic hold on my life – as soon as I could. Anger is exhausting, and by holding onto it I was in danger of becoming a version of myself I didn't want to be. After a lot of thought, I decided the best course of action would be to go on a run and, instead of being angry about, or grieving for, the relationships Graham and I had lost, celebrate both them and the ones that had endured. For this run I chose Climping Beach, a half-hour drive from Worthing, because I'd gone for a swim in the freezing English Channel here in Graham's honour a few months after he died. The swim and subsequent bacon-sarnie picnic had been my friend Faye's idea. The day had been wild and windy, and the gas burner blew out several times, but Faye persevered, so determined was she that I should enjoy what we later called 'sand-wiches' because they contained almost as much sand as bacon.

When I got to the beach, I sat on one of the few remaining wooden groynes ravaged by countless winter storms, and looked out to sea. The raging ocean had done its darndest to destroy these structures but, like me, they'd survived. My intention, now, was to build a cairn, in much the same way that Jewish people place 'visitation stones' on graves as an act of remembrance. After collecting several handfuls of chalky-white pebbles, I took each one and carefully wrote each person's initials on it before placing it in a small pile. I hoped that I'd one day be able to think of these people only with love rather than sadness or disappointment. With each name I wrote, I could feel my pain starting to lessen and being replaced with forgiveness and gratitude for what that person had contributed to our lives.

Once my cairn was complete, I started running eastwards towards Littlehampton, my feet crunching through the shingle. In the same way that I'd once taken turns with my *Women's Running* colleagues to dedicate each mile of the 2011 Brighton Marathon to the special people who'd made a big difference to our lives, I now wanted to pay tribute to the friends and family who remained. The ones who'd posted me care parcels containing thoughtful little gifts such as fluffy socks and dark chocolate. The ones who'd sent me Instagram photos of Azuki the pygmy hedgehog camping and kayaking (@uni_desu) that Graham and I dubbed 'hedgehugs' as they were so cute. The ones who sat down and wrote me letters telling me how much Graham had meant to them. The ones on speed-dial who'd always listened to me – or my voice notes, which were often so lengthy we called them 'podcasts' – when I needed advice or a chat. The ones who still thought of Graham while out cycling or running or whenever they saw a crow, and when they did, made sure they let me know. The ones who, despite having three children under two, and pumping breast milk day and night, still took the time to send me loving voice notes and amusing YouTube clips, along with much-needed advice on caring for my campervan. The ones who wholeheartedly supported me when I campaigned for assisted dying to be legalised. The ones who never failed to wish me a 'Happy Friday', championed me and reminded me of how far I'd come. The ones who still invited me round and showed concern for how I was getting on after Graham's death. The ones who placed a photo of Graham in their Thai spirit house where they commemorated all those they'd lost. Those who'd come camping with me in Bodiam, a place Graham and I both cherished, and who'd sat on folding chairs at our favourite spot

LIVING WITH LIVING LOSSES

on the riverbank, toasting Graham and scouring the ink-black sky for shooting stars.

Having turned around at the Littlehampton Harbour Bridge, I began to give thanks for the new friends I'd made since moving to Worthing. The ones who'd watered my plants and kept an eye on my flat when I was in South Africa caring for my dad. The former colleague who became the kind of friend who'd say, 'No you can't just live on biltong while writing your book, I'm coming round to give you some of my famous spaghetti bolognese,' and never said 'no' when I suggested going for a run. The ones who'd invited me to sing and dance and chat around a blazing bonfire in a washing-machine drum and then plunge into the icy sea in the dead of winter while howling at the Full Moon. The neighbours who'd bought me a squirrel garden ornament to commemorate Pecan. At my run's end, my step was getting lighter, and so was my heart.

Mermaid sighting on Worthing promenade

Zen-like peace, love and a rainbow on my balcony in Worthing

Existential question spotted in the New Forest

The answer is 'Hell yeah!'

Flaunting my Flanci activewear with company founders Alf and Nicky

The flamingo flies again at the New Forest Half Marathon

Chapter 27
'Awful, thanks for asking'

♪♪ **Mood music:** *The Closest Thing to Crazy* **by Katie Melua**
Because grief is a kind of madness

'Dead, dead, dead, alive, dead, alive.' In much the same way that Graham and I had once played the Been Game at airports, looking up at the flight-information screens and declaring which destinations we'd either 'been' or 'not been' to, now, back home in Worthing, I made a mental tally of which of my family members were dead or alive. Despite having managed to start coming to terms with my many 'living losses', in the interminably long evenings, I'd sit alone on my sofa paging through the photo albums I'd brought back from South Africa. Tracing my finger over the smiling images of my family on the Durban beachfront posing next to grinning Zulu rickshaw drivers or picnicking among the rocks at Umbogintwini Beach, I'd mutter 'dead', 'dead', 'alive'. I couldn't believe how few of us were left. Bereavement had taken a blowtorch to my life, and all that was left were ashes. I'd lost almost all the people who held my history in their hearts.

I was also plagued by another thought: 'What's the point?' I'd fought like a cage fighter to keep Graham alive and my father well looked after, but with no one left to fight for, my life seemed pointless. Being alive started to feel like a burden. It wasn't so much that I wanted to die, but that I was struggling to find reasons to live. In Viktor Frankl's seminal book, *Man's Search for Meaning*, the Austrian psychiatrist-turned-concentration-camp-inmate observed that among his fellow prisoners, the ones who tended to survive were those who'd found a greater purpose, such as completing a project or creative task. 'The prisoner who had lost faith in the future – his future – was doomed,' he wrote. He went on to paraphrase Friedrich Nietzsche, one of Graham's favourite philosophers: 'A man who becomes conscious of the responsibility he bears toward... an unfinished work, will never be able to throw away his life. He knows the "why" for his existence, and will be able to bear almost any "how".' Reading that had prompted me to start working in fits and starts on this book, but I knew I needed more to make me want to keep on living. I felt like a hot-air balloon where the ropes tethering it to the ground had been severed, one by one. With each loved one's death, I felt less and less that I belonged here on earth, and that it would be better to float off somewhere else.

Clowns give me the creeps. They're blood-curdling, not bloody adorable, and have never once made me laugh. So the fact I seriously considered attending a Sacred Clowning Retreat in Spain should give you some idea of how broken I felt. It was as if I was an amoeba with only a millimetre-thick membrane protecting me against the outside world: all it would take to utterly destroy me was the pinprick of an unkind word or action. I knew I needed to heal and rebuild my life but, bruised as I was, I couldn't figure out how. Bereavement, to me, felt like a tiring and tedious trip to Ikea: it was a long and gruelling slog, but unlike the furniture megastore, there were no handy short-cuts. The only way out was through.

Reflexology, self-help psychology, kinesiology, astrology, knick-knack buying, intermittent crying, cold-water swimming, gong-

'AWFUL, THANKS FOR ASKING'

bath healing, hot stone massage, junk-food self-sabotage: the things I tried in an attempt to put myself together again sound like the lyrics to a rap song. But none of them did the trick – although cold-water swimming, which I started doing three months after Graham died, did gift me new friendships, a sense of achievement and a small cameo in a short film called *Just Add Water: Stories from the Sea* (which you can watch on YouTube). Whereas many of my bobble-hatted co-swimmers could only withstand seawater temperatures as low as 5°C for a few minutes, I happily bobbed around in the freezing waves in my insulated sheep hat for 40 minutes, my gloved hands held out of the water like a surgeon preparing to operate, my bloodstream awash with a heady cocktail of dopamine and endorphins. Exiting the water felt like triumphantly crossing the Comrades finish line, except I didn't have to run 56 miles first to experience the headrush.

I did consider having bereavement counselling but couldn't face working with a succession of different therapists until I found the right fit. I knew therapy had helped millions of people, but it just wasn't for me because, having talked through everything many times with close friends and family members, bereavement (by now my *Mastermind* specialist subject) bored me to tears. I was well and truly done with death.

And so I took to cowering under my duvet. The more I slept, the more my mood darkened. I almost held my breath, terrified that exhaling would unleash a torrent of tears. I was no longer a wife. Or Lolly's big sister. Or a daughter. What *was* my place in the world, exactly? Again, my friend Sarah came to the rescue. She'd called me every day since Graham died following an experience she'd had while she and her family were camping at our favourite campsite near Bodiam. We'd intended on joining them, but the trip coincided with Graham's admission to the hospice.

STILL RUNNING AFTER ALL THESE TEARS

'Lisa, I know this sounds as if I made it up,' Sarah said to me soon after Graham died. 'But early one morning in Bodiam, when I was half asleep in my sleeping bag, I heard Graham say, "Look after Lisa for me." His voice was so clear, it was as if he was actually inside the tent.'

When I told Sarah how I was now feeling cut adrift from my previous identity, she understood exactly what I meant.

'You're not just starting a new chapter,' she said, 'you're starting a whole new *book*.' Sarah helped me realise that although cancer, bipolar disorder and dementia had been writing my story of late, it was time to wrestle back control of the narrative and become the author of my own life again. I was fortunate, I realised, that my default factory setting was joy. Underneath the layers of grief, I was naturally happy. And to get back there, I knew I had to seek out both old and new activities to make my heart soar.

To navigate my way back to happiness, at first I used my Compass of Excitement to guide my decisions: if the thought of doing something flooded every cell in my body with eager anticipation, it went on the list. If it didn't, it didn't. The first activity I signed up for was a gospel choir. I'd loved being a soloist in my high school choir and I'd read in Bessel van der Kolk's *The Body Keeps the Score* that singing and dancing can help heal trauma by promoting feelings of safety and relaxation. It can also *create* trauma, I soon discovered. After our second rehearsal, the choral director, an imposing woman with a personality so powerful she should have been plugged into the national grid, beckoned me over. Still fizzing from the buzz of our finger-clicking, body-swaying, side-stepping four-part harmonies, I was expecting

'AWFUL, THANKS FOR ASKING'

her to praise my performance or compliment me on my evident enthusiasm. Instead, she gave me a bollocking. My heinous crime? Using my phone to help me memorise the lyrics.

'I can't learn new songs without seeing the words in writing,' I told her, tears welling up in my eyes. 'I've got trauma-related memory loss.'

'I've taught people with *brain injuries* and *they* didn't need to refer to the words,' she snapped. I cried all the way home. The next week I went back, but only to hand-deliver a resignation letter and demand a refund.

'Maybe I should try something I loved doing with Graham,' was my reasoning for booking a solo camping trip. Sitting forlornly in my camping chair in a local farmer's field, after the third attempt to relight my fire, I experienced both intense loneliness and extreme inadequacy. No matter how much crumpled newspaper I shoved into it, it refused to ignite, leaving me with just a wisp of smoke on which to toast my marshmallows.

My next attempt at getting the old me back was equally catastrophic and involved staring at a pair of nipples for three days at a Kundalini yoga retreat. The nips in question belonged to our Italian yoga guru, a half-naked, Russell Brand lookalike in his early 70s whose sun-wizened skin was so heavily tattooed that he resembled a Persian carpet. Kundalini, I learned, involves lots of 'fire breathing', in which stale air is violently expelled from your lungs using your diaphragm. I also learned that it's wise to blow your nose beforehand or else you risk spray-painting snot onto your boobs – or your neighbour's man-bun.

Turns out The Guru was the most garrulous teacher I'd ever encountered, instructing us to get into a convoluted yoga posture before, without drawing breath, embarking on a 20-minute diatribe against unnecessarily talkative yoga teachers. Another

STILL RUNNING AFTER ALL THESE TEARS

yoga contortion, another rant, this time about unscrupulous gurus.

'Be very careful of gurus who want to charge you a lot of money,' he droned.

'Funny that *you* thought it okay to charge each of us £350 for the privilege of camping for three nights in a muddy field,' I thought, recalling that 'breakfast' had consisted of a profit-maximising teabag in a mug of hot water, justified by the fact Kundalini should be practised on an empty stomach.

'Many gurus, they is into yoga for the wrong reasons. The power, money, Rolls-Royces,' he continued.

After 40 minutes of additional droning, his monologue drifted onto the topic of holy men living in caves in the Himalayas whom, he told us in all seriousness, were immortal as they could meditate themselves into a state of suspended animation. When the mood took them, he added, they found time to do a spot of astral travelling.

'So don't be surprised if you see one in the supermarket,' he concluded.

The idea of a saffron-robed saddhu, bored of his bat-like existence, popping up in the middle of Lidl, made me lose my composure – and my balance.

'This definitely isn't for me,' I thought, suppressing a giggle.

The £350 wasn't entirely in vain, however. While zoning out as The Guru sermonised, it dawned on me that although 18 months had passed since my back spasm had healed, I was *still* only running sporadically. I also started to think about the book I'd been planning to write about the coping strategies I'd used while I was a cancer thriver's wife. I was only writing it sporadically, too. Then and there, I vowed to both run a marathon and finish my book, in Graham's honour.

'AWFUL, THANKS FOR ASKING'

That night, as I slept on my yoga mat in my tiny one-person tent, I had a very vivid dream in which Graham appeared to me for the first time since he'd died. He wasn't in his usual chinos and floral shirt but was dressed as a shaman, wearing only a loincloth and an elaborate headdress crafted from antlers, feathers, twigs and berries. He smiled approvingly as I excitedly told him about my new plans.

'It's sad that we don't know what each other is doing any more,' he said softly. I awoke with a jolt, my right hip aching from pressing into the hard ground, my heart aching even more that I hadn't had time to find out what Graham was getting up to in the spirit world.

If I was to do a marathon, I had to accept that I couldn't do a marathon. At least not right then. When you've previously lost your fear of distance, which I had when chasing my 100-marathon dream, it's really annoying to have to accept that seven years later you're not the runner you used to be. After reading James Clear's *Atomic Habits,* a book beloved by none other than the Olympic gold medallist and former world-record-holding Kenyan marathon runner Eliud Kipchoge, I came to the realisation that true behaviour change is *identity* change. That my goal wasn't in fact to run a marathon again, but to *become a regular runner* again. My dad had seldom run more than 6km, but he did so five or six times a week, and in doing so cultivated a lifelong running habit. If he could call himself a runner by doing such short distances – something that allowed him to still fit into his high school blazer in his 70s – so could I. 'The joy of life is being superbly fit, and you only become superbly fit by running every

STILL RUNNING AFTER ALL THESE TEARS

day,' Dad had told me. What's more, to my delight, Clear stated that a University College London study showed that it took an average of only 66 days to create a habit: by the time I'd written two more *Runner's World* columns I would be able to call myself a regular runner again.

And so I used one of Clear's techniques which urges readers to make habits as easy as possible to start with. In other words, he wrote, if you want to run a marathon you should start with a super-achievable 'gateway habit' such as tying your running shoes. I felt I'd moved beyond that, as I wear trainers all day anyway, so I set myself the tiny target of running a mile, a distance I used to view as 'small change' back in my marathon heyday. In *Marathon Woman*, my friend Kathrine Switzer had called the daily mile she ran as a 12-year-old her 'Secret Weapon', saying that each day she'd gone for her run, she'd won a little victory that no one could take away from her. I realised, now, that running a mile could be my Secret Weapon, too, and that regular, short runs could become a way of 'winning at life'. Hell yeah, I liked the sound of that! Until that point, I'd had more comebacks than Rocky Balboa in my attempt to reignite my flagging running mojo. I'd even gone firewalking, for pity's sake, in an attempt to reignite my passion for running by stepping outside my comfort zone.

'I've never seen you run so fast in your life!' quipped a friend after watching the video clip of me hot-footing it across flaming coals in a pub car park. All to no avail. But the one-mile run would be different: I'd finally acknowledged that before I could take even baby steps, I first had to haul my battered body into a standing position.

'AWFUL, THANKS FOR ASKING'

'I still can't believe my luck that Worthing is the place I now call home,' I thought as I set out, remembering to factor in a walking warm-up so my body wouldn't go into shock. Pressed into a strip of land between the South Downs and the English Channel, like a slick of strawberry jam between two layers of sponge, Worthing felt more enchanting the longer I lived there. Virginia Woolf loved the area, too, writing: 'The Downs… too much for one pair of eyes, enough to float a whole population in happiness, if only they would look.'

In Croydon, where I'd lived for 27 years, the sky and seasons were camouflaged by concrete and obliterated by buildings, but in Worthing I'd become acutely aware of the weather, the tides and the cycles of the moon. I was so grateful to Graham for handing me a roadmap out of my grief: by agreeing to buy a property in Worthing, he'd given me his approval to move there; by saying many years ago that he'd definitely try to find a new wife if I died, he'd given me permission to remarry or find a new partner one day, too. And even though he was a self-proclaimed 'running hater', by telling me, a few months before he died, that he'd 'forgiven' running – and acknowledging all the pleasure it had given us over the years – he'd encouraged me to find the pleasure in it again and keep on doing it.

When I broke into a run, it was obvious why I hadn't been running for a while. It was just as bloody hard as it ever was. Way worse. But I knew that if I kept going for ten minutes, the 'toxic ten' I was always banging on about, I'd feel better. It was a sign of how traumatised I was feeling that my thoughts immediately drifted to the negative, leading to the horrifying realisation that I'd spent the past five-and-a-half years fighting: fighting cancer, The Fuckers and the healthcare system. An almost inconceivable, stomach-churning *ten per cent* of my life so far. No wonder I felt

STILL RUNNING AFTER ALL THESE TEARS

like utter shite. I started to cry as a huge wave of compassion for myself and what I'd been through swept over me and through me, so much so that I had to sit down on one of the memorial benches dotted along the seafront to get my breath back. I sobbed and sobbed – in all my years of turd flushing with Graham this was by far my longest flush – and when I was done, I wiped my nose on the hem of my T-shirt, not caring if anyone saw me, stood up, and forced myself to push on.

When I got to the turnaround point at Waterwise Park, I stopped for a moment to appreciate its wooden statues, among them a flaxen-haired mermaid and a grimacing 8ft-high blue shark, planted upright on its tail, its Hollywood-white teeth making it look embarrassed rather than terrifying. Heading back, I saw another other-worldly sight: what looked like a rainbow-powered wind turbine. Like an illustration in a children's book, a rainbow had pierced through an enormous raincloud and was bathing the turbine's slowly turning blades in a luminous, multi-coloured arc of light. The wind farm's offshore power station on stilts looked just like a 1950s comic-book spaceship. I smiled at this alien landscape I was now inhabiting, where mermaids rubbed shoulders with sharks, rainbows and UFOs, and where anything felt possible, even a return to marathon running and writing another book. Before I knew it, I was back where I started, dog tired but puppy happy.

Two weeks later, I turned up at Worthing parkrun – and ran all the way, with a 74-year-old who was recovering from a knee operation. It was probably my slowest parkrun time, but I didn't check or care. Like me, parkrun started small, with only 13 runners. It now has over six million participants in 23 countries. It's incredible to think it was founded by someone who once felt as utterly broken as I did. Fellow Southern African Paul Sinton-Hewitt related in his amazing book *One Small Step* that he'd

'AWFUL, THANKS FOR ASKING'

been relentlessly bullied at school and had created parkrun in his mid-40s when he was injured, unemployed and in the midst of a nervous breakdown.

By setting myself the target of running three times a week, and going just that little bit further each time, I slowly managed to start enjoying running again. A golden rule I never once broke was to always walk for the first five minutes, which helped make the start of each run feel less like staggering straight up Everest. On my friend Sarah's recommendation, I discovered the deep joy of podcasts: with 'running buddies' such as Rick and Ben from *Runner's World*, Esther and Holly from *Women's Running* and Paul and Rob from *Running Commentary*, plus a host of fascinating speakers on all manner of things, such as David Sedaris, Elizabeth Day, Fearne Cotton and Mel Robbins, each outing became an opportunity to not only stretch my legs but expand my mind.

Three months after that super-sedate parkrun, I completed a half marathon in the New Forest, my first in over four years. During this event I vowed to follow three-time-Olympian Lornah Kiplagat's approach: 'I run till I'm tired, and walk till I'm bored,' she once told me when I interviewed her for an article in *Women's Running*. A profound sense of peace washed over me deep in those pony-filled woods as I ran-walked past a grove of 1,000-year-old giant redwoods. Running, I realised, was the only thing I'd shared with Graham that I felt entirely comfortable doing on my own. Though we'd lined up on start lines together many times, we'd almost never raced together as his speedy pace was most certainly not mine. Unlike camping and travelling, when running I didn't need Graham by my side to make it feel worthwhile. Once again, running was proving to be my salvation. How lucky was I to have found it long before I lost so many people I loved, and to have rediscovered it now, when I needed it most?

Potential dating profile pic 1:
Lisa the Flamingo Runner

Potential dating profile pic 2:
Lisa the Traveller

Potential dating profile pic 3:
Lisa the Spiritual Seeker

Graffiti message spotted in Worthing

My Slow Dating 'speeding ticket'

Potential dating profile pic 4:
Lisa the Fancy Dress Queen

Chapter 28
Love me Tinder

♪♪ Mood music: *Believe* by Cher
The anthem for those of us hoping to find love again

'Dick pics and dickheads' is the phrase that best sums up my first forays into the dastardly world of online dating almost two years after Graham died. I knew his greatest wish was for me to be happy, and that he'd want me to find a new partner as we'd discussed the subject before he became ill.

'If you died before me, I'd probably go travelling in the hope of meeting a new partner as I'm not good at chatting women up,' he once told me. Back then, I didn't even want to imagine losing Graham so I hadn't said how I'd meet someone, but when it came to the crunch I realised that despite conversing with strangers during countless marathons, I wasn't brilliant at chatting people up either – and, in this new scenario, I ran the very real and mortifying risk of flirting with someone who was already taken.

It had all been so easy with Graham: I had instinctively known he was The One and then spent the next four years before we got married confirming my initial impression. It truly was love at first sight. Now, aged 56, and no longer a student in a pool of single potential partners roughly the same age, I found myself in a seemingly bottomless ocean of women of all ages, most of whom looked no older than 36. As a picky Virgo who had loved Graham with every fibre of my being, I didn't hold out much hope of being lucky enough to find a second soulmate.

STILL RUNNING AFTER ALL THESE TEARS

'Just think of it as "people shopping",' said my friend Hannah, who was a dating-apps veteran, implying it was no different to online grocery shopping: easy, once you'd got the hang of adding items to your imaginary basket. But I knew it wouldn't be that simple, at least not for me, someone who'd last been on a date at the age of 19. I suspected dipping my toes into the dating pool was going to be more like jumping into a shark tank, summed up by an anonymous quote I stumbled across: 'People tell me there are plenty of fish in the sea. Well, that's nice and all, but I'm human and I don't date fish.'

My first inclination was to try to find a widower as I reasoned someone who'd lost the love of their life was going to be a better bet than someone who was potentially embittered by a messy divorce. Two things put me off on the sites I visited, however: they didn't seem to have solely widower members (c'mon algorithms, you had just *one* job!) and I'd read in a newspaper once that a fraudster targeted a widow on one such site and she ended up dead in a drain.

Tinder was my next option, not because I'm a hook-up kinda girl but because this dating site has a surprisingly high success rate. Besides, I knew two women who'd met very decent men on the app – and I could certainly do with some help in setting my love life on fire. Using a photo from 15 years ago because I couldn't find anything more current at short notice, I signed up for a sneak preview. The men didn't look sleazy and there sure were a heck of a lot to choose from. You also got to read a few things about their interests, rather than judging them purely on looks. I spent a happy half hour swiping and then began to notice

LOVE ME TINDER

something curious: I was getting matched at a rate of knots. The more I swiped, the more quickly the matches racked up.

'I know I look rather fetching in my purple Thai fisherman pants, and I'm posing next to a cute street dog, but this is insane,' I thought. After a while it dawned on me that something was up, so I consulted Dr Google. I was horrified to discover that swiping right, as I'd been doing intuitively on my smartphone to window shop through the profiles, actually meant something entirely different to what I'd thought. Swiping right, I found to my shame, meant I'd expressed an interest in someone. Eek! No wonder I was suddenly the most popular woman on Tinder: I'd just let the entire universe know that I'd date anyone with a pulse. Or at least a profile pic. Hastily, I deleted my account, not least because I knew Graham would not approve of me dabbling on the dating dark side. Him and I both knew that ordering hot 'takeaways' with the flick of a finger – like one did on Uber Eats – really wasn't my style.

'Less searching, more chatting,' promised the tagline of EliteSingles, the dating site that had famously found a new life partner for the popstar-turned-priest Rev Richard Coles after the untimely and sad death of his first. Chatting, as you must know by now, is my chosen Olympic discipline so I couldn't wait to get cracking. Initially I kept my profile description to one short-but-sweet sentence, but when that garnered precisely one 'smile' – the way users could indicate their interest with a single click rather than having to go to all the trouble of lifting their fingers up and down repeatedly to type a few words – I realised I had to take this dating malarkey more seriously if I wanted serious results.

STILL RUNNING AFTER ALL THESE TEARS

Annoyingly, each box had a highly restrictive word count: how could I possibly describe all my likes and dislikes in one short paragraph? It took me all morning but I think I nailed it. Judge for yourself...

> *This makes me laugh:* Myself [sorry, I have to interject here, but I'm *still* laughing about this witticism I came up with, even now]. Diane Morgan aka Philomena Cunk. *The Inbetweeners*. Ian Hislop's giggle. Peter Kaye and Sally Phillips' faces (they don't have to say a word!)
>
> *What I do not like:* Fine dining, clubbing, injustice, five-* hotels (youth hostels keep me feeling young), pretentiousness, tattoos, people obsessed with money – or who aren't good with it! Women on *First Dates* who expect men to pay: if you want to be treated as an equal, you should behave like one.
>
> *How I like to spend my free time:* Chat-running, camping, backpacking, live comedy, kayaking, seaside full moon parties & wild swimming, star-gazing, reading, writing, museums, historic walks, bookshops, box sets. I do not like cooking so hope to meet someone who does (I promise my dishwasher will wash up!)

The 'smiles' started to trickle in. First up was Greg, a smartly dressed businessman, who claimed to love reading and to loathe 'multiple piercings and tattoos'. At least we had that in common. He was after a 'well-mannered, lovely lady with a nice pretty smile and family values'. Only trouble was, besides the fact that he preferred 'nice restrants' to 'buffays' and loved 'walks on the beech' (don't get me started on bad spelling, all you 'Manageing Directors' out there), he didn't appreciate women who liked a drink.

LOVE ME TINDER

'Hi Greg, thanks for the smile!' I wrote. 'I'm a wine lover so I don't think we'd get on, but good luck, you sound really nice.'

Despite what he'd written in his profile, Greg wasn't going to let wine stand in the way of romance with a polite-smiley-faced-family-orientated lovely lady like myself.

'I do love wine too,' he replied in a text message that featured more kiss-covered emojis than a teenage girl's. 'Maybe we get on well. I love wine and kisses, cuddles after that. You have beautiful smile and hair. I love good sex after wine. I do drink with food, specially white wine Chardonnay. How about you?'

It was enough to put me off wine. For life.

My other 'smiles' were no better. There was Muscle Man, who had biceps so bulging that he struggled to hold his mobile phone when taking a selfie. Scowler, whose profile photo made him look as if he'd taken his headshot while on the loo mid-poo. Lazybones, a chap who listed his favourite pastime as 'relaxing' ('Mine's breathing,' I was tempted to message him). And then there was the Joker who thought it amusing to go for a serial-killer vibe by wearing a white shirt covered in blood. Not just a speck or two from a shaving misadventure either – we're talking large bloodstains here, the size of fried eggs.

It wasn't all duds and deadbeats, however. One profile in particular caught my eye: it belonged to a man called Dan and had me in stitches every time I read it. 'I'm 5ft 10in (6ft in Crocs), unless I don't sleep well, because then I tend to slouch. I'm a big fan of running – because nothing screams "relaxation" like pretending you're being chased by a ferret for six miles. Aiming to visit every continent… but currently still debating if Antarctica counts as "travel" or "torture" (I hate the cold). I believe in love and oxygen, even though I have no idea why. I spend my free time yodelling, attempting to finish the book that's been on my bedside

STILL RUNNING AFTER ALL THESE TEARS

for a decade, giving my houseplants CPR and trying to convince myself that donating blood to starving mosquitoes while sleeping on a slowly deflating camping mattress is fun. I need someone who enjoys silence and steak; not into arguments or salad. Let's make bad decisions together, like adopting a goat. Or wearing lederhosen as leisurewear.'

Dan sounded like the Ideal Man: athletic, intelligent, adventurous, funny, and with a fabulous turn of phrase. Except he lived miles away and was an introvert.

After just two weeks, my smiles started to dry up and the site started to send me entirely inappropriate matches: smokers, a man in New York (yeah right, but can you imagine the Air Miles!) and men who wanted to become fathers. If I were to write a thesis about online dating, the latter would be the phenomenon I'd focus on. It didn't matter if they already had four children or none, were aged 45 or 65, almost without fail they all answered the question about whether they wanted kids with a 'Yes, at some point'. Having not had any children myself, and having indicated a strong preference for sticking with my decision, not least because I'm in my mid-50s, this algorithmic matching error puzzled me until I realised that if the site didn't include men who'd said they were up for having kids, I'd have had virtually no matches and the app would've gone bankrupt. What also became painfully obvious was that most men were hoping to meet younger women – well, much younger than me at any rate. Apparently, 'young at heart' didn't cut the mustard. No wonder online dating has such a low success rate.

I've always been a feminist, so when things went quiet, I took matters into my own hands and made the first move by 'smiling' at a man in Brighton who ticked about five boxes on my 100-point checklist.

'Thanks for the interest,' he replied gallantly, 'but I don't think I could keep up with you.' He obviously didn't know how slowly I ran, I thought to myself. The other two 'smiles' I sent were met with silence.

As I'd been off the dating scene for so long, the thing I feared most was a new (as in post-1986), seriously unsavoury dating phenomenon I'd read about – the surprisingly common practice of men sending women a photo of their penis.

'Surely I'm too old for that?' I asked Hannah, the Grand Dame of Online Dating.

'Oh no, you won't believe how many you'll receive,' she said breezily.

'Really? That would totally gross me out,' I laughed nervously.

After 18 'smiles', I was convinced I'd finally been sent one. The folds of skin indicated the sender was probably uncircumcised, but why had his todger taken on such a weird, yellowish tinge? Surely he hadn't spray-painted it gold? I instantly turned into Disgusted Widow Woman of Worthing. How dare he? What had happened to common decency? And more to the point, what on earth was wrong with the poor man's appendage? I just had to take a closer look and clicked to enlarge it – the photo, *not* his penis. And then it dawned on me. Hapless Dick (yes, you couldn't make it up) was proudly standing in front of a giant statue, no doubt having selected this particular shot to signal his love of exotic travel. And what I'd assumed to be Dick's dick turned out, in fact, to be... a giant golden Buddha's big toe!

Deciding I'd probably have more luck IRL ('in real life', for those not fluent in Acronym), I signed up for speed-dating. I might have

STILL RUNNING AFTER ALL THESE TEARS

a better chance if only people could experience my 'delicious personality', I reasoned. The thought filled me with the kind of dread I'd last felt when I ran my first naked 5K at a naturist resort in Orpington, and I postponed going several times before taking the plunge. Organised by Slow Dating – a perfect fit for my running style, at least! – the event was held at an upmarket bar, and after we'd all assembled we were given a sticker badge displaying our name and number. We were also issued with a 'speeding ticket' (pun intended) on which we, like cops at a roadblock, could jot down the names and numbers of our dates and make some notes about their interests and eccentricities to remember them by.

'You have four minutes to get to know each other before the men have to move to the next table,' announced our host.

Armed with a pint of lime and soda after having been advised by Hannah that it was 'a really bad idea to drink and date', I greeted my first candidate, a charming plumber from Eastbourne whom I liked immensely. However, it soon transpired we had absolutely nothing in common except our mutual love for builder's tea.

'May I give you a kiss?' he asked when the bell rang.

'Sure,' I said, offering him my cheek.

My next date was a quiet-spoken, shy man who looked young enough to be asked for ID when buying a kitchen knife. The four minutes passed as slowly and painfully as if I was just starting out on a hilly run. I came up with question after question without him asking me any in return, and he always replied with one- or two-word answers. It was as if he'd been issued with a word ration and had to eke it out over the entire evening.

'Where do you work?' I eventually enquired in desperation.

'A pet shop,' was the reply.

'He's a Pet Shop Boy!' I shrieked, to myself, highly amused by my sharp wit, even if he wasn't.

LOVE ME TINDER

When the third man sat down, his sticker was obscured by the lapel of his jacket, making it difficult to read his name and number.

'What's your number?' I asked him.

'Don't you think it's a bit early for that?' he joked.

'You should be a comedian!' I blurted out.

'I am!' he exclaimed. The next four minutes were spent discussing the amateur comedy circuit and how some people were so desperate to get their foot in the door that they'd endure two hours on a train just to perform a two-minute gig at an open-mic night. While I learned a lot about a career in comedy, we learned precisely nothing about each other.

Date after date came and went, and the more men I spoke to, the more I enjoyed myself. By allowing me to practise chatting to strangers, marathon running had been ideal preparation for this, I realised. The only differences were the strict four-minute time limit, the fact that none of us was in pain, and that we all smelled good. The only truly unpleasant moment came when my penultimate date, a suave-looking gent in a violet suit wearing so many bejewelled rings he looked like a magician, paid me a compliment.

'You have lovely hair,' he said approvingly. 'Unless it's a syrup?'

'Now why on earth would you accuse me of wearing a wig?' I laughed.

'You're not listening to me, perhaps your hair got in the way of your hearing,' he said with annoyance. 'I didn't say you *were* wearing a wig, I *asked* you if you were.'

The next three minutes and 50 seconds lasted a long, long time.

My final date was far more promising: he had lovely brown eyes and a smile danced around the corners of his mouth, as if he were permanently recalling a much-loved private joke.

STILL RUNNING AFTER ALL THESE TEARS

After exchanging interests – by now I'd got the hang of speed dating and realised I really couldn't afford to waste a second discussing my real-or-fake lovely hair or South African accent – I asked the man what he did for a living.

'I'm a human statue,' he deadpanned.

'A what?'

'A human statue,' he reiterated, sliding a promotional postcard across the table to prove his claim.

'You mean like those people who're covered from head to toe in gold paint and only move if tourists pay them money?' I asked incredulously.

'No, in my case it's white paint,' he corrected me.

Three thoughts immediately flitted through my mind. Firstly, I hated to imagine how long he'd have to spend in the shower each evening. Secondly, I hoped he'd chosen a clothed statue to model himself on, rather than Michelangelo's *David*. And thirdly, had I finally met my perfect match? Someone who could remain silent for hours while I did all the talking? One who would never answer back? Sadly, the conversation that followed revealed no further coincidental compatibilities.

By the end of the evening, the only man I thought had any real potential was a respectable-looking gent – I prefer 'solid, stable and sane' to 'sexy, smooth-talking and self-destructive' – who enjoyed hiking and had been to Machu Picchu.

'Why are you single?' he enquired.

'My husband of thirty years died.'

'I'm so sorry to hear that. How did he die?'

I filled him in and tried to steer the conversation back to him, but he was having none of it.

'You're just so brave,' he continued. 'Was he in a hospice at the end?'

LOVE ME TINDER

Again I politely responded, thinking I didn't want to be recalling something so upsetting on a first date and instead would rather have discussed our favourite small furry animals or whether he'd rather have to sing everything he said, or dance every time he walked. Or would rather live with a messy flatmate or a poltergeist who stole his socks. Or, truth be told, me.

That night, after I'd caught the bus home, I went onto the speed-dating website and ticked Machu Picchu Man. He never ticked me back.

Mum with the daughters she adored

My parents on their wedding day

Running the Comrades Marathon in honour of Mum

Mum, me and Loren run the SPAR Women's Challenge 10K in Durban, South Africa

Chapter 29
All about my mother

♪♪ Mood music: *Fernando* by ABBA

My mother adored this song

'I don't own any underwear. Honestly, I simply don't have, or wear, underpants,' I once heard the radio presenter and legendary endurance runner Vassos Alexander confess during a National Running Show presentation. Vassos went on to say that many years ago, he'd swapped boxers for running shorts. 'So if I want to go for a quick run, I simply whip off my trousers – completely removing the need to change – which makes my runs much more likely to happen,' he told us.

I wasn't about to suddenly start 'going commando', but I did think being 'run ready' at all times might be beneficial, so I swapped my daywear for activewear and began living – and even sleeping in – my Flanci gear. I'd been made an ambassador of this colourful running brand after the Southern African owner, Nicky Chrascina, had read with amusement that a fellow running journalist had suggested that brands pay me *not* to run in their gear as I come last so often.

The crucial decision of what marathon to enter in Graham's honour was not an easy one. 'This might be my last-ever marathon, so it had better be super-special,' I thought. In the event, my biggest deciding factor, as it had been throughout my marathon career, was the cut-off time. I needed a race with the longest possible time limit as, with a PW (personal worst) of 11h40, I didn't want to be booted off the course. Looking through the options, I thought

STILL RUNNING AFTER ALL THESE TEARS

how nice it would be to choose a marathon that Graham had run with me, too. Although we'd started 30 marathons together, he was so much faster than me that we almost never ran together, so this whittled it right down to a grand total of one race: the Brighton Marathon. In 2012, Graham had attempted to pace me there when I was gunning for a Comrades qualifier, but had only run half the race with me as I'd torn my calf muscle at mile 13 and had to walk the rest of the way.

For the first time in my running career, I started training a full five months before Marathon Day and made myself publicly accountable by sticking a photocopy of the training plan from Prof Tim Noakes' *Lore of Running* on my fridge so I could mark off each completed training run. Now, if I skipped a session, I'd be reminded of it every time I opened the fridge to get out the milk for my tea – in other words, about 14 times a day. I also roped in a couple of friends to accompany me on my marathon training runs. Emma, a self-confessed 'running geek', would drive down from Pulborough with her whippet, Woody the Woodster, in tow, to chat me through my long runs, and Beth, a former colleague who lived nearby, would volunteer for the shorter ones. It helped immensely that Beth was writing a 'naughty novel' based on a relationship she'd had with a gorgeous Bradley Cooper-esque boyfriend 25 years before. Each time we met up, I'd hear another steamy instalment or have a conversation about it that would reduce us to shrieks of helpless laughter.

'I'm struggling with some of my metaphors,' Beth panted on the footpath leading to Sea Lane Café one evening. 'I'm wondering whether to compare us to horny hamsters, restless rabbits or hungry lions. On the other hand, there's an idea brewing about a *Star Wars* stormtrooper, something along the lines of allowing him to enter my chamber of secrets!'

ALL ABOUT MY MOTHER

'Stop! I can't breathe from laughing!' I told her.

'Oh yes, and then there's another bit about his pert buttocks changing speed like a set of Shimano gears.'

It was on my solo runs, however, that I found myself thinking about and observing the trajectory of my grief. In the early days after Graham died, I recall congratulating myself for surviving one whole week, then two, then three. Reaching the one-month anniversary of his death on 1 October 2021 had seemed nothing short of a miracle. But then time accelerated and all of a sudden, he'd been dead for an entire year. And then two, and three. I was amazed that I'd managed to adjust to his loss, but then I remembered that I'd managed to adjust to losing my mother, too, even though her death had felt like a bomb going off in my life. As I continued to tick off each training session, I found myself thinking about my mum more and more, and I wasn't sure why. Why was I grieving for her all over again when she'd died 17 years before?

'You can't untangle one bereavement from another,' my friend Sarah explained when I told her about it. 'Look what happened when Princess Diana died. People who'd never met her cried their eyes out because her death triggered emotions about their own losses.'

I realised, then, that I hadn't fully processed my mother's death back in 2007 when she was killed by a motorist in Pretoria while training for the Médoc Marathon we were planning to run together. In the months after her death, I'd been qualifying as a hypnotherapist while commuting to a full-time job, and had also been preparing for my first ultra, which I ran in her honour. Now

STILL RUNNING AFTER ALL THESE TEARS

I came to see that by keeping busy I'd managed to avoid thinking about her because I didn't want to be overwhelmed by grief.

But now, during these runs, my mother was often on my mind. I knew that strangers had mourned her death after reading about it in *Your Pace or Mine?* Why hadn't I taken the time, I thought guiltily, to do this, too?

And so I began doing just that. During my solo training runs, I started recalling how our mother had spent 12 months, each and every year, planning the joint birthday parties she threw for Loren and me, long before themed celebrations were 'a thing'. Our birthdays fell in spring, so our garden was always filled with a profusion of potted pink azaleas, the plants my dad adored before he fell in love with cycads. Our Umbrella Party featured a covered sandpit turned into a makeshift stage on which every guest was invited to do a short performance under a colourful canopy of decorated up-ended umbrellas. Our Animal Party was held at Pretoria Zoo and I distinctly recall that the young guests did not appreciate the salted liquorice cats my mum put in their goody bags at my request. The zoo's lawns ended up sprinkled with spat-out sweets while I rushed around assuring my nine-year-old friends that if they didn't like the liquorice cats, they could skip the intermediate stage of tasting them and give them all to me.

After being hospitalised and subsequently missing many months of school due to a bone infection she developed aged six, Mum had always felt like an outsider. Her doctors had suggested amputating her arm, but her parents had begged them to save it, something that involved taking skin grafts from her stomach and calf. It also necessitated two of her sisters dropping out of university as my grandparents couldn't afford both their tuition fees and the exorbitant medical bills. In the event, my mother's arm was saved, but the experience left deep emotional scars, and many physical ones – Mum once joked that she looked like a hand-sewn ragdoll. Knowing what it felt like to be different from her peers meant she always jumped to the defence of the underdog. In apartheid South Africa, it was my mum who taught me that everyone should be treated equally, no matter the colour of their skin. When a racist shopkeeper called her to the front of the queue, ahead of the black customers who'd been waiting their turn, she refused to be served first. And on another occasion, when the same shopkeeper rudely declined a request for a straw from a black customer who'd just paid for a bottle of Coke, Mum showed him up by asking for two before handing one to the grateful woman. Mum also frequently took what Dad referred to as 'lame ducks' under her wing. As a child I recall innumerable acts of charity and kindness: she was always visiting elderly neighbours, and championed all her children and friends, being one of those rare people who got more satisfaction from seeing others succeed than she did from her own achievements.

Having grown up in a home where there wasn't much spare cash for books or cultural activities, my mother filled our house with books on every subject under the sun: when I packed up our family home I estimated there were close on 8,000 volumes covering everything from travel and architecture to literature – she particularly adored Laurie Lee, A. A. Milne and Dylan Thomas. Growing up, my sister and I had been treated to a rich diet of at least one visit to a museum, art gallery or symphony concert a week. But Mum had been less of a role model in the healthy-eating department, often driving around Pretoria in her red-and-white Mini, and later her orange Mazda 323, with a long stick of liquorice dangling from her mouth. Her love of pizza and ice cream was legendary, as was her hatred of greens. 'Vegetables?

STILL RUNNING AFTER ALL THESE TEARS

Yuk!' she'd say after her breast-cancer diagnosis aged 61 when my sister urged her to revamp her diet.

In her later years, Mum fearlessly took up micro-lighting, bungee-jumping and white-water rafting, all terrifying things I wouldn't dream of attempting. But then she'd always been a bit of a rebel: she'd grown up in a conservative Afrikaans household and yet had wanted to be an actress, as evidenced by her love of glamorous false eyelashes, bouffant hairdos, flamboyant kaftans, statement, overly large earrings and pastel slimline cigarettes. The video we showed at her funeral celebration pictured her scrambling up a rocky path through a steep-sided gorge leading away from the Zambezi River. When interviewed by the rafting company's cameraman about her white-water experience, like the former drama lecturer she was, Mum beamed at the camera and said: 'It was gorge-ous!'

When my mum died, my friend Sarah sent me a touching message of sympathy: 'Whenever you feel sad, remember, your mum lives on in you.' This was true on so many levels: of course my mother's genes survive in me – I look like her, cackle-laugh like her and even cough like her – but so do her values and interests, the most precious and enduring of which is running. She didn't have a talent for it and, like me, was super-slow, but what she did have was the mindset of an Olympian, often going out for a casual half-marathon jog with my dad, in her 60s, before breakfast while they were on holiday. Once, aged 67, she memorably complained to her GP that she was experiencing extreme fatigue, but he could find nothing amiss despite conducting a battery of tests.

'Did you tell him, Mommy, that you walk or run up to fifteen kilometres every day?' asked Loren.

'No, I didn't think to mention that,' my mother admitted.

ALL ABOUT MY MOTHER

While my dad was the 'real runner' in the family, ironically it was Mum who enabled me to join the 100 Marathon Club. Dad didn't really approve of my silly hats and chat-running, whereas Mum couldn't wait to be told about my latest fancy-dress get-up and fully understood that the chance to connect with other runners was my main marathon motivation. Without having inherited her bulletproof, can-do mindset, I never would have achieved my Comrades Marathon dream either. The bible verse we chose to put inside her coffin summed her up perfectly: 'I have fought the good fight, I have finished the race, I have kept the faith.'

Now, almost two decades after her death, I finally understand why my mother took up marathon running aged 63. It came after a chance conversation with my father's friend Lezani, a fellow cycad lover, after his death, in which she revealed my dad's reason for embarking on a law degree in his late 60s: 'He told me he didn't want you kids to think he was just an old man, he wanted to make you proud.' Her words made me realise Mum had been doing that too with her daredevil exploits and running ambitions, something I found heartbreakingly poignant. Having spent my whole life striving to make my parents proud of me, I'd never before realised that they, too, felt the need for *my* approval. What they may not have realised, however, was that they already had it, and that by giving me running, and such an incredible start in life, they also had my undying gratitude.

'Last night I met TWO spirits with lung cancer, and another who liked lobbing marshmallows at his loved ones!' I wrote in a WhatsApp message to my cousin Anna. I'd been toying with the idea of going to a spiritualist centre for ages as a schoolfriend had said it had brought her great solace, but I'd been very apprehensive about doing so as my mother, a committed Christian, had maintained that communicating with the dead was evil and akin to witchcraft. However, after my three recent losses I thought I should at least make one attempt at contacting my loved ones, and confessed my intentions to Sarah.

'Oh, it's nothing to worry about. My mum and sister often go,' she reassured me. 'They find it comforting. They especially love the raffle where they win random bizarre gifts people have clearly dug out from their regifting boxes!'

Suitably forewarned, and having roped in my friend Rose for support, I made my way to the venue. After surveying the super-sized raffle collection displayed on a table at one end of the church hall, I bought five pounds' worth of tickets.

'I'm always lucky in raffles,' I told Rose. 'And tonight, if I'm *really* lucky, I *won't* win those!' I said, pointing to a truly hideous 3D puppy dog photo frame and a pony-sized, chintz-covered rocking horse.

'Good evening, everyone,' said the medium, a middle-aged woman dressed in a voluminous, floor-length purple kaftan. 'Thanks for coming along. I'm going to speak to the spirits tonight and if I ask you a question, all I want you to do is say "Yes", "No" or "Not sure".'

We nodded.

'I'm getting a young man, who passed into spirit of his own accord,' she continued after closing her eyes. 'Does that mean anything to anyone?'

Two hands shot up on either side of the room.

'Thanks both of you,' said the medium, 'but I get the strong feeling it's someone related to the gentleman on my right.'

ALL ABOUT MY MOTHER

The creased-faced man behind us, a dead ringer for Gordon Ramsay, smiled eagerly and rubbed a hand through his floppy blond fringe. The woman on the left lowered her hand dejectedly.

'Oh my God, they're playing tug of war over the spirits,' I thought. 'I suppose everyone wants to think that the spirit coming through is their own loved one.'

'I know this sounds odd, but I can see him throwing marshmallows at you!' continued the medium. 'He wants you to know he's safe and that no one should blame themselves for his passing.'

The medium moved on to the next departed soul.

'I'm getting the smell of chocolate,' she said. 'You know those big tins of Christmas Quality Street? It's one of those. It belongs to the relative of someone over there. He died of lung cancer and, just for placement, his name starts with the letter B.'

The woman in front of us nodded vigorously and brought a tissue to her eye.

'He wants you to know that you're loved and that he's fine. And he wants to share some Quality Street with you. He's actually laughing because he knows you think he doesn't believe in what he would have called "this crap", but he's here. He really is.'

At this point I started to suspect that the woman was wrong and that, perhaps, this was in fact *my* loved one coming through. Had the medium misheard 'B' instead of 'G'? Should I stake my claim before it was too late? All along I'd known that the only way I would give credibility to anything the medium said was if she reported Graham being extremely sceptical – and my mother utterly appalled – about being contacted in this way. But though I would dearly have loved to have been bequeathed some spectral chocolates, it soon became apparent the spirit wasn't actually Graham when he professed to loving golf. And KFC.

STILL RUNNING AFTER ALL THESE TEARS

'I'm now hearing from someone who died of an illness here,' said the medium, pointing to her chest. A shiver passed through me.

'Oh my God, that's the second ghost who's died of lung cancer,' whispered Rose.

'I don't know if this means anything to you but he wants to give you a slice of Scotch egg.'

I spluttered. Surely if people's dead relatives really were turning up they'd have more important things to talk about than a spiritual smorgasbord? I also knew that if my mother really was in the room, she'd be offering up loving words of encouragement and comfort, not liquorice and ice cream. Graham would have done the same. Realising that none of my loved ones were likely to pitch up, I relaxed and thought I might at least be lucky with the raffle. And by jove, my luck was in. I had six winning numbers and, although the insulated mug I'd had my eye on had gone, I did manage to procure a couple of boxes of chocolates, a seventh-hand Brut deodorant-and-shower-gel gift set and some very fetching silver-and-crystal dangly earrings (after being thoroughly disinfected, they're now affectionately known as my 'spiritualist earrings'). Even though my departed relatives had stayed away, at least the spiritualist evening reassured me that I'm still *very* lucky at raffles.

Meeting my friend Nadia at the start

Zone G baggage drop

Mark and Rose say 'Go Lisa!'

All smiles with Peter at the 2025 Brighton Marathon finish

Medal moment

Admire the bling – and spot the toilet logo!

Chapter 30
The flamingo rises from the ashes

🎵 **Mood music:** *Tubthumping* **by Chumbawamba**
The song for anyone who keeps getting up again

It's a tad disheartening to be told by your physiotherapist, two months before your first marathon in seven years, that you have glutes lazier than do-as-little-as-possible, doughnut-eatin', nap-lovin' Homer Simpson. What's more, Cathy told me after thoroughly investigating the hip niggle that had driven me to seek out her professional help, my other muscles were pretty workshy, too. I hadn't darkened the door of a gym in well over a year and the closest thing I'd got to strength training was lifting up the heavy mattress on the divan I'd bought, so I suppose this shouldn't have come as a surprise.

Unfortunately, my body did not take kindly to the exercises Cathy prescribed me, nor the YouTube strength training I began doing, and after the first few sessions, every inch of my body ached as though an elephant had trampled all over me. Even getting up from the loo involved hanging on to my towel rail for dear life.

As I sat tearfully on my sofa feeling extremely sorry for myself, I took stock. Was I actually going to be able to run the bleedin' Brighton Marathon or would I have to drop out, as I'd done for various reasons from no fewer than five marathons since 2018? When I reported my physical disintegration to Cathy, I was secretly hoping she'd say strength training – which I had dodged like a rugby scrum-half almost my entire life – just wasn't for me,

STILL RUNNING AFTER ALL THESE TEARS

but no, she said my reaction proved I needed to do more, not less of it. Holy shitbiscuits! I'd read in Vassos Alexander's book, *How to Run a Marathon*, that only seven per cent of people actually do their physio homework, and knew if I was going to finish Brighton, I'd better not land up in the 93 per cent. Thankfully my running buddy Beth was keen to tone up her 'bumble' as she called her bottom, so she dutifully came round twice a week for exercises with yukky-sounding names I'd never heard of, such as inchworms, banded bird dogs and deadbugs. Night after night, Beth and I continued to head out for a run after work, and I realised why she was my ideal training partner: she hated running even more than I did.

'I can't go on,' she said melodramatically during a 30-minute run one evening, going to lie flat on her back on the low wall fronting Worthing beach and hiding her face in the crook of her arm.

'What's wrong?' I said, extremely concerned.

'I think it's because I didn't eat my banana before I came out,' she whined. 'Besides, I really don't like running, you know.'

'Beth! You're a disgrace!' I laughed. 'I'm going to take a photo of you having a snooze in the middle of our run and post it on Facebook to show everyone how incredibly lazy you are.'

'I don't care!' she retorted defiantly. 'I don't do Facebook!'

Hating running aside, Beth never once chickened out of any of our runs. Like me, she was a woman of her word, and if she said she'd meet me on the promenade, she always did, rain, frost, hail or shine, thereby eliminating any of the 'Shall I? Shan't I?' thoughts that had seen me ducking out of so many training runs in the past. Even the Met Office's gale warnings didn't deter her: on a night so brain-freezingly cold that we wished we'd worn balaclavas, she dutifully turned up at our designated meeting point, and merely

THE FLAMINGO RISES FROM THE ASHES

laughed as a particularly violent gust almost swept us off our feet and into the English Channel. Meeting up so frequently had another unintended but delightful consequence: Beth went from being a former colleague to a close friend; someone whom I'd once only occasionally chatted to in the office kitchen to someone I could share life's trials, tribulations and triumphs with. The kind of friend who'd not only bring me a 'pensioner's portion' of fish and chips most Fridays, but would volunteer to climb out of my sixth-floor kitchen window to scrape seagull and pigeon poo off the glass! I'd be lying if I said I looked forward to our runs, but knowing we'd be spending the whole time having a catch-up meant I didn't spend the entire day dreading them as I had in times gone by. As we chugged courageously through the miles, the words of Mel Robbins, one of my favourite podcasters, sprang to mind: 'If you only ever did the things you don't want to do, you'd have everything you've ever wanted.'

Five weeks before marathon day, I did a trial run: the Brighton Half Marathon. I bumped into Kate, a stellar runner I knew from my Croydon days, at the train station. 'I recently turned sixty-one, so I'm officially an OAP now,' she told me, 'but that won't ever stop me running marathons. I'll only give up when something vital drops off or fails irretrievably!'

As we walked to the start on Hove Lawns, Kate told me that although she was on her A game, 2025 would mostly be a 'B year' for her as she was running marathons in Bognor Regis, Boston, Berlin, Beachy Head and... bloomin' London. After a quick catch-up with Jenny, a runner alongside whom I'd once struggled

STILL RUNNING AFTER ALL THESE TEARS

through the Beachy Head Marathon, but who now inspired me with her plans to do the Boston Marathon and the Ironman World Championship in Kona, Hawaii, later in the year, Kate and I lined up in the Portaloo mega-queue.

'My start's in ten minutes, I'll have to find a toilet on the course,' said Kate a little while later, giving me a hug before bounding off.

'You're lucky you're behind me in this queue,' I told the smiling 50-something woman who stepped forward to take Kate's place. 'I can be in and out in under a minute – I've actually gone so far as timing myself!'

'Yes, when people take ages I've often wondered whether they remove all their clothes before taking a pee,' she laughed.

When, with a door slam, a loo became free, I rushed into it, calling good luck to the woman as I did so. When I emerged, exactly a minute later, she was gone, and I made my way to the start, my stomach fluttering with excitement as I watched the tail-end of the 9,000-strong field shuffle slowly forward to the start line.

Eventually a marshal let me through the barrier onto the course and I was off, warning myself to take it easy in case my hip injury flared up. I was right at the back, and anticipating a very lonely three or four hours, when I thought I saw the woman I'd chatted to earlier.

'Are you the Loo Queue Lady?' I asked, just to be sure.

'I am indeed,' she said, smiling. 'My name's Marian.'

'And I'm Lisa. Mind if I run with you?'

'Not at all, though I should warn you that I'm going to run one lamppost and walk the next. If you want to go on ahead at any point, please do.'

'I can't believe you just said that,' I told her. 'Twenty-one years ago, I wrote a book called *Running Made Easy* that popularised

THE FLAMINGO RISES FROM THE ASHES

run-walking in the UK, long before the Couch to 5K app. I'd almost forgotten that's an option. Yes, let's follow your plan.'

'Just one other thing,' said Marian, 'I can't really run and talk.'

'That's not a problem,' I laughed. 'As long as you don't mind, I've got enough anecdotes for both of us!'

The pleasures and perils of speed dating, how much we loved living by the sea, and how uncannily like a toilet, in Marian's opinion, the logo on the race medals looked, was the calibre of conversation that got us round. Eventually, at around the ten-mile mark, we came across a young runner crying at the side of the road.

'Are you OK?' I asked.

Her face blotchy from crying, the young woman told us she was there with her older sisters but she didn't feel she could continue. After checking she wasn't injured and was merely having a mental speed wobble, I made her an offer: 'Just call us Runner Rescue,' I told her. 'If you come with Marian and me, we can guarantee that you'll sleep with a medal round your neck tonight. Deal?' The young girl nodded tearfully.

With me chatting away merrily, and Marian adding one-sentence-long words of encouragement, we pushed on, passing Hove Lagoon and finally looping back towards the finish line, along the way learning that Emily was running her first half, and that she was only 17 years old.

'*Seventeen?*' I puffed. 'You should be incredibly proud of yourself – I was *thirty-one* before I ran my first half marathon.'

'I'm feeling much better now, do you mind if I go on ahead?' asked Emily a little while later.

'Sure,' I said, 'but only if you and your sisters promise to wait for us at the finish so we can pose for a photo together.'

STILL RUNNING AFTER ALL THESE TEARS

In the final kilometre I could see Marian was flagging slightly, whereas I felt as if I'd just gulped down rocket fuel. I'd never, in all my previous 43 half marathons, felt this good after 13 miles. Radio presenter and running convert Chris Evans was right, I thought, when he wrote in his book *119 Days to Go*: 'The fewer gaps there have been in your [training] plan, the more you will want to kiss your own face on the start line.' Training really does pay off.

In the final 200m, a runner with what looked like a fridge on his back but what was actually an enormous sound system, trundled past. The music he was playing – Beyoncé's *Texas Hold 'Em* – was so foot-stompingly catchy that I just had to dance to it, and so I began zig-zagging back and forth across the course, flapping my elbows like a hoedowning cowboy, because, by now, there was no way I could stick to our run-walk plan, I simply *had* to run.

'Thanks to you, I've never finished stronger in a half marathon in my whole life. And I've certainly never danced across a finish line!' I wrote to Marian the day after the race, having just been informed by the organisers that my time was 30 minutes faster than the year before.

'I think that works both ways,' she wrote back. 'You lifted me the whole way round. I've never finished with such a big smile on my face.'

I may have triumphantly conquered the Brighton Half Marathon – gaining a new runner friend and a medal with a picture of Brighton Palace Pier and a tiny toilet on it in the process – but there was no time to revel in my success. What lay ahead was

THE FLAMINGO RISES FROM THE ASHES

the real deal: the 2025 Brighton Marathon I'd vowed to run in Graham's honour, 26 years after my first marathon in London when I'd cried uncontrollably at the finish, fully expecting blood to gush out of my battered feet.

For the next five weeks, I fitted in as much training as I could but, because I was writing this book, I ran out of time to do all the long runs, which as any marathoner knows are the ones you really shouldn't skip.

'Oh well,' I told myself, knowing I simply couldn't afford to spend one day a weekend running from dawn till dusk, 'it is what it is. I know I've done my best in the time I've had available.' This was not the time to start beating myself up. The one thing I made sure to do, however, was attend my weekly physio and sports-massage appointments as I knew keeping my hip happy was going to be key to marathon success.

The night before The Brighton Big One, Gaby, a magazine editor I'd met on a press trip in St Andrews 20 years before, came to stay so that we could travel to the marathon together. After carb-loading on sourdough pizza and white wine at a neighbourhood bar, Gaby and I headed home to stick to our strict 10pm curfew. As I laid out my flamingo hat and Day of the Dead Flanci skort, and pinned my race number to my well-stocked bumbag, I thought of Graham and how proud he would be of me. Gazing down at the T-shirt I'd had printed with photos of us at home, at the 2010 FIFA World Cup in South Africa and at the Piglet Plod Half Marathon in East Sussex's Ashdown Forest just days after he'd been diagnosed (he'd driven me there and cheered me on), my heart was filled with gratitude and love for the wonderfully supportive man I'd been so lucky to share so much of my life with.

During the train journey to Brighton, I reminded Gaby of how she'd inadvertently embarrassed me in St Andrews. I'd been

STILL RUNNING AFTER ALL THESE TEARS

working at *Zest* magazine at the time, and she'd arranged to meet me on West Sands beach at dawn to re-create the iconic slow-mo *Chariots of Fire* running scene that had been filmed there. Except she'd overslept, leaving me to run on the famous, deserted beach alone. I'd followed the run with a dip in my undies in the frigid North Sea, and returned to shore only to find that all the clothes I'd so carefully placed on top of my trainers were bobbing about in the waves, having floated off on the incoming tide. My hotel key card, however, had disappeared. Dripping wet and barefoot, I had to sneak into the marble-clad reception of the five-star Old Course Hotel to ask for a replacement. And who should be standing there, all suited and booted at 7am, but the General Manager we'd had dinner with the night before.

'I blame you for that whole cringe-worthy debacle,' I teased Gaby as our train, jam-packed with the excited, nervously chattering runners we'd picked up en route, pulled into Brighton Station. 'Well I blame you for getting me into marathon running,' she laughed. 'I read your books and now, here I am, doing two in three weeks! If I don't get a PB here, I'll have another go in London in three weeks' time.'

During the walk up to the start in Preston Park we chatted about pacing strategies, just as, I thought with a pang, my Aunty Rosie and I had once done on our way to our first marathon. My aunt and I had gone on to run seven more marathons together before she died of lung cancer in 2011 and I'd really missed her at the start of every marathon since. It occurred to me that Gaby and I were nervous for different reasons: she was aiming for a PB (personal best), while I was aiming for a PBEE (personal best experience ever)... or perhaps just to finish, come what may.

In the park we met up with my dear friend Nadia, who'd been such a rock to me during Graham's illness. She'd also been a

THE FLAMINGO RISES FROM THE ASHES

source of running inspiration when my mojo was at its lowest ebb, and once emailed me, 'Just stop talking about it and start running again!' Gaby and Nadia had been assigned earlier start times, so after hugging them good luck, I made my way to the baggage drop on my own. I'd been assigned to zone G, so from the get-go I knew that Graham, whom I often called G, was smiling down on me.

'Please can you take a photo of me next to this giant letter G?' I asked a random runner strolling by, before telling her why I was posing against that particular backdrop. Five photos and three hugs from her later, I headed to the start, sobbing, as I desperately missed Graham's presence beside me.

'I'm doing this for you,' I whispered to him. 'Please take care of me today.'

Cheers of 'Go! Go! Flamingo!' from the clapping crowd rang in my ears as I set off, my entire body buzzing from the thrill of taking part in a marathon again. Where the course turned sharp left at the bottom of the park, near the Rose Garden, I recalled Graham cautioning me to keep a steady pace back in 2012.

'I know it's tempting, and that you love the cheers from your fans,' he'd said, 'but you shouldn't speed up every time someone shouts out your name.'

As I'd asked Graham to watch over me, I was on the lookout for signs that he was doing his job, and he didn't disappoint. Near the Brighton suburb of Withdean, at around the two-mile mark, I came across a block of flats called Cliveden Court, a name strikingly similar to Clevedon Court, the small mansion block Graham had been living in as a student in Cape Town, and where he'd once read me poetry in front of a crackling log fire. A mile later, back in central Brighton, a trio of giant flamingos painted above a café shopfront made my spirit soar – Graham couldn't be there, so he'd arranged for my own personalised cheer squad.

STILL RUNNING AFTER ALL THESE TEARS

My policy of run two lampposts, walk one, worked amazingly well for the first few miles, and I was really in my groove when I spotted my running buddy Emma and her whippet Woody the Woodster on a patch of grass at the side of the road, near the Brighton Gay Men's Chorus, who were harmoniously belting out show tunes in the sunshine. Next my friend Iona gave me a good luck hug outside Itsu, having dashed out of her sushi-making class to wish me well. Another mile, another hug, this time from a beaming 100 Marathon Club member called Martin, who gave me an update on his latest marathon tally: a jaw-dropping 1,200 marathons.

'Holy smokes, Martin!' I exclaimed. 'I could swear the last time I saw you, you were on about five hundred! That's just awesome!'

'Time for a Jellyatric,' I thought a mile or so later, digging the little foil parcel of jelly sweets out of my bumbag. My friends Sarah and Anthony had sent them as a good luck gift, along with a crow-shaped lapel pin, and it tickled me to think even Jelly Babies get old, in their case, very old, as the packet proclaimed they were celebrating their centenary. My running-hating training partner Beth was with me in spirit, too, and kept sending me encouraging WhatsApp voice notes: 'Hurry, hurry, chicken curry,' she chanted. 'Winner, winner, chicken dinner.'

Just then, a brilliant sign, held up by a spectator sporting a rainbow-patterned hat, caught my eye.

'Touch here: it'll turn you gay,' it read.

'Only in Brighton!' I thought. In the seven years since I'd last run a marathon here, the spectators had really upped their poster game: 'Pain is just a French word for bread,' proclaimed one; 'You've trained so hard, today is your victory lap,' read another near the distinctive onion-shaped domes of the Royal Pavilion.

The switchback section where the course cut inland towards the tiny village of Ovingdean and then returned along the same

THE FLAMINGO RISES FROM THE ASHES

road to the seafront turned into an episode of *This Is Your Life* as I kept spotting 100 Marathon Club members I'd shared many smiling miles with in the past, among them the incredible Vanessa (racking up her 414th marathon), Donna the Marathon Gypsy (who's run 195 marathons in over 30 different countries), Davey (whom I'd last seen when we attended a mutual friend's wedding midway through the Las Vegas Half Marathon) and Debbie (who'd once selflessly donated a kidney to a schoolfriend).

'Funny running into you here,' called out my pun-loving journalist friend Rose when I ran past her and her boyfriend Mark on Marine Parade near Kemptown. Seeing the flamingo poster she'd gone to the trouble of making for me saying 'Go Lisa! Just keep going!' brought a lump to my throat.

Everything went to plan until about 15 miles – not coincidentally the same distance as my longest run-walk training outing with Emma – but then the wheels came off. The Navy SEAL maxim 'the more you sweat in training, the less you bleed in battle' sprang to mind: it was patently obvious from this sudden loss of va-va voom, that I hadn't sweated – or trained – quite enough. Or, as the former FBI hostage negotiator Chris Voss put it: 'When the pressure is on, you don't rise to the occasion – you fall to your highest level of preparation.' Two lampposts of running became one, and then I ground to a full-time walk. Fortunately, another 100 Marathon Club member, Kirsty aka 'Crustie', came to the rescue by offering me plenty of entertaining catch-up chat. Brighton was her 380th marathon so I knew if I stuck with her, I'd be fine. But then, four miles later, I made the mistake of stopping to photograph a poster tied to a tree saying, 'We don't know you, but we know you are awesome', and just like that, Crustie was gone.

We were now on Hove's New Church Road, surely the world's longest, straightest suburban avenue, and I was suddenly reminded

STILL RUNNING AFTER ALL THESE TEARS

of how brutal running 26.2 miles can be, especially when the sun is blazing down. I'd experienced the ecstasy of marathon running, now it was time for the agony. Even the kids handing out sweets ('You are so sweet,' I said to a toddler proudly offering me a saucer of jellybeans, only afterwards realising what a great pun that was) and the man offering me sausage-rolls-on-a-stick couldn't mask the misery.

'It's going to be really grim from here until the finish,' I thought, gritting my teeth at the thought of still having six miles to go.

At that very moment, I was joined by a runner who'd cheered for me by name a couple of times on the switchbacks. Because his name was printed on his T-shirt, I thought he was Peter, another friendly 100 Marathon Club member I hadn't seen for many years, but it turned out that although they looked very similar, he was a different Peter entirely.

'How did you know my name?' I asked him. 'It's not on my T-shirt.'

'I listened to the audiobook version of *Your Pace or Mine?* – twice – on the treadmill during my training,' he told me.

'That's a pity, because now you already know all of my best marathon stories,' I replied.

Peter was an incredibly encouraging and engaging runner, with many a tale of his own to tell.

'We had to cancel our honeymoon when my wife Dominique was diagnosed with breast cancer,' he told me. 'That's why I'm running for Cancer Research UK.'

'I'm fundraising for Marie Curie,' I said, pointing to the back of my T-shirt where I'd printed the words: 'In honour of Graham, for Marie Curie' above a photo of Graham at the Karlovy Vary Half Marathon in the Czech Republic.

'A Marie Curie nurse cared for my dying husband one night so I could get some sanity-saving sleep.'

THE FLAMINGO RISES FROM THE ASHES

When I spied two jet-black crows sitting on the roof of a gaily painted bathing hut alongside Hove promenade, their feathers ruffled by the breeze skimming the sparkling ocean, I told Peter that Graham's spirit animal was a crow, and how much he'd supported all my dreams throughout my life.

'Your life with Graham sounds like such an amazing adventure – two kindred spirits who found each other. Lucky you!' said Peter.

When I met Peter, I was dreading every single one of the remaining miles, but with his enjoyable company those six miles magically went by. I didn't think about how hot it was, or how much the crowds had thinned out, or how achy my hip was. All I could think about was what Peter was sharing with me and that I'd soon be wearing a fabulous medal round my neck – and sleeping in it soonish, too. And then, with just a mile to go, who should pop up like a chequered flag to wave us home? Marian, the big-hearted woman who single-handedly made me fall in love with long-distance running again during the Brighton Half Marathon.

'Marian!' I cried out. 'I can't believe you've come along specially to see me finish! I almost didn't recognise you in your normal clothes.'

'I promised I'd be here to support you, so here I am! Well done you!' she said as I gave her a very sweaty hug.

Dominique was waiting for Peter at the finish and greeted me warmly. As Peter and I swapped contact details, he told me that his surname was Rooke. As in the birds. The ones that are often mistaken for crows. My skin was covered in goosebumps as it occurred to me that not only had Graham sent me a cancer thriver's husband to help me get to the finish, but he'd made sure it was someone with a very special surname so that I'd know, without a shadow of a doubt, that he was by my side.

STILL RUNNING AFTER ALL THESE TEARS

Afterwards, with my medal proudly in place around my neck, Emma, who'd waited around all day, came to congratulate me and capture the magical moment when I sprinkled the tiny pouch of Graham's ashes that I'd carried with me for 26.2 miles into the ocean. Graham had truly been with me in spirit every step of the way, and now it was time to bid farewell to another little part of him and let him know that he'd always hold a very special place in my heart.

When I look back on the 26 years I've been running, it's interesting to observe how my relationship with it has changed. As a child, running was something I utterly detested and associated with hot-faced humiliation. Then, when I took it up again as a 30-something, it became a 'hall pass' to achieve things I once thought were highly unlikely for someone like me – running a marathon and becoming a running writer and author. And then it became a way to make friends and travel the world as I chased my 100-marathon goal. Still later it became an escape from the horror of Graham's diagnosis, a way to blot out emotional pain by giving me physical pain to focus on instead. At other times it was a way to burn off the anger that threatened to consume me. My sporadic runs also afforded me time to gain clarity about our situation and gave me the courage to step back into the bare-knuckle boxing ring that was our cancer experience. It was, as my friend Nadia put it, 'a way to suspend time and take a step away from real life where nothing mattered but Graham and his journey towards dying'. Emerging from my bereavements, running became a way for me to feel like 'me' again.

THE FLAMINGO RISES FROM THE ASHES

After the 2025 Brighton Marathon, I wrote to all the people who'd sponsored me. 'On Sunday, I ran my 109th marathon in my husband Graham's honour and cried uncontrollably on the way to the start line as I was carrying a small packet of his ashes with me. Everything – and more importantly – everyone, was a reminder of why I love marathons and the running community so much.'

That final sentence neatly captures why Brighton won't, after all, be my last marathon. I have to confess, I've already entered next year's event – but going forward I'll mostly be focusing on my goal of doing 100 half marathons and embracing my dad's running philosophy, which was to run a relatively short distance almost every day. Yes, he once beat the Springbok international marathon runner Jon Lang, but when Dad stopped running competitively, he just ran for the sheer hell of it. The joy of it. One thing I know for sure is that I'm not going to let running slip from my grasp again by setting myself unrealistic targets. In the lingo of Cognitive Behavioural Therapy (CBT), I'm going to 'stop should-ing on myself'. There are no distances I 'should' be able to run: I'm going to let my Compass of Excitement be my guide. If I don't feel like doing 5km, I'll do two. Or even one. And I'll walk whenever I need or want to, just like I advised my readers 21 years ago.

Simply put, running gave me hope and purpose, and when I did it consistently, it forced me to keep moving forward. One small step at a time.

'You are such a happy bunny! Don't ever stop being one,' my darling husband Graham wrote to me in an email four months before he died. With running firmly back at the centre of my life – and all the lessons I've learned during my many journeys around the grief block – I know for sure that I have everything I need for Graham's wish to come true.

Campaigning for the Assisted Dying Bill in the Houses of Parliament

The day the Assisted Dying Bill was passed

Epilogue

🎵 **Mood music: *End of the Line* by The Traveling Wilburys**
To remind us that the line ends for all of us and that's why we need
to experience as much joy as possible along the way

Congratulations, you've nearly made it to the end of my sad book! I do hope that there were at least some smiles along the way. Before you go, here's a summary of the life lessons I've learned since Graham was diagnosed, the 'unlikely gifts' of cancer that Sophie Sabbage talks about in *The Cancer Whisperer* – and of the other challenges I faced. I've grown stronger and wiser over the past eight years, and I hope that by sharing my journey with you, you've discovered many of the tools you'll need to fearlessly navigate life's trials and tribulations – whatever they may be.

What I wish I'd known about regaining my running mojo

Forget Imposter Syndrome. Trash talking to yourself is never going to spur you into action if you've lost your running mojo. Remember, once you're a runner, you're *always* a runner – even if you haven't run for months or years. Ditch the guilt and tell yourself you were 'taking a sabbatical'. I was amazed to find that even *Jog On* author Bella Mackie, whose book has inspired thousands of people to run, has felt like a fraud because she's never run much further than 15km, checked her PB, or run a half or full marathon. Remember, running's not about time, or distance, it's about you! And if you're worried about being slow, take some advice from Bart Yasso, an inductee of the Running USA Hall of Fame: 'I often hear someone say, "I'm not a real runner."

STILL RUNNING AFTER ALL THESE TEARS

We are all runners, some just run faster than others. I never met a fake runner.'

Don't compare or you'll despair. Yes, your fitness will have headed south but you'll be amazed at how quickly it returns if you run regularly. Whatever you do, don't berate yourself for not being capable of what you were before. Instead, take stock and acknowledge that while you may no longer be able to run 5km without stopping/hit your old time targets/run marathons or ultras, you're taking the first step towards being able to do those things again.

You don't have to love running to do it. As Bryony Gordon, renowned for running the 2018 London Marathon in her underwear, writes in *Eat, Drink, Run*, 'nobody actually wants to run, unless they are quite, quite strange. Believe me when I tell you that initially, absolutely everybody feels as if they are about to die when they so much as break into a light trot. Even those people who regularly go out for jogs will tell you that they don't actually want to beforehand – the difference between those people and the rest of us is that they have realised they never regret going for one afterwards.'

Think 'baby' not 'big'. My successful comeback started with a single mile. If you set yourself a target you can easily manage, rather than one that's a daunting leap, you'll be more likely to stick with it and not throw in the towel the minute things get challenging. I used to think I wouldn't get out of bed for anything less than 5km, but now I know that going for really short runs is way better than not running at all.

Consistency is key. Run twice a week and you'll retain your fitness, up that to three times, and you'll get fitness gains. Choose a do-able, realistic training plan that features plenty of rest days, and make skipping a run matter by putting a copy of the plan on

EPILOGUE

your fridge and marking off each completed session, or using the NHS's Couch to 5K app. If you're aiming for a marathon, use a training journal such as Chris Evans's *119 Days to Go: How to Train for and Smash Your First Marathon*.

Juice up your joints. Warm-ups aren't a waste of time – they're essential as they give your joints time to produce the synovial fluid that will act as a shock absorber and lubricant by allowing the ends of your bones to move without friction. Ease yourself into every session with a five-minute walk and research dynamic stretches online (leg swings, hamstring scoops, walking lunges, squats, inchworms, high knees, butt kicks).

Remember the 'toxic ten' is a thing. Your body needs time to adapt to the stresses running puts on it, so if you're feeling horrendous at the start of a run, tell yourself that you only need to survive the first ten minutes. If you check in with yourself after 600 seconds you'll be amazed at how much better you're feeling.

Walk the walk. Walk breaks aren't for the weak, but the smart. Run-walking means you can keep going for longer, reduces your injury risk and means you'll recover from sessions more quickly.

Save the speed sessions for when you're fitter. Be cautious about including speedwork after a long lay-off as it increases your risk of injury. Run on grass and trails where possible as it's gentler on your joints.

Make every step count – and give yourself a 'medal moment'. I'm a self-confessed Medal Maniac: my impressive collection is a feature in my kitchen where it's displayed on a two-metre-long curtain pole. That's why I find The Conqueror Virtual Challenges (theconqueror.events) so rewarding – their medals, which often feature 'bits that move', are the most blingtastic out there, and have inspired me to increase my daily step count as well as go

STILL RUNNING AFTER ALL THESE TEARS

for my training runs. I've already been awarded their gorgeous Camino de Santiago medal for virtual running 480 miles across Spain and, at the time of writing, I'm currently a fifth of the way from Land's End to John O'Groats.

Use your ears to ease your aches. Distraction is the best way to swerve your attention away from any niggles or lactic acid build-up, so invest in some bone-conduction headphones (which are safer than conventional headphones as they allow you to remain aware of your surroundings) and set up a podcast playlist. On the topic of running, I love listening to *Runner's World*; *Women's Running*; *Running Commentary*; *The Running Channel* and *Band of Runners*. Non-running favourites include *How to Fail/... Date/... Write a Book* (all by Elizabeth Day); *The Life of Bryony*; *Young Again*; Mel Robbins; *The Happy Place*; *Woman's Hour*; *Desert Island Discs*; *Diary of a CEO*; *The Rest is History/Politics/Entertainment* (three different podcasts). On the subject of grief, I've found the following invaluable: *Grief Works*; *The Lessons from Loss*; *The Art of Dying Well*; *What's Your Grief* and *Terrible, Thanks for Asking*.

Buddy up. Find a running buddy, or run with a club – you'll find running with friends always puts smiles into the miles and will ensure you run, whatever the weather or no matter how lazy you're feeling. Always try to think of a story you can't wait to tell your running companions: one of my most memorable was the time when, while preparing veggies for my air fryer, I held my new oil sprayer the wrong way round and inadvertently gave myself an olive oil mini-facial.

There's no such thing as a bad run, only a bad attitude. Get out there, do what you can and make for home, even if you have to cut a run short. Graham loved to paraphrase Voltaire with, 'Don't let the perfect be the enemy of the good,' reminding me to

EPILOGUE

prioritise progress over perfection and embrace a 'good enough' mindset.

Don't skip the stretches. Like elastic bands, when muscles are warm, they're more flexible. Stretching after a run can accelerate recovery, improve your muscles' range of motion and reduce post-run muscle and joint soreness. You'll find plenty of inspiration online.

Find your own 'why'. Whether it's to boost your health, stave off cancer or Alzheimer's, train for an event in aid of a charity, or to give yourself headspace, me-time, stress relief or a sense of control or achievement, keep reminding yourself *why* you run – and remember, it really doesn't have to be all about achieving PBs. Oh, and never forget that according to one 2017 study, a single one-hour run may add an additional seven hours to your life, and that people who run tend to live about three years longer than those who don't. By running regularly, you can increase both the quality *and* quantity of your life.

Use self-hypnosis to turbo-charge your motivation before a run. Simply close your eyes and breathe yourself into a hypnotic state by slowly counting down from ten to one and focusing on relaxing your entire body with each exhalation. Next imagine your ideal training run, one in which everything feels effortless and running feels like pure, unadulterated joy. Fully experience the exhilaration of movement using all of your senses: feel the wind playfully tousling your hair, hear the rhythmic sound of your footfalls, smell the crisp freshness of the air and visualise the fallen leaves underfoot or the neighbourhood you're passing through. Now focus on the 'why' of your run for a few seconds (see above). Finally imagine how incredibly invigorated – and smug – you're going to feel post-run, a feeling that's going to last for the rest of the day. When you're done, open your eyes and set off on your run.

STILL RUNNING AFTER ALL THESE TEARS

Reward yourself after every training session. My Dad adored his post-run ice-cold can of beer whereas I favour copious amounts of tea. Fill your kettle before you head out, so you can speedily make yourself a steaming hug in a mug when you get back.

Enter races or attend parkrun. Races can feel intimidating, but once you're there, you'll remember how energising, exciting and downright exhilarating it can be to run with other people. Remember that parkrun not only has tailwalkers who're tasked with bringing up the rear, but has introduced parkwalkers, too, after a 2022 survey found that some people still didn't feel comfortable attending if they weren't running. The volunteer role of parkwalker involves walking the entire route (in front of the tailwalker) to encourage other walkers. So if you're keen to start running again, but don't think you can manage 5km quite yet, it's now perfectly acceptable to walk the whole way at these free, weekly timed events held in parks around the UK and abroad.

Book recommendations

- *How to Run a Marathon* by **Vassos Alexander.** Written by the most enthusiastic runner you're ever likely to meet, this book has it all: inspiring stories and marathon exploits around the world, plus training tips and plans.
- *Marathon Woman* by **Kathrine Switzer.** Part memoir, part historical document, part love story, it's my all-time favourite running book.
- *Running Made Easy* by **Lisa Jackson and Susie Whalley.** The most beginner-friendly running book on the block (even if I do say so myself!), *RME* will teach you the '60-second secret': how you can build up to doing 5km by interspersing walk breaks with running for a minute at a time.
- *Your Pace or Mine?* by **Lisa Jackson,** yours truly, who's come last in 25 marathons.

EPILOGUE

- *The Courage to Start* by John 'The Penguin' Bingham. How John, a smokin', drinkin', overeatin' non exerciser like me became a waddling marathon runner and beloved *Runner's World* columnist.

- *Atomic Habits* by James Clear. The book that teaches you how to get one per cent better – at anything, including running – every day. I'd also suggest signing up for Clear's super-brief 3-2-1 newsletter, which claims it's 'the most wisdom per word of any newsletter on the web'.

- *One Small Step* by Paul Sinton-Hewitt. The fascinating – and by turns heartbreaking and hope-inspiring – story of parkrun by the visionary man who founded it.

- *The Ultimate Guide to parkrun* by Lucy Waterlow. Everything you need to know, from how parkrun started to how you can get involved, plus real-life stories from those whose lives – and health – it has transformed.

- *Eat, Drink, Run* by Bryony Gordon. The hilarious account of how a woman with 'boobs like beach balls' ran the London Marathon to prove that 'overweight, imperfect people can do exercise, too'.

- *Jog On* by Bella Mackie. This memoir by a journalist battling crippling anxiety and depression is the most useful – and well-researched – book I've read on how and why running boosts mental health.

- *There Is No Wall* by Allie Bailey. To quote ultra-legend Damian Hall's endorsement, this is 'a bum-squirmingly honest, heartbreaking, brave, funny... stealth-help book'.

- *26.2 Miles to Happiness* by Paul Tonkinson. The comedian and *Running Commentary* podcaster's moving account of what it takes to run a sub-three-hour marathon – and his incredibly sad reason for wanting to do it.

- *Wild Running* and *Short Runs in Beautiful Places* by Jen and Sim Benson. Two inspiring books by a couple of avid adventurers that are guaranteed to make you fall in love with trail running.

STILL RUNNING AFTER ALL THESE TEARS

- *Dead Man Running* by Kevin Webber. How Kevin used running to beat his 'two years to live' prostate-cancer prognosis and live his best life.
- *Run Mummy Run* by Leanne Davies and Lucy Waterlow. A fantastic beginner-friendly book on how to fit running around family life co-authored by Leanne Davies, the founder of Run Mummy Run, a supportive, super-friendly online running community for women (you don't have to be a mum to join!).
- *In It for the Long Run* and *We Can't Run Away From This: Racing to Improve Running's Footprint in our Climate Emergency* by Damian Hall. Anyone who ran his first marathon dressed as a toilet gets my vote of approval, and when it's someone who writes as well as fellow *Runner's World* columnist, ultrarunning legend and The Green Runners co-founder Damian, you know you're in for a great read.
- *The Power Within* by Sophie Power. Written by someone who came second to last in her school cross country, this is the incredible story of the breast-feeding ultrarunner's world records, her campaign to make races more female-friendly, and how running truly is her superpower in life's toughest moments.
- *Lore of Running* by Tim Noakes. History, advice and science all in one very readable, enormous tome!
- *When Running Made History* by Roger Robinson. Funny, heart-warming, informative and thought-provoking, this is a compelling account of our sport and the way it has shaped and changed lives – from a front-row seat.
- *Run Well* by Dr Juliet McGrattan. An accessible, incredibly well-researched book written by a keen runner and former GP that brilliantly answers the most common health questions runners ask.
- *119 Days to Go: How to Train for and Smash Your First Marathon* by Chris Evans. A training log like no other, it's part Gratitude Journal, part cheerleader, part funny, wise-cracking

EPILOGUE

Wisdom Dispenser, and makes the marathon distance feel distinctly do-able.

- *Ultra Women: The Trailblazers Defying Sexism in Sport* by **Lily Canter and Emma Wilkinson**. An inspiring insight into the world's toughest endurance challenges and the incredible women who participate in them.
- *The Path She Runs* by **Jen Benson**. A fascinating exploration of the science, stories and history of women's ultrarunning, alongside the author's journey to running her first 100-mile race.
- *The Pants of Perspective* and *Barefoot Britain* by **Anna McNuff**. Join the fearless force-of-nature adventurer as she runs 3,000km through the wilds of New Zealand and then makes her way from the Shetland Islands to London – barefoot!
- *Just Run* by **Merili Freear**. This book reminded me that running isn't just about the miles, the pace or PBs, it's about the messy, funny, humbling moments in between.
- **Websites:** parkrun.org.uk; 5kyourway.org; runnersworld.com/uk; womensrunning.co.uk; thegreenrunners.com; facebook.com/groups/runmummyrun
- **Films and TV series:** *Brittany Runs a Marathon*; *Run Fatboy Run*; *Chariots of Fire*; *Free to Run*; *Forrest Gump*; *Unbroken*; *Lorena: Light-footed Woman*; *The Finisher: Jasmin Paris and the Barkley Marathons*; *Spine*; *Dragon's Back Race*; *Skid Row Marathon*; *The Unknown Runner*; *Totally FKT*; *Sprint* (TV series)

What I wish I'd known about living with a cancer diagnosis

Don't feel you need to comfort people to whom you've broken bad news. Graham and I were the ones in need of reassurance, but we often found ourselves comforting people who'd reacted badly to the news of his terminal diagnosis. Now, whenever I'm told upsetting news, I remember it's not about me, and save my tears for when I'm alone.

Expect the unexpected. Graham's cancer journey had more unexpected twists and turns than a Chessington World of Adventures rollercoaster, but we dealt with each setback by doing research, seeking out expert advice and discussing things with Prof Hope.

Remember how beneficial it is to stay active. Not only does moving boost mental health and combat fatigue but it helps people cope better with the side effects of chemo and radiotherapy. But, and it's a big but, there are many people undergoing cancer treatment who, like my runner friend Jackie, simply can't exercise, no matter how much they want to. 'It's not always an excuse, it's just sometimes impossible,' she told me. So be compassionate with yourself and don't feel guilty: if you can only manage a little walk round the block or to the post box that's fine. Do as much as you can.

Be kind to yourself. Again, my friend Jackie had this to say: 'The advice from many is that whatever gets you through – running or not, box sets, eating chocolate – is allowed. Frankly, during chemo and radiotherapy, all bets are off as it's not for ever.' As a cancer thriver's wife, fistfuls of Beacon milk chocolate marshmallow Easter eggs got me through a particularly challenging patch early on: yes, I wish my 'drug of choice' had been running, but at the time, only South African chocolate would do.

Realise that the cancer world is full of snake-oil salesmen. To this day I swear I have PTSD from ploughing through impenetrable books promising miracle cancer cures and trying to figure out why a nutritionist we consulted had suggested we take sackloads of supplements, some of which were prescribed in dangerously high doses or were contraindicated for the meds

EPILOGUE

Graham was on. Be wary of forums where you get cancelled for daring to ask questions. And before trusting someone, do an internet search of their name followed by 'fraud', 'scam' or 'controversy' – you'll often discover that so-called experts have 'knowledge' of a subject, rather than 'qualifications' in it, much as I could claim to be a theoretical physicist just by having read *A Brief History of Time*. Even in some of the books I've recommended, there are things that just don't sit right with me, so please don't take them as gospel: keep questioning and researching everything thoroughly before making decisions. For example, John of God, a Brazilian self-proclaimed medium and psychic surgeon, is unfortunately mentioned in *Radical Remission* – he was also featured in *Oprah's Next Chapter* but is now jailed for life after multiple claims of sexual abuse. Several books I bought made me feel uneasy, so I got rid of them. Trust your gut. The Netflix series *Apple Cider Vinegar* is a cautionary tale I think everyone with cancer should watch as it will help you become aware of the dangers of blindly following 'cancer influencers' – but also accurately portrays the kind of blunt, non-compassionate oncologist that drives people with cancer to seek out help elsewhere.

Ask if you can have chemo at home. According to Cancer Research UK, this is possible if you're taking tablets or capsules, your hospital or private healthcare company has home-care chemo nurses or you're having low-dose, continuous chemo through a pump that you can wear at home. Even if you can't have chemo at home, plan little treats: I always changed our sheets on chemo days so Graham would have a fresh bed to come home to; my friend Cynthia bought new shoes at the end of each treatment cycle.

Consider fasting during chemo. Some studies show fasting might protect healthy cells from chemotherapy, make cancer cells more vulnerable to chemo, and could reduce chemo side effects such as fatigue. Be aware that it can also lead to malnutrition and muscle loss. Prof Hope recommended it, but Cancer Research UK doesn't, advising that it 'may be harmful if you have other health problems like diabetes, heart disease and weight loss or low weight', so do your own research, and if you decide to do it, do so under medical supervision.

Don't feel obliged to do penance and put on a scratchy hair shirt when it comes to your diet. Many cancer thrivers will do absolutely anything to aid their recovery and start cutting out entire food groups and eating weird foods. We initially tried brewing our own kefir, daily juicing and going vegan, but in the end, we decided it was more important to enjoy life – and our meals – as all of this was just too time-consuming and I'm a hopeless vegan cook. Our diet was really healthy anyway, as most of our meals were packed with veggies and salad, but we made sure we limited foods high in sugar, saturated fat and salt. We also reduced our intake of processed and red meat, as they can increase bowel-cancer risk, and upped our intake of turmeric (taken with black pepper to aid absorption) as it has an anti-inflammatory effect and Cancer Research UK says 'there is some evidence that curcumin, a substance in turmeric, can kill cancer cells in certain cancers'. See bit.ly/42I0Lou for Cancer Research UK's dietary guidance.

Don't ignore certain chemo side effects as they can indicate a life-threatening illness (sepsis) or blood clot. Graham's chemo had so many side effects that if we'd called up his medical team every time he experienced one, we'd have been on the phone 24 hours a day. These are the side effects, according to Cancer Research UK, that you really do need to respond to urgently: feeling generally unwell and not able to get out of bed; a change

EPILOGUE

in your temperature – 37.5°C or higher or below 36°C (buy a good-quality thermometer); flu-like symptoms; coughing up green phlegm; a sore throat or mouth or painful tooth; peeing a lot or pain when peeing or having cloudy or foul-smelling pee; diarrhoea; skin changes; a fast heartbeat; feeling dizzy or faint; vomiting; a headache; pain, redness, discharge, swelling or heat at the site of a wound or intravenous line; pain anywhere in your body that wasn't there before your treatment.

Accept that not all 'help' is helpful. Gifts of food and chocolate were what we were most thankful for, along with thoughtful care parcels containing feel-good goodies such as novelty socks and fluffy blankets. Constant requests for updates on medical appointments, often just when we'd emerged from hugely upsetting ones, sometimes made us feel more stressed than our many battles with the medics ('I'm not Reuters!' I once exclaimed. 'When we come out of those medical appointments we feel as if we've been run over by a bus. Please can you give us the chance to process everything first before we have to broadcast the latest?'). Setting up a WhatsApp group can be a useful way to update everyone with a single message, rather than having to repeat often upsetting news over and over again.

Say something. If you have a loved one or friend going through a hard time, saying or writing something is always better than doing nothing, even if you don't know what to say. Even a simple 'Thinking of you and sending love' is enough. What I craved most was the chance to speak to my friends in real time, rather than via WhatsApp message – most of them worked full time, so it was difficult finding convenient times to speak, but when we did, it was immensely helpful. I found it challenging and draining listening to stories of how others' relatives had died or undergone cancer treatment, though I sometimes learned very useful information this way. What I really wanted was for people to listen to what Graham and I were going through, and to talk about things other than cancer. I also appreciated other people asking how I was coping occasionally, as often people only asked after Graham.

Use the words 'No need to reply' to take the pressure off. We appreciated every supportive card, text and email we received, and included them in our Positivity Book, but sometimes the need to respond felt like a burden – yet another thing on our to-do list when there were days I was so busy caring for Graham that I didn't have time to take a shower. Being told we were in people's thoughts but that they didn't expect a reply really helped and I always do this now whenever I message someone who's going through a difficult time.

Book recommendations

- *The Cancer Whisperer* by **Sophie Sabbage.** The heart-warming story of a fearless cancer thriver, this book also gave us many practical tips including how to deal with medical professionals and loved ones wanting to help.
- *Surviving Mesothelioma and Other Cancers* by **Paul Kraus.** Written by a long-term mesothelioma survivor, this book's holistic approach encouraged us to live in the present, overhaul our diet, heal our emotions and love, laugh, exercise and meditate regularly.
- *Not That Kind of Love* by **Clare Wise and Greg Wise.** A funny, touching tale of sibling love and loss, this book charts both Clare's journey through breast cancer and her brother Greg's role as her 24/7 caregiver.
- *Do No Harm* by **Henry Marsh.** A brutally honest account of working as a neurosurgeon in an often-chaotic hospital

EPILOGUE

environment, this book gave me an insight into the pressures doctors face and the agonising decisions they have to make.

- *When Breath Becomes Air* by **Paul Kalanithi**. The story of a neurosurgeon's transformation from brilliant doctor to lung cancer patient at the age of 36.
- *The Emperor of All Maladies* by **Siddhartha Mukherjee**. Winner of the 2011 Pulitzer Prize for Non-fiction, this book bills itself as 'a biography of cancer' and examines the history of the disease and the desperate battle to cure it.
- *How Not to Die* by **Dr Michael Greger**. A highly readable, science-based guide to the foods proven to prevent and reverse disease.
- Websites: cancerresearchuk.org; macmillan.org.uk
- Films & TV series that will help you understand what cancer patients experience: *The Cancer Conflict*; *Apple Cider Vinegar*; *50/50*; *The Fault in our Stars*; *My Oxford Year*; *Living*; *Wit*; *Me and Earl and the Dying Girl*; *The Bucket List*; *Love Story*; *Shadowlands*; *Terms of Endearment*; *My Sister's Keeper*; *Firefly Lane* (TV series)

What I wish I'd known about living in hope, not fear

Don't leave anything unsaid. Very soon after Graham's diagnosis we went away for a weekend to agree on our approach to treatment, and have full and frank discussions about our relationship and our priorities. We used the questions in the '6 Steps to Healing Yourself' chapter of *Mind Over Medicine* (see below) as prompts to unburden ourselves and find closure and forgiveness about past hurts. It also gave us the chance to reaffirm our love for each other, meaning that when Graham died, neither of us had any regrets as everything that needed to be said had been said.

STILL RUNNING AFTER ALL THESE TEARS

Find joy and contentment in the simple, often overlooked, everyday things. As the author Robert Brault once wrote: 'Enjoy the little things, for one day you may look back and realise they were the big things.'

Use the STOP/Whack-a-Mole and Waterfall Techniques. The 'thought-and-emotion management' tools I wrote about in Chapter 7 are tricky to master and take lots of practice, but they really do work.

Make time for fun. Remember that laughter really is the best medicine. We regularly took ourselves off to the Banana Cabaret comedy club in Balham where for two hours cancer didn't exist and we laughed until we wept happy tears.

Distraction can and does work. Not always, and perhaps not for long, but it does. Try books, box sets or chatting and laughing with other people. An art lesson, where our only thoughts were 'What colours do I mix to make brown/purple/pink?' made us forget about cancer for two hours.

Add 'but luckily…' to the end of a negative statement to shift your focus towards the positive. If you're facing a distressing situation, whether that's a death, redundancy or divorce, this technique is a game-changer. 'I'm devastated that I'm going to lose Graham,' I told myself, '*but luckily…* we've spent most of our adult lives together – very few people are fortunate enough to do that.'

Breathe yourself calmer. If you've had upsetting news, try breathing in through your nose for a count of four, pausing briefly, and then breathing out for a count of eight. Even three of these can quieten your stress response.

Don't feel obliged to join support groups or online forums. I very soon came to the conclusion that Graham and I would be the most positive people in any group we attended, and feared that I'd end up thinking I'd have to support and encourage others, as well

EPILOGUE

as Graham, which I didn't feel strong enough to do. I also didn't want to be given advance notice of how Graham's illness would play out, or grieve those who'd died before him. I did join Inspire (inspire.com), an American health forum, but only read the posts where lung-cancer patients had survived for many years.

Stay in the now. Cancer journeys are like marathons. In other words, you need to run the mile you're in. This means living in the present – and dealing with cold, hard *facts* – rather than catastrophising and dreading things that might never happen. Two of my greatest fears were seeing Graham in an oxygen mask and witnessing him suffocating to death, neither of which happened. In the event, Graham's cancer spread to his brain. This is a remote possibility in mesothelioma, and so we didn't give it a second thought until it actually happened, sparing ourselves four years of anguish in the process. Likewise with Prof Hope saying Graham's cancer had spread to his oesophagus and diaphragm – I took a mental note of that but didn't allow myself to speculate that Graham might eventually not be able to eat or breathe.

Stay as active as you can to help ward off depression. In a 2017 American study of almost 34,000 people with no symptoms of mental-health issues, those who did no activity were 44 per cent more likely to experience depression than those exercising for one to two hours per week. In 12 per cent of cases, if the participants had done just *one hour* of exercise *a week*, the research suggested that depression could have been averted. The take-out message here: you don't have to run yourself into the ground, or even run all that regularly, to help prevent depression.

Book recommendations

 Radical Remission by **Kelly A Turner.** My inspiration for our 'marginal gains' approach. By studying over 1,500 cases of radical remission – where people recovered from cancer either without using conventional medicine, or after it had failed – Kelly came up with nine factors all of the cases had in common. She found they had strong reasons for living; had radically changed their diet; had taken control of their health; had followed their intuition; had used herbs and supplements; had released suppressed emotions and increased positive ones; had embraced social support and had deepened their spiritual connection.

- *Mind Over Medicine* by **Dr Lissa Rankin.** Graham's favourite cancer book explores how trauma and our emotions can make us ill, and how we can use our mind to help us heal. Dr Rankin, herself a medical practitioner, also offers the most wonderful advice I've ever read on how medics can communicate honestly with their patients without depriving them of hope.

- *Love, Medicine and Miracles* by **Dr Bernie Siegel.** Dr Siegel, a former paediatric surgeon, emphasises how important it is for doctors to treat their cancer patients holistically, and with empathy.

- *And Finally* by **Henry Marsh.** A retired neurosurgeon navigates the bewildering journey from doctor to patient when he's diagnosed with advanced prostate cancer. Henry also makes an impassioned argument in favour of assisted dying.

- *Friendaholic: Confessions of a Friendship Addict* by **Elizabeth Day.** A life-changing examination of the joys of friendship with one key message: value quality rather than quantity.

- *The Joy of Small Things* by **Hannah Jane Parkinson.** From buying new trainers to the runner's high and clean bedding, this book celebrates 108 'through leaves' experiences the author describes as 'pockets of pleasure' in her everyday life.

- *The Comfort Book* by **Matt Haig.** Each uplifting page is the equivalent of getting a 30-second hug.

EPILOGUE

- *The Art of Not Falling Apart* by Christina Patterson. Funny, uplifting and informative, this book explores how the author – and those she interviewed – managed to bounce back after devastating life events, including redundancy and breast cancer, that threatened to drag them under.
- Websites and newsletters: heartleap.substack.com; melrobbins.com/newsletter; theredhandfiles.com
- Funny and distracting TV series: *Cunk on Earth/Life/Britain/Christmas*; *Mandy*; *Grace & Frankie*; *This Is Us* (my all-time favourite American TV series); *Motherland*; *First Dates*; *Gogglebox*; *Peep Show*; *Below Deck*; *Fresh Meat*; *Schitt's Creek*; *Parenthood*; *The Change*; *Colin from Accounts*; *Fisk*; *Derry Girls*; *Kath & Kim*; *The Inbetweeners*; *Extraordinary*; *Ted Lasso*; *Big Bang Theory*; *Austin*; *Shrinking*; *The Morning Show*; *Ugly Betty*; *Detectorists*; *Emily in Paris*; *Superstore*; *And Just Like That...*; and *Sex and the City*
- Funny, uplifting and distracting films: *Central Intelligence*; *The Castle*; *The Peanut Butter Falcon*; *Little Miss Sunshine*; *The Shawshank Redemption*; *Cool Runnings*; *The Dish*; *Eddie the Eagle*; *Spy*; almost any film starring Will Ferrell, such as *Elf*, *Anchorman: The Legend of Ron Burgundy*, *Eurovision Song Contest: The Story of Fire Saga*; almost any film starring Ben Stiller, such as *Zoolander*, *Meet the Parents*, *Blades of Glory*; all of the Bond and Jason Bourne films

What I wish I'd known about dealing with medical professionals

You can't be a passenger in the back, get in the driving seat. Cancer tends to make patients and their loved ones feel powerless so it's vital not to hand over all your power to your doctors, no matter how much you trust or like them. Instead, become an equal partner in your treatment plan by researching all your options and be thoroughly prepared with a list of questions before every appointment. This means you won't regret decisions because you'll have been fully informed when you made them. We had one chance to make the right choice about Graham's surgery, and we aced it. There wasn't much Graham could control about his illness, but the things he could – such as eating well, running and taking supplements – he did. Day in, day out.

Make audio recordings and take notes at all medical appointments. We found ourselves in a state of shock and unable to think straight at appointments, so the recordings were invaluable when we had to make difficult treatment decisions, and also proved useful when I wrote letters of complaint. You're fully within your rights to do so, though it's only polite to ask permission first.

Never, ever be too embarrassed to ask for a second opinion. If we hadn't done so, we'd never have met the doctor who became not only Graham's surgeon but our CMC (chief medical cheerleader). And don't hesitate to question medical staff if what they're saying doesn't make sense – keep asking until it does.

It's incredibly helpful to work as a team, if you can. Graham signed all his letters to his doctors 'Warm regards, Graham and Lisa' which let them know that we took decisions jointly and made me feel that he valued my opinion. He wrote in our Positivity Book: 'Lisa guides me and educates me, but she does not force me. The decisions are ours, rather than mine or hers alone. This is how it needs to be, and this is the most beautiful and soothing and yes, inspirational thing.'

No one cares about your loved one more than you do, so keep a close eye on their caregivers and speak up when you notice something's amiss. When Graham had surgery, the nurses, who in every other aspect were amazing, forgot to give him a prescribed

EPILOGUE

nebuliser and also didn't plug his drain back in overnight. Mistakes are made and you'll never have a more important role in life than advocating for a loved one when they're vulnerable and can't speak for themselves.

Find doctors you can trust. If you can't trust your doctor, it's 'intolerable', wrote the renowned neurosurgeon Henry Marsh in his book *And Finally* when he himself was diagnosed with terminal prostate cancer. Many people on cancer forums admit to lying to their oncologists – this can be very dangerous as, for example, taking antioxidant supplements may interfere with the effectiveness of chemo by protecting cancer cells as well as healthy ones. Despite what I've written about some doctors in this book, there are many truly wonderful, caring, compassionate, highly talented doctors out there – make it your mission to locate them. In the UK, you have the legal right to choose which hospital you go to and are also able to choose which consultant-led team will be in charge of your treatment. See the NHS's overview at bit.ly/42UnQmo for more on this.

Keep an updated list of medications and their dosages on your phone. It will save you a lot of time and stress at appointments, especially if prescriptions and doses keep changing.

Take the time to write letters of complaint, if you feel you need to. It can help you process what happened and will hopefully ensure better care for future patients. Gather all the evidence you have – notes you took and the emails and WhatsApp messages you sent to the clinicians and friends or relatives – and put them into bullet points under specific headings such as 'Medication administration errors' or 'Concerns regarding X's professional behaviour'. Double check the dates when things happened, and your facts, as you don't want to undermine the accuracy of your complaint by making errors that can easily be disproved by those you're complaining about. Then get someone to read through your letter, paying particular attention to its tone, so that it comes across as rational and objective rather than an emotional rant.

Be clear about the outcomes you want: do you want the staff to be informed about their errors and held to account? Are you seeking an apology? Do you want to try to avoid others having similar experiences? Keep your expectations realistic and prepare yourself for both positive and negative outcomes. If you decide to pursue legal action, make sure you will be able to cope with the process. In a grief webinar I attended, the psychotherapist Julia Samuel cautioned that taking caregivers to court can often lead to 'complicated grief' (when strong feelings have a significant impact on your daily life for more than 12 months after a bereavement), so carefully consider whether you're really prepared, or in the right place emotionally, to spend several years fighting a court case you may very well lose. Even if you just make a complaint and get the brush-off, you can sleep well at night knowing that you've raised a concern. It may well go in a file somewhere and, if others make the same complaint, may be used to build a case. At the very least, even if staff are exonerated, hopefully you will have made them reflect on their actions.

Take the time to write letters of thanks. Caring is a tough job, so it was important for me to let Graham's caregivers know how much they'd been appreciated by writing them thank-you cards and sending them gifts. The handmade card I received from Graham's district nurses and the home-made doughnuts Morine, Graham's carer, gave me in response to my gestures touched me deeply and brought me great comfort.

EPILOGUE

What I wish I'd known about palliative care and dying

Make getting your affairs in order your first priority.

Write a Living Will – also known as an Advance Decision – which is a legal document that specifies what medical treatments you would like to refuse in the future (such as mechanical ventilation, CPR, antibiotics and artificial feeding and hydration) should you become unable to communicate or make decisions yourself. It also allows you to state the circumstances in which you'd want to refuse these treatments. A Living Will differs from a Lasting Power of Attorney (LPA) for health and welfare (see below), which appoints someone called an attorney to make broader health and care decisions on your behalf if you're no longer capable. A Living Will is legally binding in the UK (and plays an important role in decision-making in Scotland) if it meets certain criteria, and it takes precedence over decisions made in your best interests by other people. Compassion in Dying (cdn.compassionindying.org.uk) provides clear guidance and has a downloadable form (it's free to set one up, but it does need to be signed and witnessed).

Set up Lasting Power of Attorneys – one regarding how you'd like to be treated if you became seriously ill and were unable to make your own treatment decisions, and the other how you'd like your finances to be handled. It takes a bit of admin effort, but once it's done, it gives you incredible peace of mind. You can write and register them cheaply and easily yourself at gov.uk/power-of-attorney (for England and Wales), mygov.scot/power-of-attorney (for Scotland, where they're known as Power of Attorneys) and nidirect.gov.uk (for Northern Ireland, where they're known as Enduring Power of Attorneys). There's no need to use a lawyer.

STILL RUNNING AFTER ALL THESE TEARS

Don't put off writing a will. Many charities offer free will-writing services without insisting that you leave them a legacy, though doing so – even a small one – is a lovely gesture of gratitude if you can afford it.

Learn as much as you can from your partner. Some people jokingly call this 'widow/er training' but it really can be useful when your loved one's gone. Graham had taught me how to hang pictures on my own, but there were many other things, such as getting the car taxed and MOT'd and inflating the tyres that I hadn't a clue about which caused me untold stress.

Make a note of the passwords to everything from your laptop, iPad and mobile phone to your bank accounts and investments and keep this somewhere safe or encrypt the information: Which? recommends Bitwarden, which is free and can sync across an unlimited number of devices, as well as paid-for options such as Dashlane and 1Password. Also make sure your loved ones and Executor/s know where all important documents are filed. If you have online accounts and social media, and store photos, videos, music and other media on digital devices, you may want to plan what happens to these accounts after you die. The Digital Legacy Association (digitallegacyassociation.org) has very useful, free-to-access materials (including a Social Media Will template), tutorials and support.

Don't avoid discussing palliative care. I used to abhor the term 'palliative care' as whenever anyone mentioned it to me I associated it with 'dying', because I didn't understand its true aims: improving the quality of life of terminally ill patients by preventing and relieving suffering. I now wish I'd had the courage to properly discuss Graham's end-of-life care with him as I wasn't always 100 per cent certain of his wishes or what was important to him. In *Being Mortal*, Atul Gawande cites a 2010 study from Massachusetts General Hospital where all of the patients with

EPILOGUE

stage four lung cancer received standard oncology care but half of them also saw a palliative care specialist who discussed their goals and priorities for if and when their condition worsened. The result? The second group 'stopped chemotherapy sooner, entered hospice far earlier, experienced less suffering at the end of their lives – *and they lived 25 per cent longer*. In other words, our decision making in medicine has failed so spectacularly that we have reached the point of actively inflicting harm on patients rather than confronting the subject of mortality. If end-of-life discussions were an experimental drug, the FDA would approve it.' Atul goes on to provide a brilliant question to ask someone who's terminally ill that is direct but not blunt: 'If time becomes short, what is most important to you?'

For help with end-of-life discussion with loved ones, visit The Conversation Project (theconversationproject.org), an American initiative that believes it's important to start having these conversations at the kitchen table – not in the intensive-care ward or hospice. The Conversation Starter Guide is a free resource to help guide you through the process. Marie Curie also has a very useful guide to planning ahead: mariecurie.org.uk/information/planning-ahead.

Have a discussion about assisted dying. If this option is legal where you live, talk about it as soon as you can, to avoid you or a loved one dying in pain. Even with the best palliative care, some dying people experience severe pain and other symptoms (according to the campaign group Dignity in Dying, 17 people with a terminal illness will die in pain every day in the UK, even with the best palliative care, showing that 6,394 people a year would have no effective relief of their pain in the final three months of their life). This is why I'm strongly in favour of assisted dying. As I, and many others, believe, assisted dying is not about ending life, it's about shortening death.

STILL RUNNING AFTER ALL THESE TEARS

Going to Dignitas to end your life costs an average of £15,000 and you may need to do so much earlier than you want or need to because you have to be well enough to fly to Switzerland for the procedure. According to the UK campaign group My Death, My Decision, in Oregon, US, where assisted dying is legal, 'on average a third of people approved for assisted deaths decide not to take their life-ending medication. In most cases, that's because having the security of knowing they can end their suffering if it ever became too much to bear is enough.'

Remember, in the UK you have the right to die at home. Palliative care is not limited to a hospice, hospital or care-home setting. According to the NHS, 'People who are approaching the end of their life are entitled to high-quality care, wherever they're being cared for.' The health and social care professionals looking after you or your loved one (your hospital/hospice team, district nurse, specialist nurse, care-home staff or GP) can refer you, and the service is free of charge. The end-of-life charity Marie Curie can help with this. According to Rachel Clarke's *Dear Life*, 'only one in five of us will die at home, despite two thirds of us expressing the wish to do so.' If this is your loved one's wish, I'd strongly suggest doing whatever you can to make it happen to avoid regret down the line, though for some people it may not be possible due to emergency admission or their care needs.

There's no need to go it alone. I had only the vaguest idea of what the end-of-life charity Marie Curie does until two of its nurses cared for Graham. If you're living with a terminal illness or have been affected by dying, death or bereavement, Marie Curie can help. Visit mariecurie.org.uk or call the free Support Line on 0800 090 2309 or email support@mariecurie.org.uk.

EPILOGUE

Book recommendations

- *Dear Life* by Rachel Clarke. Written by a wonderfully caring palliative care doctor whose own GP father was diagnosed with terminal cancer, this very personal and profound memoir demystifies dying and death.
- *With the End in Mind* by Kathryn Mannix. A brilliant explanation of the dying process and the lessons we can learn from the dying.
- *Being Mortal* by Atul Gawande. In this moving book the surgeon not only explores the death of his own father but shines a light on what ageing entails, revealing that it's not just about illness and decline, but can also be a time of putting things into perspective and concentrating on what's *really* important in life. Atul also has some profound things to say about end-of-life care.
- Websites: mariecurie.org.uk; mydeath-mydecision.org.uk; compassionindying.org.uk; dyingmatters.org; hospiceuk.org (it has a Hospice Care Finder); goodfuneralguide.co.uk; dignityindying.org.uk; artofdyingwell.org; deathcafe.com; mydeath-mydecision.org.uk; theswitzerlandalternative.com; digitallegacyassociation.org; lifecircle.ch; dignitas.ch
- Films and TV programmes: *Endgame*; *The Room Next Door*; *The Farewell*; *Extremis*; *You Don't Know Jack*; *Prue and Danny's Death Road Trip*; *Me Before You*; *Euphoria* starring Eva Green and Alicia Vikander

STILL RUNNING AFTER ALL THESE TEARS

What I wish I'd known about death

Educate yourself about the dying process long before you need to so you won't be ill-prepared and anxious when it happens. This knowledge will help you understand that, like birth, dying has recognisable stages. Both Kathryn Mannix's *With the End in Mind* and Rachel Clarke's *Dear Life* have detailed, but gently explained, information on what to expect. The podcast *The Art of Dying Well* is also a very useful resource.

I've attended two natural births, and after Graham died it struck me how similar birth and death are. All of us are guaranteed to experience both and yet they're often shrouded in mystery and inaccurately portrayed on screen. In the movies, both are usually depicted as rapid and dramatic. In reality, both can often take a lot longer than expected and be surprisingly calm. Babies, especially ones whose parents have taken hypnobirthing classes, can slip into the world just as beautifully as my dad departed it. Kathryn Mannix makes a similar observation in her book: 'We know what the processes of both birth and death look like when they are proceeding smoothly – clear phases, predictable progression, needing companionship and encouragement but not interference... We also know when extra action is needed – when should the midwife ask the mother to push, or pant and wait?... Likewise, our skilled and experienced nurses know when to summon a family, when to offer pain relief or treat anxiety, when simply to reassure that all is normal, that the dying is progressing as it should.'

A 'death rattle', which can be distressing for loved ones to hear, is a normal part of the dying process. In the last days of someone's life, saliva and mucous may accumulate in their

EPILOGUE

mouth and throat which can cause a gurgling or rasping sound when they breathe. This occurs because they can no longer cough to expel the fluid. It's sometimes possible to dry up these secretions using medications, or by repositioning the patient. See mariecurie.org.uk/information/symptoms/noisy-chest-secretions for more on this.

Consider saving nine lives by becoming an organ donor. According to the NHS, a single organ donor can save up to nine lives by donating their organs and tissues, but organ donation will only go ahead with the support of your family, so it's a conversation worth having with your next of kin or loved ones. In the UK, most adults over 18 (and most people over 16 in Scotland) must opt out of organ donation, rather than opt in. However, organ donors do need to die in hospital. See organdonation.nhs.uk.

Realise that a body deteriorates really quickly after death. If you want to keep the body of a loved one at home for quite some time, like I did, or you want to bring their body home from the hospital or hospice – which you're legally entitled to do – you need to keep it cool using reusable freezer blocks (see goodfuneralguide.co.uk).

Don't step inside a funeral home if you don't want to. Most funeral directors will be willing to arrange details by phone or pay you a home visit. And your loved one's ashes can be delivered to your home.

Plan the funeral you want. Direct cremation is a much cheaper option than cremations that include a funeral ceremony. You may also want to consider eco-friendly aquamation aka resomation, which involves the use of heat, water and an alkaline solution. Goodfuneralguide.co.uk has info on natural burials, which take place in woodlands or meadows, and usually involve a shallow grave in a biodegradable coffin or shroud, with no permanent memorial. They aim to improve biodiversity and create beautiful landscapes. For ideas on what you might want, listen to Mel Giedroyc's brilliant podcast *Where There's a Will, There's a Wake* where she interviews celebrities about their death wishes and afterlife beliefs.

A good death allows you to have happy memories. But a traumatic death, like the one Graham had, has the potential to blot out happy memories for those of us left behind. Remember, too, that death is only a very small part of a person's life. Make it a priority to remember how your loved one lived, rather than how they died.

Learn not to fear death. As Matt Haig put it in *The Comfort Book*: '... death forms the basis for so many of our deepest concerns. And it is a part of life. It helps *define* life. It raises the value of our time here, and the value of the people we spend it with. The silence at the end of the song is as important as the song itself.'

Be aware that banks and building societies freeze a deceased person's accounts after they've been notified of their death, meaning you may find it difficult to pay your bills (they will, however, generally release funds to pay for funeral costs, but will send the money to the funeral director directly once they've been sent an invoice). If you have a joint bank account, the funds automatically belong to the surviving partner and the bank will change the account to a sole account in your name when they receive a copy of the death certificate – in the meantime, you have full and immediate access to all the funds. Make sure you have enough money in your joint account or, with your ill loved one's permission, transfer money from their sole account to your joint or sole account. For more on this, see which.co.uk/money/wills-and-probate.

EPILOGUE

What I wish I'd known about grief and grieving

Get a clear understanding of what grieving entails. I found Tonkin's Model of Grief – which grief experts call 'growing around grief' – most accurately described what I experienced, but everyone experiences grief differently. The model involves seeing your grief as a circle that's surrounded by a layer of life. While many people expect their grief to get smaller over time, this model sees the size of the circle staying the same, but what's outside the circle growing larger as you make new friends, gain new interests, have new experiences, learn new skills and come to terms with your loss. See the charity Sue Ryder's brilliant explanation here: bit.ly/4hoEq3I.

Many people think that grief shrinks over time...

... but what actually tends to happen is that our grief remains the same but we grow around it

STILL RUNNING AFTER ALL THESE TEARS

Move forward. Something else I found useful in dealing with my three losses was using the term 'moving forward' rather than 'moving on'. The former implies actively taking steps to rebuild my life and focuses on the future, whereas 'moving on' has connotations of detaching from the past and not looking back, which I didn't want to do. On the contrary, I wanted my departed loved ones to still be part of my life.

Realise that depression is par for the course. According to an article published by *Psychiatry Times*, a month after a loss, about 40 per cent of bereaved people experience a major depressive episode. This reduces to 24 per cent after two months, 15 per cent after a year and seven per cent after two years. Remember, time really does heal all wounds, but you may need a little – or a lot of – help from your friends, a bereavement counsellor, a bereavement app such as Grief Works, or a support group (such as The Loss Foundation, the UK's only charity supporting those bereaved by a loved one's death from cancer, or the weekly Grief Works meet-ups hosted by Julia Samuel; juliasamuel.co.uk). Please seek out professional help if you feel you need it.

Put a suicide-prevention strategy in place. I had suicidal thoughts several times after Graham's death, often following what I now realise were the most trivial things, which felt terrifying. Never before had I encountered a setback and found my default response to be: 'Well Lisa, you can always end it all – you don't have to deal with this pain if you don't want to.' I realised I needed to suicide-proof my life and so I did some research. Most sites advise talking to a close friend or family member, so I asked my friend Sarah and my cousin Anna (who was on maternity leave), whether I could call them when I was feeling very low (Anna, bless her, told me that if I wasn't able to reach her immediately, I should call her partner Alan who was on his phone day and night and would always stand

EPILOGUE

ready to alert her to a crisis). I reminded myself, too, that taking my own life wouldn't punish anyone but myself, and that Graham would be horrified if I took my own life while I'd fought so hard to save his. Without fail those thoughts and feelings passed, and I'm beyond grateful I didn't act on them. Please remember that there are a host of organisations that can offer support, including the Samaritans (freephone 116 123; get free, 24/7 support by phone, letter, email and in branches); Stay Alive (prevent-suicide.org.uk; an app with help and resources for people who feel suicidal); and Shout (giveusashout.org; a free, confidential and 24/7 text messaging service run by volunteers for anyone in the UK who needs support). You can also dial 999 for immediate help.

Run, but don't expect it to be a cure-all. For me, as someone who's run for close on 30 years, running was most definitely my salvation and provided me with invaluable coping skills but, as Bella Mackie puts it in *Jog On*: 'Running is not magic beans and I now know that I can't expect it to inure me to the genuine sadness of life.' That said, Bella did cite a 2016 Harvard study that showed that aerobic exercise changes the way that people respond to their emotions. In it, the researchers asked volunteers to either jog or stretch for 30 minutes before showing them an incredibly sad clip from the 1979 film *The Champ* (a film so sad, I've yet to watch it, having been warned by my primary school friends to 'take a box of tissues with you or else you'll get snot all over your popcorn'). Participants who said they usually struggled to handle negative emotions were more intensely affected by the sad clip, but crucially the impact was lessened if they'd completed the 30-minute run rather than the stretching.

STILL RUNNING AFTER ALL THESE TEARS

Follow the dos and don'ts. Grief is a kind of madness, and you're really not 'in your right mind' for a very long time, so it's important to heed this advice.

> **Do:** spend time with people you feel safe with; try to stick to a simple daily routine; do things you enjoy or that give you a sense of purpose (even small 'winning at life' tasks like tidying your sock drawer); get enough exercise, sleep, healthy/soul food, water, rest and touch (through massage, self-massage and hugs, which all release the feel-good hormone oxytocin; in the early days, I aimed for six hugs a day from anyone willing to give them); keep a journal where you can explore any negative emotions but also note down the things you've done well and are grateful for; find ways to commemorate your loved one through creating a memory box, writing about them, setting up a memory nook with objects that were meaningful to you both, planting a tree (see woodlandtrust.org.uk) or creating a photobook.
>
> **Don't, or try not to:** drive in the first few days or weeks after a bereavement as you'll be permanently distracted; make big decisions such as moving house (I know, I know!) or changing your job – many experts advise waiting for at least a year; self-medicate by sleeping or eating too much or with drugs, or alcohol; feel you need to socialise if you just don't want to; tell yourself you should be 'back to normal' within a certain time frame – everyone grieves differently and there's no 'right' or 'wrong' way to 'do' grief.

Know that it's common for grief to make you question if you've lost your mind, along with everything else, as it profoundly affects your short-term memory and can make it hard to concentrate. It helps to know that this 'grief fog' or 'grief brain' is normal, and

EPILOGUE

will get better over time. I gave up pretending I could remember things and just told people 'I have trauma-related memory loss' or wrote everything I wanted to say down before attending medical appointments. I also made more use of lists, Google Calendar and my Filofax to help me remember things. My sense of taste changed, so all my food tasted funny and I temporarily had to switch from drinking tea to coffee as my previously favourite beverage tasted like milky dishwater.

Realise that you literally can be broken hearted. It's believed that the surge of stress hormones that follows a bereavement can cause Broken Heart Syndrome aka acute stress-induced cardiomyopathy, resulting in the intense chest pain, palpitations and shortness of breath that mimic a heart attack. It usually doesn't leave lasting damage but always get it checked out, just in case.

Tell people that you love hearing the name of the loved one you've lost. People are often frightened to mention Graham, Loren or my dad for fear of upsetting me, but every time someone talks about them, I feel a surge of gratitude, even if it results in tears. If someone you know is bereaved, give them the chance to reminisce about the person who died and tell them you miss that person, too: nothing is worse than thinking they've already been forgotten. The end-of-life charity Marie Curie told me that many people say that talking about your losses can help you to start processing your thoughts and emotions.

Ask the right questions. If you're speaking to someone who's bereaved, it's no use asking them, 'How are you?', because most of the time the honest answer would probably be 'Awful, thanks for asking.' It's far better to acknowledge their loss by saying 'How are you feeling/doing?' and then taking the time to listen to their answer. Likewise with the question, 'Is there anything I can do to help?' I hate asking for assistance, so I hardly ever replied in the affirmative, whereas I really appreciated people who just took matters into their own hands and came up with truly wonderful ways to support me. After Graham's death, a neighbour offered me the use of her off-street parking space for visitors while another neighbour's daughter arrived with an armload of sunflowers and sat talking with me about life, love and loss for several hours, which brought me great comfort. When my mother died, it was the gift of a huge pot of home-made soup and crusty bread that sticks in my mind, plus the offers from relatives to drive Loren and me to appointments.

Accept there may well be 'living losses', too. The online article '10 ways to let go of someone you love', by an American psychologist, is one of the best I've read: bit.ly/4lFD2Mu. Comfort yourself with this thought by the American author Roy T. Bennett in his book *The Light in the Heart*: 'Life is too short to waste your time on people who don't respect, appreciate, and value you. Spend your life with people who make you smile, laugh, and feel loved.'

Beware of 'promiscuous honesty'. A common symptom of raw grief is to want to share it with anyone who'll listen. This was certainly true in my own case: I found myself blurting out my story to people I hardly knew. The problem with 'venting all our feelings to all people', as psychotherapist Julia Samuel puts it, is that it can feel overwhelming for those around us as it triggers thoughts of their own losses and vulnerabilities. This puts them into 'fight or flight' mode, where their ability to reason and respond sensitively is impaired. 'When we indiscriminately express unfiltered feelings, we can disturb those around us, and not receive the empathic response we need,' she said in an interview with the *Daily Express*. Remember that having emotional boundaries is healthy and that oversharing with strangers won't necessarily garner a supportive response, so try

EPILOGUE

to only talk about your feelings with people you know you can trust.

Remember that grief is exhausting, both emotionally and physically. Extreme fatigue is normal. Schedule in early nights, and nap if you need to.

Know that it's fine to laugh. I felt very guilty laughing in the days after my mother's death, but then I realised I was laughing because I was sharing fond memories of her with her two sisters so it wasn't a betrayal, but rather a celebration of Mum's life. After my other three significant losses, I actively sought out opportunities to laugh by recounting funny stories about them and attending live comedy.

Set aside time to grieve. I found it enormously helpful after my dad died to schedule a few minutes each day to lean into my feelings of sadness. This allowed me to confront the reality of my loss in tolerable doses. In my mind, I likened it to inserting a Grief DVD into a DVD player – I'd watch only as long as I felt able to do so, a few minutes perhaps, and then eject the DVD when my feelings became too much to bear, and I always felt an enormous sense of relief afterwards. Remember that running – when you're untethered from your computer, phone and social media – can afford you distraction-free pockets of time during which you can grieve.

Make time to celebrate your lost loved one. 'You heal when you can remember those who have died with more love than pain,' the grief expert David Kessler wrote in *Finding Meaning: The Sixth Stage of Grief*. One way to do this, he suggests, is to choose a special moment you've shared, fully re-create it in your imagination using all of your senses, and then replay it over and over again, aiming to deepen the experience. Because of the trauma of what happened during and after Graham's death, I was initially unable to remember a single positive thing about the 35 years I spent with him, even though we'd been soulmates. Writing this book forced me to retrieve those positive memories because I figured if I couldn't convince you to love Graham as much as I did by sharing them with you, you wouldn't be able to join me in celebrating his life. From now on, I've vowed, I'm going to memorialise the monthly anniversary of Graham's death by lighting a candle and spending ten minutes magicking up something like our poltergeist moment at university, imagining me in my yellow fez, him in his John Lennon spectacles (that Loren and I took to calling 'nerd glasses'), the noise of the canteen, the sour-tasting coffee we drank from our polystyrene cups and our conversation as I continued falling deeper in love with him. As George Eliot wrote, 'Our dead are never dead to us, until we have forgotten them.'

Make anniversaries special. I anticipated feeling especially sad on milestones and important anniversaries and so planned enjoyable activities for those days. I spent my first birthday without Graham with close friends and went on a scenic run in his honour. And on our 31st wedding anniversary, my first without him, I organised a day full of treats – a run along the seafront, a long massage and a potter around a homeware store – so I wouldn't only feel anguish at his loss but would have a day punctuated by happy happenings.

Continue to make new memories with your lost loved one after they've died. Graham had never been up Cissbury Ring or the reputedly heavily haunted Chanctonbury Ring – two iconic hill forts near Worthing – so I ran to them along ancient country roads and tracks and shared the experience with him by taking along a pinch of his ashes to scatter there (bit.ly/44NpWa4).

Write your lost loved one a letter after they've died. If there are things that were left unsaid before someone died, it's never too late – you can write them a letter, and even go so far as to write a letter back on their behalf. Julia Samuel suggested this in one of our online Grief Works meet-ups and it was a revelation. I never got to say goodbye

EPILOGUE

to my little sister, and didn't get the chance to tell her how much she'd enriched my life, so I wrote and told Loren about the chapter in this book celebrating her life, which I'd written as her eulogy as she never had a funeral. In her letter back to me, she said that she was delighted that I have such happy memories of her, and that I was a pretty awesome big sister, too.

Get specialist support after 12 months if you need it. Ten per cent of bereaved people experience 'complicated grief', also known as 'traumatic grief', 'prolonged grief disorder' or 'persistent complex bereavement disorder'. This is when strong feelings of pain, anger, loneliness, guilt, blame, relief, sadness, resentment or emptiness have a significant impact on your daily life for more than 12 months, and stay intense or get worse over time, according to the end-of-life charity Marie Curie. For example, day after day you may not be able to get out of bed, have a shower, see friends, go to work or participate in hobbies. You may also yearn intensely for the person who died and have suicidal thoughts. Find out more, and how to access help at mariecurie.org.uk/information/grief/complicated-grief.

Book recommendations

- *Grief Works* by **Julia Samuel**. Grief psychotherapist Julia Samuel tells the stories of people who are facing their own imminent death or who've lost a partner, parent, sibling or child, and gives practical suggestions on how, with the right approach, grief and anticipatory grief aren't something to be endured but can in fact heal us.
- *Grief and Loss: A Guide to Preparing for and Mourning the Death of a Loved One* by **Harvard Medical School**. Can't face reading long books? This 51-page special report summarises helpful advice from a host of grief experts.

STILL RUNNING AFTER ALL THESE TEARS

- *On Grief and Grieving* by Elisabeth Kübler-Ross and David Kessler. An explanation of the grieving process by two world-renowned grief experts.

- *Finding Meaning: The Sixth Stage of Grief* by David Kessler. A roadmap explaining how to move forward in a way that honours our departed loved ones.

- *The Body Keeps the Score* by Bessel van der Kolk. Discover how trauma rewires the brain and how activities such as being physically active, mindfulness, deep breathing, yoga, singing and dancing can help with the recovery process.

- *Outside, the Sky is Blue* by Christina Patterson. A beautifully crafted, heartbreaking but hopeful memoir about the many challenges the author's family had to overcome, including illness, multiple bereavements and her sister's schizophrenia.

- *The Red of My Blood* by Clover Stroud. An unflinching exploration of what it means to lose a beloved sister – and how hard it can be to find hope in the aftermath of a death.

- *The Year of Magical Thinking* by Joan Didion. One of America's most acclaimed writers grapples with her feelings of intense loss after the death of the husband she adored.

- *A Grief Observed* by C. S. Lewis. The renowned author reflects on his struggle to come to terms with his wife's death.

- *Leftover Life to Kill* by Caitlin Thomas. The poet Dylan Thomas's widow questions what her life means without him.

- *Man's Search for Meaning* by Viktor Frankl. A psychiatrist examines the coping strategies he and others used to survive the Nazi concentration camps.

- **Websites:** juliasamuel.co.uk; whatsyourgrief.com; cruse.org.uk; sueryder.org; emdrassociation.org.uk; traumaresearchuk.org

- **Films & TV series:** *Bridget Jones: Mad About the Boy*; *Truly, Madly, Deeply*; *P.S. I Love You*; *Ghost*; *After Life* (TV series)

EPILOGUE

What I wish I'd known about dementia

Get a Lasting Power of Attorney (LPA) for finances and health. Having LPAs in place for my dad would have saved a lot of worry and guesswork, so too would setting up an Advance Statement (detailing his preferences, beliefs and values regarding his future care) and Advance Decision (a written statement about refusing specific types of medical treatment). For more on this, see nhs.uk/conditions/dementia/care-and-support/legal-issues.

Focus on what your loved one can do, rather than what they can't. At my dad's care home, the residents danced, sang, played carpet bowls and enjoyed quizzes – and they often knew more of the answers than I did!

Stick to a regular routine. People with dementia thrive on routine as it provides stability and reduces confusion. They also tend to become easily overwhelmed by too much stimulation, so creating a calm environment and reducing noise is key. We gave my dad noise-cancelling headphones to wear when we were blending his smoothies, for example.

Understand 'sundowning'. People with dementia often experience increased confusion, agitation or behavioural changes at dusk. Physical activity, maintaining a consistent routine, exposure to bright light during the day, creating a calm environment, limiting caffeine, alcohol and sugar and providing reassurance can all help to reduce the intensity or frequency of these episodes. Distraction is also a key strategy in managing confusion.

Don't feel guilty about 'fiblets'. White lies are a helpful technique when caring for someone with dementia because they help them to feel calm and safe – and can spare your loved one enormous pain, and you a lot of frustration.

Book recommendations

- *50 Things Every Carer Should Know About Dementia: Helping Carers Cope* by Christina Neal. A very short but incredibly helpful book by a runner friend of mine who cared for her now late mum Hazel for almost ten years, it offers invaluable advice to carers on all aspects of coping with the condition. See also Christina's free-to-download magazine at dementiahelpuk.com/magazine.
- *What You Really Want to Know About Life with Dementia* by Karen Harrison Dening, Hilda Hayo and Christine Reddall. Based on the real stories and real questions brought to the Dementia UK helpline, this book gives those affected by dementia – and the people who care for them – the tools and expert advice they need to live better with dementia.
- **Websites:** dementiauk.org; dementiahelpuk.com
- **Films:** *The Notebook*; *On Golden Pond*; *The Iron Lady*; *Still Alice*

What I wish I'd known about bipolar disorder

Understand bipolar.

People living with bipolar experience fluctuating periods of elevated mood and energy, and periods of depressed mood and energy, that can last for weeks or months at a time. It's a common misconception that they're happy one moment and sad the next – it is more episodic in nature and far more complicated than just mood swings. Manic episodes involve elevated or irritable mood, increased energy and a reduced need for sleep, while depressive episodes are characterised by feelings of sadness, hopelessness and a loss of interest in activities.

People with bipolar should not be prescribed antidepressants

EPILOGUE

without a mood stabiliser, as they can trigger harmful mood episodes.

It can take time to get someone's bipolar medication right. Several different combinations of medications are used depending on the nature and degree of symptoms and the phase of the condition someone is in.

Alongside medication, there are many other aspects to keeping well with bipolar, such as having a good support network, specialist psychological therapies and self-management techniques.

Know the bipolar facts.

Bipolar is common. About four per cent of people globally will develop bipolar disorder in their lifetime, and about 45 million people live with bipolar disorder globally.

People with bipolar face significant health disparities, with higher rates of obesity and a 10- to 15-year reduction in life expectancy.

There is a high risk of suicide in those with bipolar. Globally, about 15 to 20 per cent of people with bipolar disorder die by suicide, with 30 to 60 per cent making at least one attempt.

With the appropriate treatment, support and self-management tools, someone with bipolar can live a long and meaningful life.

Book recommendations

- *Bipolar Disorder: The Ultimate Guide* **by Sarah Owen and Amanda Saunders.** Written in a reader-friendly, Q&A format by two cousins who share a family history of bipolar disorder, this fab book draws on a broad range of expert opinion as well as personal experiences from people with bipolar.
- **Anything by Kay Redfield Jamison.** Diagnosed with bipolar in early adulthood, Kay is a clinical psychologist and the

STILL RUNNING AFTER ALL THESE TEARS

author of bestsellers *An Unquiet Mind*, *Night Falls Fast: Understanding Suicide* and *Touched with Fire*. She is also the Dalio Professor in Mood Disorders and Psychiatry at the Johns Hopkins University School of Medicine.

Websites: bipolaruk.org; samaritans.org

Films and TV series/programmes: *Silver Linings Playbook*; *Sylvia*; *Mr Jones* (starring Richard Gere); *Modern Love* (Season 1, Episode 3); *Big Mood* (TV series); *In My Skin* (TV series); *Euphoria* (TV series starring Zendaya); *Homeland* (TV series); *Heston: My Life with Bipolar* (TV programme)

Well, dear readers, this really is The End. My main aim with this book was to show how running helped me through the darkest times of my life, and I sincerely hope it will help you, too, no matter how bumpy the road ahead. Happiness is a choice: choose wisely. I wish for you to live heartily, love passionately, laugh uproariously – and run as often and joyously as you can. Then, when your own finish line looms into view, you'll be able to look back on your life and say in all honesty: 'I stayed the course. I lived and loved well. I ran my personal best.'

Acknowledgements

Heartfelt thanks to…

… Debbie Chapman, my extraordinary editor, whose sensitive and insightful editing of this book has made it immeasurably better. I can't think of anyone I'd rather have worked with on this labour of love. Debbie also drew the delightful book illustration on page 411.

… Claire Berrisford, the intrepid, meticulous and very patient editor who took over from Debbie and cheered this book across the finish line.

… the incredibly talented Matthew Hams, for once again designing a gorgeous cover that makes my heart sing and that's the perfect 'sister' to *Your Pace or Mine?*

… Rob Ward, for his amazing creative input into the cover and book design, and Ben Ottridge for his help with the photos throughout this book.

… Hannah Hargrave and Jasmin Burkitt, two tireless publicists, who secured this book such fantastic media coverage.

… the Summersdale editorial team – Sophie Martin, Imogen Palmer and Vicki Vrint – whose eagle eyes honed and toned my manuscript.

… legal reader Nicola Thatcher, who took such care with my book.

… Kathrine Switzer and Vassos Alexander, for championing this book and writing two incredibly touching Forewords that made me cry.

… Sarah Owen, who walked every step of my journey with me, called me every single day for a year after Graham died, and then relived it all again when she deftly edited several drafts of this book. Sarah shared every trial, tribulation and triumph, sent me

STILL RUNNING AFTER ALL THESE TEARS

care parcels and offered me wise counsel every time I broke down in tears – I owe this dear friend my life.

... Rose Shillito, my first British friend, who rode to the rescue whenever I was struggling with the most challenging sections of this book. Her wit and flair for language are truly extraordinary.

... Julia Samuel (juliasamuel.co.uk) and Kristen M Stanton (uniguide.com), for so kindly allowing me to quote from their remarkable writings.

... Fallingwater photo courtesy of the Western Pennsylvania Conservancy (Fallingwater is located in Mill Run, Pennsylvania; 00 44 7243298501), Action Photo (actionphotosa.com; photo of me at the Comrades Marathon finish), UK Running Events (photo at Inflatable 5K), Humanists UK and Simona Sermont Insta @simona.sermont (photos of the Dignity in Dying rally), Yong yi Chen (photos of The House), Faye Slater (portrait of Lisa the Flamingo Runner), Lyndel Costain (photo of the bench in Hermanus), Liz Liston (photo of me at Climping Beach), Angie Govender (photos of my dad and I), Anthony Jackson (photo of our wedding day) and Justine Desmond (justinedesmond.com; publicity shots) for shooting or providing amazing photographs.

... the artist Glenn Badham (glennbadham.com), for so generously granting permission to reproduce our favourite painting *Solitaire*, and the sculptor and artist Alan Wallis (alanwallisceramics.com; Instagram @alan.wallis.sculptures) for so kindly allowing me to reproduce his *Crow* painting. I failed to track down the Ludlow artist Mr Hawkin who painted *Midday Carillon* but would like to thank him for creating a painting that brought Graham and I so much joy over the years.

... the *Runner's World* team – Andy Dixon, Joe Mackie and Rick Pearson – who made a lifelong dream come true by inviting

ACKNOWLEDGEMENTS

me to become a columnist, and who believed someone slow like me had something valuable to say about running.

... Esther Newman, the award-winning editor of *Women's Running*, who has been a joy to work for over many years.

... Suzy Walker, the founder of the wonderful Heart Leap Writing Hour (heartleap.substack.com), whose twice-weekly meet-ups with fellow writers kept me motivated through the ultramarathon that this book turned out to be.

... Nicky and Alf Chrascina, for inviting me to become an ambassador for their funky activewear brand Flanci (flanciactivewear.co.uk). They not only commissioned the amazing Jan Olive to design a special flamingo-and-crow-themed print called Flamboyance in honour of this book, but hosted my book launch at The National Running Show.

... Mike Seaman, founder of The National Running Show, for his unwavering support.

... Claire Carroll, this book's Fairy Godmother, who not only came up with its brilliant title, but persuaded Flanci to create a special flamingo-themed print to celebrate its publication.

... my courageous team of beta readers who helped me shape this book: Anna Britz, Alan Madine, Claire Carroll, Nadia Dawson, Rose Shillito, Angie Govender, Hilary Ivory, Suzy Walker, Saskia Starbook, Chris Collison, Penny Southall, Jackie Graveney, Faye Slater, Liz Liston, Ian Beach, Darian Jeffs and Inez Britz.

... Nadia Dawson, a rock, a runner and a truly wise friend.

... Angie Govender, Cheerleader-in-Chief to both Loren and I, for her endless encouragement, help and support.

... Anna Britz and Alan Madine, for always being 'on standby'.

... Hilary Ivory, for taking the time to encourage me from my very first day as a journalist, and for her unstinting help in campaigning for the Assisted Dying Bill.

STILL RUNNING AFTER ALL THESE TEARS

… Professor Loïc Lang-Lazdunski aka Professor Hope and his wonderful wife Alexandra – without you we would have had no hope.

… Lourdes Durán, Georgia Henson, Zoran Aman, Dimitris Kanakis, Laura Garcia, Tara the physiotherapist, Makho Mthunzi, Adewunmi Okuboyejo, Morine Nantongo, Dr Shannon Odell, Melinda du Toit, Angela Van Heerden and Catherine Bumhudz, for the compassionate care they gave Graham and my dad.

… the doctors, GPs, surgeons, oncologists, radiologists, physiotherapists, nurses, Marie Curie nurses, paramedics, hospice nurses, care assistants and receptionists who went above and beyond for Graham and my dad.

… Lacey St James and Catriona McGregor from the legal firm Irwin Mitchell (irwinmitchell.com), for their kindness and tireless efforts on our behalf.

… Bryony Gordon and Headline Book Publishing, Henry Marsh and Vintage, Julia Samuel, Elizabeth Day and Mel Robbins.

… The MP Kim Leadbeater, MP Dr Becky Cooper, the teams at Dignity in Dying (especially Sarah Wootton and Sadie Kempner), Compassion in Dying and Humanists UK, Prue Leith, Dame Esther Rantzen, Rebecca Wilcox, Jonathan Dimbleby, Dr Jacky Davis, Dr Sonia Adesara, Ian S Colley, Elizabeth Reed and Sue Biggerstaff, who have all campaigned so tirelessly to get the Assisted Dying Bill passed. Also to Rachel Smith from *The Lessons in Loss* podcast, Francine Wolfisz from Mail Online and Nick Ferrari of LBC, who all helped me tell Graham's story.

… Cathy Atkinson and Mike Turner from Core Fitness (corephysiofitness.co.uk), whose expertise and encouragement got me across the Brighton Marathon finish line in one piece.

… Beth the Running Buddy, Emma Simpson and Woody the

ACKNOWLEDGEMENTS

Woodster, for their stellar company during training runs.

... my friends from the running community and 100 Marathon Club who have shared so many smiling miles with me: Peter Rooke, Marian Tipler, Gaby Huddart, Nikki Campbell, Sally Brown, Roger Biggs, Traviss Willcox, Rachel Smith, Rik Vercoe, Sue Cesarini, René Kujan, Juliet McGrattan, Kirsty 'Crustie' Winwood, Vanessa Brewster, Kate Custiss, Martin Bush, Donna Dawn, Debbie Stirling, Jenny Evgenia, Cecy Montes, Victoria Legge, Mailynne Woolley, Emily Robinson and Davey Green.

... Antoinette Strapp, Ian Beach, Joan Steyl, Yvonne Jackson, Angie Govender, Lezani Calitz, Petru Wessels, Carel Trichardt, Sandy van Lingen, Barry Jackson, Piet Bredell, June Clarkson, Arline Scott, Deirdré van Biljon and Rika, for the enduring friendship and love they gave my dad, sister and me.

... all my many friends, both those mentioned above, and Yong yi Chen, Anthony Varela, Joan Ciacciofera, Michael Thomas, Sanober Sheikh, Chris Sell, Roger Robinson, Wayne Davies, Iona Gunning, Grace Lamb, Helena Charles, Marissa Charles, Ruth and Paul Boughton, Lyndel Costain, Helen Brown, Jane Donovan, Cynthia Walley, Andy and Marianne Schaffner, Madeline Gillies and Joan McCrea who were, and always have been, in it for the long haul.

... my beloved soulmate and husband Graham Williams, whose catchphrase 'This book won't write itself' inspired me to keep writing whenever I felt I just couldn't go on. You are the reason for this book, and live on in my heart and its pages.

About the author

Lisa Jackson is a clinical hypnotherapist, running writer and *Runner's World* columnist, and the author of the best-selling books *Your Pace or Mine?* and *Running Made Easy*. Lisa is also *Women's Running*'s hypnotherapy expert, and her work has been published in *Psychologies, Red, Prima, Top Santé, Healthy, Cosmopolitan, The Guardian, The Independent* and Mumsnet. Originally from South Africa, Lisa is based in Worthing, UK, and is a veteran of over 100 marathons and two 56-mile ultramarathons – but often comes last!

Lisa has presented talks at numerous events including The National Running Show and RunFestRun. She was one of 40 people featured in *The Sunday Times*'s Alternative Rich List aka The Enriched List, as someone whose life has been 'rich in experience, rich in spirit, rich in life'. She was nominated in the 2020 Women of the Year Awards, and in the 2018 *Women's Running* Awards in the 'Influencer of the Year' category. Lisa is an ambassador for the multi-award-winning fitnesswear brand Flanci Activewear.

Contact Lisa if you enjoyed this book, or want to try online hypnosis to boost your running motivation (www.quiet-medicine.co.uk). If *Still Running After All These Tears* has inspired you to regain your running mojo – or to give running a go – Lisa would love to hear from you. Drop her a line at quiet.medicine@gmail.com and she may even end up including you in a future book or magazine article. Follow Lisa on Facebook at facebook.com/LisaFlamingoJackson; Twitter/X at @LISAJACKSON43 and Instagram at @lisaflamingojackson.

Book club questions

Questions on running

Have you ever lost your running mojo? And how did you get it back?

Has reading about Lisa's experiences during her 100th marathon and the Brighton Marathon made you want to run a marathon, too?

Lisa says running was her salvation. Has running been a lifeline for you, too, and in what way?

How did Lisa's attitude towards running change over the years?

Questions on relationships

Why do you think Lisa and Graham lost so many relationships during his illness and after his death?

Lisa had a challenging but very close relationship with her sister Loren. Are sibling relationships always complicated and if so, why?

How do you feel about the decision not to tell Lisa's dad that he had terminal prostate cancer or that his daughter Loren had died? If you were Lisa's dad, would you like to have been informed of those things or not?

Questions on living with a terminal diagnosis and attitudes to death

Graham's cancer journey was a rollercoaster of emotions – which part of his story stirred up the most emotion in you?

How do you think you'd react to receiving a terminal diagnosis?

Do you think you'd be able to overcome fear in order to live in hope?

How do you think you can best support a loved one who's been given a terminal diagnosis?

Has this book made you think differently about dying? In what way?

What did you learn about end-of-life care, dying and death that you didn't know before?

What are your views on assisted dying? And has reading this book changed them?

Should people who are not terminally ill but wish to die – such as those with incurable conditions such as motor neuron disease or multiple sclerosis, or those with unendurable disabilities or severe and long-lasting depression – be allowed to seek help to end their lives?

What do you fear most about dying and death?

We are all born and we all die – why does our society avoid talking about death?

Questions on grief

Lisa contrasts the agonising death of her husband with the pain-free, peaceful death of her father – how did these vastly different deaths affect her mental state afterwards?

Lisa doesn't sugar coat how it feels to face the death of a loved one, or the ensuing grief. Has this book stirred up difficult emotions regarding your own past losses?

BOOK CLUB QUESTIONS

Anger and guilt are two emotions commonly experienced by the bereaved. Has this been true for you and if so, why?

What do you think of Tonkin's Model of Grief – which grief experts call 'growing around grief'? Do you think it's true that a person's grief stays the same over the years but that their life outside their grief grows larger as they make new friends, gain new interests and come to terms with their loss?

General questions

How did Graham and Lisa's relationship change over the years?

Does the book have any relevance to your own experience of love?

What incident in this book made you laugh out loud?

Lisa believes in poltergeists and signs from the Universe. Do you? And if so, why?

Perversely, Covid was a blessing in Lisa and Graham's life as the lockdowns enabled them to spend more time together and gave them the opportunity to write their travel memoirs. Covid also resulted in a peaceful death for Lisa's dad. What effect did the pandemic have on your family?

What will you do differently after reading this book?

Have you enjoyed this book?

If so, why not write a review on your favourite website?

If you're interested in finding out more about our books, find us on Facebook at **Summersdale Publishers**, on Twitter/X at **@Summersdale** and on Instagram, TikTok and Bluesky at **@summersdalebooks** and get in touch. We'd love to hear from you!

Thanks very much for buying this Summersdale book.

www.summersdale.com

Also by Lisa Jackson

- *Running Made Easy* (co-authored with Suzy Whalley)
- *Adore Yourself Slim: Eat, Exercise and Hypnotise Yourself to a Healthier, Happier You*
- *Your Pace or Mine? What Running Taught Me About Life, Laughter and Coming Last*
- *Travel Seekness: In Search of Places to Be, People to See and Strange Stuff to Eat* (co-authored with Graham Williams)
- *Travel Agents: More Scrapes, Japes and Narrow Escapes* (co-authored with Graham Williams)
- *Quit For Ever! Stop Smoking and Vaping the Super-quick, Easy and Fun Way*